Storehouse of Treasures

Storehouse of Treasures

Recovering the Riches of Chan and Zen

NELSON FOSTER

消雲

SHAMBHALA

Shambhala Publications, Inc.
2129 13th Street
Boulder, Colorado 80302
www.shambhala.com

Cover calligraphy: "Bao" by Bob Speiser
Cover design: Daniel Urban-Brown
Interior design: Michael Russem

9 8 7 6 5 4 3 2 1

First Edition
Printed in the United States of America

Shambhala Publications makes every effort to print on
acid-free, recycled paper.

Shambhala Publications is distributed worldwide by
Penguin Random House, Inc., and its subsidiaries.

LIBRARY OF CONGRESS CATALOGING-IN-PUBLICATION DATA
Names: Foster, Nelson, 1951– author.
Title: Storehouse of treasures: recovering the riches of Chan and Zen /
Nelson Foster.
Description: Boulder: Shambhala Publications, 2024.
Identifiers: LCCN 2023039347 | ISBN 9781645473107 (trade paperback)
Subjects: LCSH: Zen Buddhism—Essence, genius, nature. |
Zen Buddhism—Doctrines. | Buddhism—Essence, genius, nature.
Classification: LCC BQ9265.4 .F675 2024 | DDC 294.3/927—dc23/eng/20231026
LC record available at https://lccn.loc.gov/2023039347

Contents

Preface

The storehouse of treasures will open of itself,
and you may use them as you please.

—Dōgen Kigen, *Fukanzazengi*

The storehouse of treasures that Dōgen Zenji invites us to enjoy is as wide as the world, its riches infinite. The contents range in kind from a rooster's shriek at sunrise or the fragrance of jasmine to a plastic bag fluttering in the wind, a lover's touch, a single word, the rings of Saturn, the tartness of a plum. But the treasure house is even larger than that. It has a second level, you might say, holding a collection of priceless items that Dōgen and other masters of the tradition cherished, protected, and expanded with their own contributions—a cache of expressions that illuminate the *dao*—the *tao*, that is, in the spelling more familiar to many of us.

Treasures of the first sort have been discovered and celebrated since the dawn of time by artists, poets, mystics, visionaries, and others of a myriad peoples; no one person or tradition can rightly claim them as theirs alone. The chapters that follow deal with such treasures, but this book is devoted chiefly to wonders of the second type, retrieved from the fabulous literary assets of the Chan and Zen tradition and, so far, very little known among practitioners in the cultural West.

Before explaining what motivates me to dust off and display these old treasures, I feel a need to address what I mean when I refer, as I just have, to the "Chan and Zen tradition." I don't intend to imply that Chan and Zen, much less the two of them together, can rightly be reduced to a unified institution or even to a consistent set of traits and certainly not to an abstract essence; I intend only to recognize the historical relationship that made the amazing Chinese development of Buddhism known as Chan the principle source for the later Japanese phenomenon Zen. Even referring to the two of them with singular nouns vastly oversimplifies actuality. Look beyond the rubrics Chan and Zen, and one soon sees that these tidy labels mask a slew of subtraditions past and present and, what's more, ignore family ties and resemblances linking them to longstanding, diverse Korean and Vietnamese evolutions of Chan.

So to write of the "Chan and Zen tradition" is grossly inaccurate from a historical standpoint, yet this shorthand seems justifiable for present purposes because the treasures in question are, without a doubt, elements of a common heritage. Stored away in the enormous textual vault of the tradition mainly by medieval Chan masters and scribes, they've been in continual rotation and refinement by teachers and writers in China and Japan ever since. Pinpointing the origins of these gems or crediting one or another wing of the Chan and Zen complex for their creation and beauty matters much less to me than the gems themselves.

As for my motivation in writing, I can honestly say that this book is born of ignorance, mainly my own. In the first chapter, I tell the story of the afternoon I happened to learn suddenly, shockingly, how superficially I knew my beloved tradition. After this initial surprise, fortunately, came many more discoveries of a pleasant variety, as study yielded greater and greater access to the family legacy. I realize that it's impossible to reproduce the astonishment and sometimes glee I felt when, in the course of my often haphazard investigations, the storehouse "opened of itself" and revealed one of its gleaming treasures, but I like to think that at least a little of the wonder of my serendipitous finds will survive retelling.

It seems obvious to me that what I've stumbled across so far represents only a small fraction of what further exploration will reveal, and I hope that this book, as a sort of preliminary report and reconnaissance project, will encourage others to venture into recesses of the storehouse I haven't visited and to turn up more of its Dharma jewels. As a service to such future investigators—you, perhaps?—I've added notes throughout the book supplying Chinese characters omitted from the text, indicating variant translations, and of course crediting sources I've used. But don't let those little numerals hovering over the text deceive you into mistaking this for a scholarly treatise. It's not. I'm no scholar, and my purposes in writing are far from academic.

I hope this book is well *informed* by scholarship, however. Immersion in the languages, cultures, history, and literature of our tradition means that scholars know it in some important respects much better than those of us who've entered through the gate of practice. If my own experience is at all representative, even we Westerners who've spent decades training in Chan or Zen have just *begun* to assimilate the incoming Asian tradition and so can't possibly receive or pass along its benefits as fully as we'd like. This is an awkward observation, since it could be construed as criticism of my late teachers, of good friends and colleagues, and of everybody else working to establish a version of the tradition that might prove viable in societies outside East Asia. Please! I know at first hand the commitment, generosity, care, intelligence, and creativity that have gone into, and continue to go into, rooting and sustaining vital training in the Americas, Europe, and elsewhere. My intention isn't to criticize existing efforts but rather to support them.

As more of our precious legacy comes to light and is brought into circulation and fresh use, I think it'll become evident that gems from our tradition's Asian past, hitherto unsuspected, hold exciting potential for us moderns and English speakers. They're interesting as artifacts, yes, but beyond that, they may be valuable to us today in negotiating the slippery path of practice. They may prove useful in expressing the infinite subtleties of the dao, in enabling us to touch the heartmind, and in suggesting ways to consider and respond to inescapable issues of our time.

Often these treasures are hidden in plain view. With the very word *treasure*, in fact, we've already stepped into the storehouse. Even newcomers to Buddhism know of the Three Treasures or Three

Jewels of Buddha, Dharma (teachings), and Sangha (community), but even veterans in Buddhist practice are rarely aware of the new shades of meaning that the incoming Sanskrit term *triratna* acquired in China. Of the several options available for translating it, 三寶 *sanbao* (or *san-pao*; J., *sanbō*),[1] was selected, tapping into rich implications of the latter word, originally used in reference to imperial treasures considered to possess mystical power. Such *bao* were physical objects—a remarkable piece of jade, a tablet bearing an inscrutable inscription, a rhinoceros horn or a "dragon" scale, an ancient sword or tripod cup, and in one famous case a finger bone reputed to be Śākyamuni's.

Believed to signify the blessings of heaven, these treasures conferred authority on a ruler and his (very rarely her) regime and were thought to provide divine protection from malevolent forces. In fact, the earliest Chinese historical narrative linked the word *bao* that means "treasure" 寶 with its homophone, 保, a *bao* that means "to protect," thereby bonding the two words and their implications. In adopting *bao* for *ratna*, translator-priests implied that the Three Treasures of Buddhism, too, held mystical power and that Chinese rulers who respected the sanbao could put that power to use for their own purposes.

A second canny word choice followed from the first. An emperor's bao were kept safe in a treasury or storehouse known as a 藏, *zang* (or *tsang*; J., *zō*). Buddhist translators took that term to render two more key Sanskrit words—*garbha*, meaning "womb" or "matrix," and *pitaka*, meaning "basket" as in Tripitaka, the Three Baskets of early Buddhist teachings.

The scholar Robert Sharf points out that these Buddhist uses of *zang* refer both to "repositories or embodiments of truth" and to "the fount of bodhi," or awakening.[2] It's no coincidence that the famous twelfth-century master Dahui (or Ta-hui; J., Daie) incorporated *zang* into the title of a compendium of kōans, dialogues, and commentaries that he compiled, promoting his text as the 正法眼藏, *Zhengfayanzang*, the Treasury of the True Dharma-Eye. A century later, positioning his own magnum opus, Dōgen chose exactly the same words, pronounced *Shōbōgenzō* in his native tongue.

Appropriation of *bao* and *zang* permitted crafty Buddhist translators also to put to good use the compound *baozang*, which originally designated the emperor's storehouse of treasures but, prior to Buddhism's arrival, had migrated into figurative use. In Chinese shamanism and in some forms of Daoism, *baozang* had come to refer to reservoirs of occult power that masters of these schools could tap to perform healings, commune with spirits, and work other such wonders for the benefit of their adherents. Many members of the Chinese elite, ranging from emperors to local officials and wealthy families, concluded that Chan's baozang might have similar powers and attempted to harness them by bestowing their largesse upon selected teachers. Some of these benefactors took personal interest in the contents of the Chan *fazang*, its Dharma storehouse, but others undoubtedly merely awarded patronage in the hopes of getting ahead.

Baozang eventually came to serve as a metaphor for buddhanature, also referred to as original nature and self-nature—the as-is buddhahood of you, me, and other beings of all kinds, animate and inanimate. Texts of the Chan tradition and later of Zen sometimes refer to this as the 無盡藏, *wujinzang* (or *wu-chin-tsang*; J., *mujinzō*), the inexhaustible storehouse, encouraging a fruitful ambiguity between the treasury of Chan and Zen teachings per se and the treasury of buddhahood that people inherently share with worms and wasps, orioles and oaks, mountains, rivers, stars, cars, and assault rifles.[3] This calls us to realize that a hurricane or a fart belongs to the storehouse of treasures no less than the words "Wash your bowl!" uttered by the great master Zhaozhou (or Chao-chou; J., Jōshū). Alas, treasures of both types tend to escape our notice or, if noticed, our appreciation. Rushing through life, attention riveted on doing and making, getting and spending, or distracted by the latest clickbait or text message, we persistently overlook the riches arrayed before us.

—

I don't delude myself that I'll ever fully absorb the tradition we've inherited; I got a late start, after all, and have worked at an immense language handicap. But it's delight, not greed or a fantasy of completeness, that's motivated my explorations of the treasure house, delight joined with a desire to make myself responsible to the tradition, to both its present and future as well as to its past. Beyond ongoing Zen practice, becoming responsible to it has meant studying its heritage, which in turn required gaining at least enough ability to ploddingly decipher passages from original Chinese sources. Although some of the treasures on display in the chapters ahead trace back to Indian Buddhism, all of them entered our tradition via medieval Chinese, and some were borrowed from Chinese classics, particularly from texts attributed to Laozi, Zhuangzi, and Kongzi (or Lao-tzu, Chuang-tzu, and Kung-tzu, a.k.a. Confucius) but also from legends, poems, folktales, commerce, government (e.g., baozang), and the like.

While Chan and Zen writings glitter with these jewels, even the most dedicated reader has difficulty discerning them in translation unless annotations make their presence explicit and unpack their meaning. Compounding the problem is the hyper-allusive nature of Chinese, where a word doesn't so much "mean" something (conveniently encapsulated in a dictionary definition) as set loose a cascade of cultural and sensory associations that a reader has to register in order to recognize the word's connotation in a given sentence. Anyone lacking a grounding in East Asian language and literature reads Chan and Zen texts as if at least half blind.

Asian masters introducing Zen to the West have, of course, understood this and opted to put first things first, expounding fundamentals and usually refraining from intricate explanations that would enable their audiences to grasp and savor images or cultural references appearing in the tradition's great texts. That order of priorities fit their circumstances and, even today, may be appropriate when instructing beginners, but with this book I wager that many of us are ready for more and will tolerate, if not actually relish, the work necessary to gain access to the ownerless wealth of the baozang.

To members of the Chan and Zen tradition who would dismiss this book as a wholesale example of "descending into the weeds"—descending, that is, into the endless folderol of ideas rather than going straight to the heart of the Great Matter of birth-and-death—I politely return the criticism. Anyone who thinks in such terms has "fallen" headlong into conceptual snares of high and low, superior and inferior, while imagining that they dwell in some lofty "higher" world of a wisdom that excludes ideas. Too bad!

Really, where will we locate the heart of birth-and-death if not in the untidy particulars of birth-and-death? At the beginning of his teaching record, the feisty and influential ninth-century Chan master Linji (or Lin-chi; J., Rinzai) declares, "If I presented the Great Matter as required by the ancestors of this house, I couldn't open my mouth at all, and you'd have nowhere to plant your feet."[4] No words, no weeds. No weed patch, no traction for the teaching.

So into the luxuriant weeds we go. The essays gathered here got their first airings before the Buddhist communities, or sanghas, that I serve on a more or less frequent basis—groups that know me well and that nearly always had spent at least a day or two doing zazen, seated Zen practice, before I spoke. I've revised those presentations for publication, both to incorporate subsequent ideas and to compensate for the major differences of setting and medium. Even as first delivered, though, they were deliberately weedy, departing from the norm for addresses from the teaching seat.

In print form, they float free of virtually every shred of context they once had, so here I want to furnish a little background to anchor them in time and place. These essays emerge from a period of Zen training classically known as "nurturing the fetus of sagehood." That sounds pretty highfalutin, but it refers to a stretch of years, typically a decade, when a promising but still green practitioner lives alone in fairly humble circumstances, seasoning through solitary practice and study on the chance of someday receiving the summons to serve as a master. The emphasis in the phrase belongs on the word *fetus* (or *embryo*, an equally valid translation), connoting as it does the beginning of a long developmental path from birth through infancy, youth, and adolescence and on to maturity in the Zen way.

Few people of any age or country get this opportunity, and it's especially rare outside of Zen monastic institutions. To the extent that I've had such an experience, it's a result of moving, at the age of thirty-seven, from urban Honolulu, with its still-active claim upon my interest and affections, to a forest home in the Sierra Nevada foothills. It's been informal and ad hoc and has necessarily gone on much longer than a decade. If I knew anything about "fetus nurturing" when I got here, I certainly didn't yet know how badly the fetus in question needed nurturing or how one might go about it. I'd come to marry, not for isolation or study, and was working full time as a writer and editor to help pay a mortgage while also learning to live off the grid, run a chainsaw, drive in snow, and meet other requirements of my new environs.

As I look back, all that seems like good preparation for the role I'd already begun to play as a lay Zen teacher, but it didn't further my understanding of the tradition. Fortunately, once our debt on the land and house was paid, I had a chance to dig into our tradition in a way I never had before, improving my grasp of its history, reading more of its literature, taking closer stock of its luminaries, and soon recognizing the scope of my ignorance (again, for details see chapter 1). Come to find out, I was just beginning to catch up to an observation the author Gary Snyder—a friend, neighbor, goad, and inspiration—had made twenty-five years before. After a decade-plus in Kyoto, training in one of the great Zen monasteries and working with the outstanding team of scholars that Ruth Fuller Sasaki employed to translate classical Zen texts, Gary had this to say:

> How much scholarship goes into Zen study is little realized by most American Zen students. The ordinary Japanese person can't understand a Zen Master's lecture any more than you and I can. The transmission of the whole rich tradition and history of Zen with its thousands and thousands of accounts of individual men, built up generation after generation, requires a very special and difficult study for everyone, and it is going to require a lot of painstaking work for any of that historical and traditional richness to come to the West.[5]

> Someone who is going to do long-term Rinzai study would do well to thoroughly acquaint himself with the great Chinese

T'ang- and Sung-dynasty poets because the kind of imagery and language and nature of the insights that are used in Chinese poetry are borrowed by the Zen world for talking back and forth about their understandings. Chinese proverbs are often made into koans or used as part of koans with just a slight twist. So much of the culture becomes involved in ways that we don't realize.[6]

Hear that? A *lot* of painstaking work. For *any* of that historical and traditional richness to come to the West. So much of the culture becomes involved in *ways that we don't realize*. My experience has borne out each of these statements.

———

In exploring this cultural nexus, I've benefited immensely from published works listed in the back of the book and, in addition, have had the profound good fortune of live assistance from a set of generous, scholarly friends. When I ran into issues requiring linguistic, textual, historical, or iconographic expertise or needed counsel on how to present this sometimes intricate material, I've been able to depend on help from Wendi L. Adamek, Benjamin Brose, Thomas Yūhō Kirchner, Norman Waddell, and Peter Wong Yih Jiun. I'm deeply grateful for their counsel. If these essays occasionally stray from factuality, it's not because I've ignored their advice but probably because I haven't asked for it as often as I should have.

My principal Zen teacher, Robert Aitken, always encouraged my studies and relished some of my early findings; I regret that he died before this book was even begun and hope that it will, in some small measure, requite my boundless debt to him. I owe infinite thanks also to my wife, Masa Uehara, who's graciously endured my decades of sedentary "fetus nurturing" and has always stood by to rescue me when an obscure Chinese character was giving me fits. As noted, I tried out early versions of these chapters on the Zen communities I've had the honor of serving—primarily Ring of Bone Zendo but also the East Rock Sangha, Honolulu Diamond Sangha, and Maui Zendo. Their members' staunch practice, lively engagement, criticisms, encouragement, questions, and prodding have inspired my work.

Of course, I own all the errors and omissions herein and will simply plead, as Tōrei Zenji once did, "Don't laugh at my careless commentaries. I've only opened the way, waiting for wise people to come in the future!"[7] Even that may be too much to ask. Go ahead and laugh. I'll rest in this line from the Zen phrase books: "Old and infirm, pointlessly I enter the weedy wastes."[8]

Storehouse of Treasures

1 | Getting to the Spring— and Beyond

Calligraphy supplies in hand, Yamada Rōshi was shuffling briskly toward the porch of the sprawling, dilapidated building in rural Maui that our sangha was gradually making over into a temple when I stopped him to pose a question. Only twenty-three that sunny afternoon in 1974 and barely two years into practice, I was intrigued by Zen's relationship to poetry and wanted to know if he had a verse in mind that day, on the momentous occasion of authorizing his American disciple, my own teacher, Robert Aitken, as an independent master. "Yes, I do," he answered, without hesitation. Fixing his gaze on me, he delivered words that I've never forgotten: "I go to the place of flowing water, sit, and watch the clouds rise." Then, abruptly, he asked, "Do you understand?" I thought I did and said so. End of interaction.

All masters of our lineage receive teaching names that conclude with the word, the Chinese character, *cloud*. That morning, Yamada Rōshi—or Kōun Zenshin, to use his proper name as a deceased master—had designated his successor Dawn Cloud, and I understood the lines he'd recited as the mind that he'd carried into that consequential ceremony. The words seemed banal, unpoetic, but I assumed they were an off-the-cuff translation from Japanese, and whatever their faults, they conveyed a vivid image. I imagined Yamada Rōshi beside a mountain spring, sitting stone-still as he did before the altar in the zendo or in the little chamber where he received us for *dokusan* (individual instruction). Except, of course, now he was sitting alone, near dawn, as mist lifted off the pool's shimmering surface, assuming strange, fleeting forms. What a lovely image, I thought, for observing a teacher's mysterious emergence!

This all came back to me unexpectedly, with seismic impact, one afternoon in 1995 as I worked at my desk in the California foothills, struggling to meet the deadline for submission of a king-sized compendium of Chan and Zen literature. I was comparing translations of work by the famed eighth-century poet and calligrapher Wang Wei when suddenly a couplet leapt out at me, differently worded but obviously translating the very same lines I'd heard from Yamada Rōshi's lips two decades before. Never, in all that time, had I any inkling that he was quoting someone else's verse—longer, renowned, written in Chinese by a Chan layman par excellence:

終南別業
中歲頗好道
晚家南山陲
興來每獨往
勝事空自知
行到水窮處
坐看雲起時
偶然值林叟
談笑無還期

Zhongnan Country Residence[1]

At middle age I took delight in dao;
later I retired to the flanks of Mt. Nan.
Inspired, I often go wandering alone;
exquisite matters an empty self knows!
Walking, I reach where the waters end,
and sitting, see when the clouds rise.
By chance, I run into a forest graybeard,
gab and laugh, forgetting about time.

Though learning the source of Yamada Rōshi's verse wasn't a great revelation in itself, it rocked me as a measure of my ignorance. There I sat, under the responsibility of assembling an anthology on a subject close to my heart, a subject I thought I knew well, staring at irrefutable evidence of how thin my knowledge really was. That seemed bad enough for a person compiling such a collection but much worse for a person who, by that time, had served as a Zen teacher for twelve years, the second half of them as a Dharma heir— "grandson" to Yamada Rōshi—charged with conveying the tradition faithfully to members of the next generation.

I got the book finished, but that afternoon's discovery propelled me into the new phase of study that underlies this book and all of my subsequent teaching. One of the things I learned first was that many masters besides Yamada Rōshi, past and present, have held Wang Wei's couplet in high esteem. When jurist, diplomat, and philosopher John C. H. Wu published *The Golden Age of Zen* in 1967, joining D. T. Suzuki's effort to promote Zen to English speakers, he described Wang Wei's words as "the most favorite lines among the Zen masters."[2] That may be so. The important thirteenth-century teacher and literatus Wansong (or Wan-sung; J., Banshō) quotes them repeatedly in his commentaries. They appear in the collections of capping phrases for Rinzai kōan study. Zen calligraphers often have selected one or both lines to complement a painting or as a stand-alone inscription. In short, there's no question that they rank among the best-known, most-cherished treasures in the family storehouse, conspicuous to anyone well versed in our tradition.

That these very famous lines escaped my notice for so long says less about my powers of attention, or so I like to think, than it does about the formidable obstacles involved in transferring an old, complex, and subtle tradition between civilizations. Parties to such a transfer inevitably enter into it with differences extending far beyond language and literary heritage, differences that range from diet to manners to music to conceptions of nature, art, society, self, history, causality, science, and so on—conceptions that, whether consciously or unconsciously held, condition our experience (and our interpretation of experience) from cradle to grave. Although we stood face-to-face on the zendo porch that long-ago afternoon, unquestionably Yamada Rōshi and I spoke across a huge cultural divide.

Since that day, the socioeconomic-technological phenomenon known by the infelicitous name of "globalization" has narrowed the divide somewhat, but it won't be eliminated anytime soon, if ever. Whether or not you consider cultural differences a good thing (as I do), it gives us some work to do on our side of the chasm if we want to make reasonably certain that we've laid hold of Zen traditions as our Asian forebears knew them and hoped to pass them on. Indeed, we have a good deal more to discover about Wang Wei's poem itself, beginning with the couplet so highly prized in Chan and Zen.

The line I translate "Walking, I reach where the waters end" entails a delicious ambiguity. The following line makes it clear that the water doesn't end in the sense of being exhausted, of running out; clouds of mist don't rise from dry ground. Wang Wei requires readers to intuit that he's walked upstream to where the water "ends" at a spring. Steeped in the Chinese classics as he was, Wang Wei unquestionably knew the strong historic association of dao with water and knew, more specifically, that he could count on his words to bring to mind an image of tracing dao to its source. Depicted metaphorically as a spring, this source marks the inevitable upper limit of human wisdom: dao issues from unknown depths, invisible and mysterious.

Upon reaching his stream's supposed source, though, when Wang Wei sits, what strikes him is the mist rising, the clouds forming. His attention, and the reader's, turns skyward, not to the water flowing downstream or to what lies out of sight in the depths of the pool but to what's visible above. With this observation, he evokes the water cycle as a whole, a continuum clearly recognized in China for at least a thousand years by Wang Wei's time. A Daoist text dating from that era and actually titled "Tracing Dao to Its Source" contains this passage:

Ebbing, flowing, diminishing, replenishing,
It permeates beyond estimation.
Rising to the heavens, it becomes rain and dew;
Descending to earth, it becomes life-giving moisture.[3]

With the ten simple words of his couplet, Wang Wei explodes the notion of dao having a fixed or discernible beginning or end, springs it from confinement in a dark "below" as opposed to a light "above," and complicates any conception that it moves in a single, downstream direction.

His perspective is consistent with longstanding Chinese interpretations of the world as a realm of total flux, where a multitude of seamless, ongoing processes exert mutual influence. In keeping with Chan and Zen teachings, he presents a view not limited to dichotomous—dualistic, binary—perspectives. His words gesture to the nebulous character of experience and of existence itself. All of us are clouds, shifting forms in an interplay of more or less mysterious processes, not the independent, self-contained agents that many of us fancy ourselves to be.

Seen in this context, the couplet's implications for an occasion of Dharma transmission reach far beyond those I imagined on first hearing. Yamada Rōshi's recognition of Robert Aitken as an independent teacher could be viewed, from one perspective, as an ending: it concluded the formal course of training that they'd done together and fulfilled his task of passing the Dharma on to the next generation. From another vantage point, it could be seen as a beginning: it initiated a new phase in his successor's life, renamed him, settled upon him the responsibility to convey the Dharma, and even suggested the arrival of a new day for Zen itself, its dawn in the West.

An event like that 1974 transmission ceremony—but any event, really—is a point of no dimension in dynamic processes that have no conceivable beginnings or ends. Take dawn itself, for instance. At your house and mine, dawn definitely happens, but if you ask when dawn begins, you'll find the answer difficult to pin down. Is it when the sky starts to grow light? Is it when the sun's first rays become visible? Isn't dawn actually continual, since somewhere on the little blue planet dawn is breaking every moment?

Ending, beginning—what sense does it really make to class the appearance of that Dawn Cloud as one or the other? Some will want to call it *both*, but that drains the words of meaning; if you equate beginning and ending, the ordinary sense of those words goes out the window. Yet to call it *neither* seems fallacious, too, belying the fact that something consequential did happen that day. Thus the dichotomizing habit inflicts its wounds on reality. Chan and Zen, in common with other Chinese-born traditions, construe the world less in terms of beginnings and endings than as a continuous unfolding or, better yet, a multiplicity of interacting processes.

—

Wang Wei's poem has other Dharma facets not readily apparent in translation and worth noticing, beginning with the title, which intimates the poem's themes. In combination, the words 別業 denote a residence in the country, but by itself, the first of them means "to separate or detach" and, adjectivally, "separated or detached." His residence and his residing there, Wang Wei implies, encourages or even enables him to step away from normative social constructs and to understand the world differently.

This shift of perspective is stressed in a line invariably obscured in English translation—"exquisite things an empty self knows." Taken individually, the words 空自 mean *empty* and *self*, but in Wang Wei's time, they often functioned as a compound, meaning *personally* or *alone*, and have been justifiably translated that way. For Wang Wei, however, as for other students of Chan and Zen, they resonate with teachings about the empty and illusory nature of the self. He invites, and no doubt intended, both readings. Wandering alone and disencumbered of selfhood, he receives an exquisitely beautiful vision of the world.

His meander upstream to the spring exemplifies such experiences. Witnessing the clouds emerging as he sits—meditating, we may suppose—is an instance of the exquisite perceptions an empty self receives, and his chance encounter with a fellow forest elder closes the poem on a soft but clear note of liberation. In their jovial meeting, the two elders "forget about time," and again Wang Wei's word choice is subtle and evocative. The characters 無還 may be translated as "without remembering," thus "forgetting," but another meaning of 還, important in Buddhism, is to *repay* or *requite*, as in these lines from "Song of Realizing the Way," a seminal Chan doctrinal poem attributed to Yongjia (or Yung-chia; J., Yoka):

> With understanding, karmic obstructions are empty from
> the start;
> without understanding, one's karmic debts still must be
> repaid [還].[4]

The overtone he obtains with this phrasing accentuates the freedom Wang Wei expresses in the poem as a whole. He and the other old man haven't forgotten time in the ordinary sense of losing track of minutes; they've slipped out of time's regime altogether. The graph 期 he chose for *time* refers specifically to strictures of time—appointments, fixed terms, set dates, that sort of thing. Having served many years in government bureaucracy, Wang Wei knew that version of time very well, and with this poem, he celebrates a retirement from time in which before and after, beginning and end, have lost their hold.

Now it's my turn to ask the question Yamada Rōshi asked me: Do you understand?

2 | The Taste of Water

Can you taste the taste of water? I don't mean the taste of stuff *in* the water. If it has a bit of salt or lemon or sugar in it, sure, you can taste that. We do that all the time. But what about the taste of just water itself—can you taste that? Tap water tastes different from place to place due to the trace elements it contains, a little iron here, a little clay there. Again, those we can easily taste, and clever people have made sizable fortunes by bottling naturally pleasant-tasting water, coming up with elegant names and labels, and marketing the results. Good for your health, they say.

What taste do such waters and all other watery substances—wine, watermelon, green tea, blood, sweat, orange juice—have in common? The taste of pure water, you might say. Great, but what is that? Two atoms of hydrogen joined to one of oxygen must have some taste, but can you actually taste it in your coffee? How do you *know* that you can taste it? Can you prove to me that you've tasted it? Can you tell me its flavor? Can you tell me how to taste it myself?

We could pose much the same set of questions about perceptual experiences of other sorts—fragrance, darkness, pain, pleasure, confusion—and we could plunge into the thickets of epistemology and communication theory. Let's acknowledge instead that I've borrowed the taste of water as an imperfect metaphor for what, in this tradition, has long been referred to by names such as buddha-nature, the unborn, the original face, and the One Great Matter—the all-pervading, indescribable "flavor" that everything and every-one has in common. This includes phenomena usually classed as intangible, inanimate, or dead: beauty, boulders, corpses, cars, wind, ideas, sorrow, and so forth. Philosophers seeking to sound this sort of bass note in the music of being and nonbeing have tried other designations, typically of a sort more abstract and less metaphorical than flavor—suchness, *ding an sich*, the Absolute, the self-so.

As an alternative to Chan and Zen's traditional expressions, speakers and writers in the West have often applied the term *essential nature*, which mistakenly insinuates into Buddhist teaching the originally Aristotelian notion of essence—a characteristic constellation of qualities that makes a thing what it is, as opposed to its incidental features. (By this account, for example, chickens have an essence, a chicken-ness, that remains intact whether or not a particular member of the species clucks, has feathers, or lays eggs.) The nature Zen points to could scarcely be less essential in this Aristotelian sense. Its pervasiveness makes it impossible to isolate and useless as a marker of uniqueness or difference, and its so-called emptiness curdles the question of whether anything or anyone "has" it. You can't even say it "takes" a myriad of forms. You and me, a hot tire iron, a crested honeycreeper, the falling of rain, last year's belch, next year's asteroid—Zen classically associates buddha-nature with all natures and, in a seeming paradox, with no-nature but doesn't recognize any essential nature. Leave that to the Greeks.

Strangely, remarkably, our predecessors managed to create and sustain a great tradition centered on this ungraspable, inalienable call-it-what-you-like. A capsule version of its doctrine, not fully formulated until the twelfth century but credited to its sixth-century, legendary founding figure, Bodhidharma, boldly pronounces its stance:

> A separate transmission outside teachings,
> not predicated upon words and letters,
> directly pointing to the human heartmind:
> seeing nature, becoming buddhas.[1]

Besides setting Chan apart from Buddhist schools premised upon textual study, this declaration in just sixteen Chinese characters makes a stunning threefold claim: that it holds and conveys a wisdom handed down exclusively to and through it, that its instructional method illumines the heartmind without mediation, and that it can deliver a firsthand, transformative experience so potent as to set one on a par with the buddhas themselves.

Here we return to the problem of tasting water, writ large: to "see nature" is to experience what we've unconsciously known and taken for granted our whole lives—in ourselves, in others, in all fields of endeavor, all activities, all situations. Can you actually taste it? Can you prove to me that you've tasted it? Can you intimate its flavor to me? Can you show others how to taste it themselves? Chan and Zen have confidently answered Yes, Yes, Yes, and Yes again.

By so "directly pointing to the human heartmind," the tradition promises, it will enable us to savor the exquisitely subtle flavor of reality. The whole school—its rigorous training regimen, rituals, countless temples, and voluminous literature—rests on this assurance that it can convey the incommunicable. No structure sits on a less palpable foundation, I suppose, yet it's proven sturdy enough to support the tradition for a millennium and more.

Although it has eschewed any basis in words and letters, this tradition unquestionably owes much of its longevity and robustness to a stock of colorful stories exemplifying its methods and efficacy. A particularly evocative one describes the fraught encounter between Huineng (or Hui-neng; J., Enō), a supposedly illiterate layman who had privately received sanction as the Sixth Chan ancestor, and a senior monk who'd pursued him to recover the robe and bowl that signified transmission of the Buddha's teaching, the Dharma.[2] When this monk, a retired general named Ming, caught up with him, Huineng laid the robe and bowl on a rock, declaring that, as emblems of the Dharma, they should never be fought over and that Ming could carry them away. Attempting to lift them, the story says, Ming found them immovable as a mountain.

> Frightened and uncertain, he said, "I came for the Dharma, not the robe. I beg you, lay worker, please open the Way for me."
> Huineng responded by pointing directly to Ming's heartmind:

"Not thinking good, not thinking bad, at this very moment, what is the original face of senior monk Ming?"

At once Ming awakened profoundly. In tears, his whole body dripping sweat, he bowed and asked, "Besides these arcane words, beyond their arcane significance, is there something of even further significance or not?"

The ancestor said, "What I've just expounded to you isn't arcane. If you reflect on your own face, the 'arcane' actually lives right there with you."

Going on to express gratitude, Ming acknowledged that his years in the monastery hadn't enabled him to see his original face. But now, he commented, "I'm like a person drinking water, knowing for myself whether it's cold or warm." His sweat and tears, his bow, and his follow-up question all indicate that Huineng's arrow had hit the bull's-eye, but this statement in particular makes plain the personal impact of their encounter. Having "seen nature," Ming now had found unmediated knowledge of the Dharma. He'd tasted the water and "become a buddha."

Notice that Huineng's "direct pointing" entailed no information transfer, no explanation, nothing but a penetrating question—a question made all the more penetrating by its point-blank delivery and by Ming's distress. No doubt the story plays up a master's role in catalyzing such a breakthrough experience, but teaching records from medieval times to our own day confirm that interventions of this kind do trigger awakenings or, much more often, help to prime a student for a subsequent stimulus that sparks realization.

Inspiring as such stories may be, in their emphasis on dramatic moments they have the unfortunate effect of obscuring the difficult, unglamorous process of training and the invisible workings through which practice and realization affect one's character and day-to-day conduct. Coming to the West on the wings of these stories, Zen shed evidence of the long transformation it requires, seeming to confer buddhahood on a presto-chango basis. A few early exponents of Zen in the West went so far as to declare zazen, the iconic seated practice basic to the tradition, unnecessary or even delusory. We've had to discover for ourselves, sometimes at high cost, that insights like Ming's do indeed occur suddenly but that they arise almost always out of extensive training and then need to be absorbed, tested, opened out, and refined over a similarly protracted period before they truly come to fruition.

The miracle of this practice isn't that it can turn a frog—bing!—into a prince or princess but that it can give us frogs a sense of the water that we share with all beings and a means to plumb its depths and to investigate its far-reaching implications. Our forerunners' diligent practice, close interaction, skillful negotiation of political circumstances, and adaptation of their cultures' aesthetic resources enabled them to communicate the delicate taste of water from one generation to the next in Asia and beyond, to other cultures. On the receiving end of this transmission, we in turn have to discover or devise ways to keep that tradition alive, and some of the ways we hit upon may bear scant resemblance to those of the past. It can't hurt, though, and may well help, to acquaint ourselves with the expressive tool kit of our predecessors.

With this in mind, let's go back to that elusive taste. Chinese has a word for it, 淡 *dan* (or *tan*; J., *tan*), which my favorite dictionary defines as "bland, tasteless, insipid; mild."[3] The *dan* character has the water radical 氵and might also be translated as "watery." Unfortunately, with the possible exception of *mild*, all these English words carry negative connotations, whereas *dan* in some contexts is positive. In the sense of "insipid," it refers to poor food and drink, uninteresting conversation, slow business, and the like, but its valence reverses, making it a very favorable quality, in Daoist and Confucian texts, poetry, and art.[4]

In those contexts, *dan* points to the indefinable, inescapable quality of a phenomenon in itself—the whatness that makes it that, so to speak. It relates closely to another term important to both Daoism and our tradition, *ziran* (or *tzu-jan*; J., *shizen*), meaning self-so. In the following specimens of its use, for consistency's sake and for lack of a better option, I've translated it as "plain" or "plainness."

The first example, a passage from the *Daodejing* (or *Tao-te ching*), presents dan as a quality of wise speech:

> When the dao comes forth in words,
> how plain, light as air, without flavor!
> Look for it, and you don't see anything;
> listen for it, and you don't hear anything.
> Use it, and you can't exhaust it![5]

The *Zhuangzi* (or *Chuang-tzu*) calls dan a determining factor in human relations:

> The friendship of a noble person is plain as water, that of a petty person cloying as young wine. But the plainness of a noble person leads to closeness, while the too-sweetness of a petty person leads to revulsion.[6]

A concurring, even broader statement of dan's importance and effect appears in the *Zhongyong* (or *Chung-yung*), a central Confucian text commonly referred to as *The Doctrine of the Mean*, the regrettable title of an early translation:

> The dao of noble people is plain, not tiresome,
> to the point and refined, cordial and reasonable.
> Knowing the nearness of the faraway,
> knowing the origins of reputation,
> knowing the eminence of the humble—
> such people may enter into virtue.[7]

Not surprisingly, poets and critics also considered dan a desirable and hard-won quality, resulting in poems whose lines feel ziran, natural—inevitable and direct rather than forced or showy.[8]

All this made dan a nearly inevitable selection for the treasure house. A verse by ninth-century Chan monk Qiji (or Ch'i-chi) applies the term while also exemplifying the virtue:

Don't ask my reason for shutting the gate.
From the start, not much has come or gone.
Dao must return to plainness and tranquility;
the body says yes to emptiness and ease.
On all sides, moss surrounds me with green;
on the sole window, rain spots and streaks.
In my dream explorations, where do I go?
Autumn dyes the hills at water's edge.[9]

Chan masters incorporated dan into their teachings proper from an early date. It comes up for mention in a set of cautions ascribed to the Caodong (or Ts'ao-tung; J., Sōtō) lineage founder Dongshan (or Tung-shan; J., Tōzan) who calls the path of monastics "plain and detached,"[10] and it found ready application in major kōan texts, too. In *The Blue Cliff Record*, for example, a master questioned about what Buddha is answers tersely, "Three pounds of hemp." Commenting on that kōan, the great Linji master Yuanwu (or Yuan-wu; J., Engo) declares it "hard to chew, since there's no place to sink your teeth. Why? Because it's plain, unflavored."[11] A verse by the noted Caodong teacher Hongzhi (or Hung-chih; J., Wanshi) lauding an answer even terser (in fact wordless), offers the observation, "In plainness, there's flavor; it goes subtly beyond emotions or speech."[12] Later generations paid tribute to the master Zhaozhou for his consistently "unflavored words."

Thus dan came to serve as a pointer to the immediate, vital something-or-other that our tradition has historically promised to reveal. Alas, given the negative tenor of such translations as *bland* and *insipid*, this jewel of the ancient storehouse may receive little use where English is the dominant tongue. Happily, over the centuries Chan and Zen have found other ways of alluding to this same plain, ever-present, hard-to-perceive reality, some of which work nicely in English. Finally, though, no word or image in any language can ever capture it, as Wumen (or Wu-men; J., Mumon) acknowledges, indeed celebrates, in his poem on the kōan about Huineng and his pursuer:

Descriptions incomplete, depictions imperfect,
plaudits inadequate....Ah, quit agonizing about it!
Before our eyes from the start, with nowhere to hide,
when the world goes to ruin, it still won't decay.[13]

3 | To Mingle with Friends

Monks of the two halls were having an all-out brawl;
Old Master Wang capably probed truth and falsehood.
His keen blade cut decisively, never mind appearances,
bringing people to revere him as a leader for the ages.
Since this dao still hasn't died out,
the one who knew the tune deserves praise.

So begins Hongzhi's poem on the ninth case of the *Congrong lu* (or *Ts'ung-jung lu*; J., *Shōyōroku*), the notorious kōan in which the master Nanquan (or Nan-ch'uan; J., Nansen) beheads a cat.[1] I take it as a point of departure for exploration of much a happier subject— those who "know the tune" like the person celebrated in the sixth line. In Thomas Cleary's translation, that line reads, "A connoisseur is to be lauded," which obscures the sort of person Hongzhi meant to indicate by the words he chose: 知音 *zhiyin* (or *chih-yin*; J., *chiin*). Since this compound translates literally as "to know sounds" or "to know tones," Cleary's "connoisseur" is perfectly justifiable, but it misses a set of connections brimming with significance in the cultures of China and Japan.

The rich implications of *zhiyin* stem from a brief story in a Daoist classic still not much read in the West, the *Liezi*:

Bo Ya was a good zither-player, and Zhong Ziqi was a good listener. Bo Ya strummed his zither, with his mind on climbing high mountains; and Zhong Ziqi said: "Good! Lofty, like Mount Tai!" When his mind was on flowing waters, Zhong Ziqi said: "Good! Boundless, like the Yellow River and the Yangzi!" Whatever came into Bo Ya's thoughts, Zhong Ziqi always grasped it.

> Bo Ya was roaming on the north side of Mount Tai; he was caught in a sudden rainstorm and took shelter under a cliff. Feeling sad, he took up his zither and strummed it; first he composed an air about the persistent rain, then he improvised the sound of crashing mountains. Whatever melody he played, Zhong Ziqi never missed the direction of his thought. Then Bo Ya put away his zither and sighed: "Good! Good! How well you listen! What you imagine is just what is in my mind. Is there nowhere for my notes to flee to?"[2]

Thus the term *zhiyin* came to signify a friend who "knows the tune" in a very specific sense: unlike a connoisseur, who has expert knowledge of some field—of oolong teas, say, or Baroque sculpture—a zhiyin knows another person's heartmind. In attempting to convey a sense of the expression, translators have made do with approximations like "good listener," "understanding friend," and "intimate friend," none of which go very far toward capturing the full connotations of the Chinese term.

Hongzhi's verse about the cat kōan salutes Zhaozhou as a zhiyin for the immediate, wordless response he made to Nanquan's account of the cat's beheading, a response matching Nanquan's intention so perfectly that the master exclaimed, "Had you been there, I could have spared the cat!" Their interaction beautifully parallels the transparent understanding between Bo Ya and Zhong Ziqi, and it had great consequences, as Hongzhi points out. Because Zhaozhou knew the tune when called upon, this dao, the path of Chan and Zen, has continued beyond him. We owe him thanks as well as praise.

As so often happens, once I recognized *zhiyin* as a term and its value as a metaphor, I noticed it cropping up in Chan and Zen texts besides the *Congrong lu*. This was not unique to our tradition; throughout Chinese culture, *zhiyin* became a password for an exceptionally close relationship and, in effect, a model for such relationships. China's first great treatise on literature, published circa 480, hundreds of years before Chan began to flourish as a school of Buddhism, contains a chapter titled "Zhiyin," which extends the metaphor to reading:

> In composing literature, emotions quicken and decline; bursting forth, they manifest in words. In contemplating a text, one enters the [writer's] emotions.... In our distant age, no one sees their faces; getting a look at their writings, we see their heartminds instantly.[3]

Words' potential to unite people across vast expanses of time and space held tremendous appeal, of course, to writers as well as readers, and direct allusions to the zhiyin theme occur in many texts. Among those I could quote, one by the famed eighth-century poet Li Bai, an example that plays the metaphor both forward and backward, will have to suffice. In "A Moonlit Evening, Listening as Lu Zishun Plucks the *Qin*," Li Bai put himself in the position of Zhong Ziqi, listening to a friend play the same instrument that Bo Ya played, a qin, often called a lute in translations but closer to a zither:

> An idle evening, sitting around, the moon bright,
> a man in shadow plucking an unadorned qin—
> suddenly I heard grief gusting in the notes,
> much as pines moan in the winter winds.
> White clouds, fast-flying slender fingers....
> Foaming waters, clear, a vacant heartmind....
> Granted us for a time but long since died out,
> today we have no one who knows the tune.[4]

Li Bai first presents himself as a zhiyin responding empathically to his friend's music, but his grief overflows to end the poem on an opposite note: the absence of people who possess that sort of acute, intimate sensitivity. Like many an author then and now, Li Bai felt misunderstood by his contemporaries, and he lands his poem on its final word, *zhiyin*, with an unmistakable thud of disappointment.

By the time Li Bai died in 762, Chan had begun to coalesce as a Buddhist tradition and to stake out a reputation for continuing the teaching of Śākyamuni with its "separate transmission" independent of texts. In doing so, our predecessors adopted the zhiyin as a readymade image of what they called "heartmind-to-heartmind transmission." The first such transmission took place, according to Chan legend, when the Buddha wordlessly held up (or perhaps twirled) a flower before a throng of disciples. As the *Wumenguan* tells the tale,

> At that moment, the assembly kept entirely silent. The honorable Kāśyapa alone broke into a faint smile. The World-Honored One said, "I have the treasury of the true Dharma-eye; the marvelous mind of nirvāna, whose true form has no form; the subtle wonder of the Dharma gate, not predicated on words or phrases, a special transmission outside the teachings. I entrust it to Mahakāśyapa."[5]

Kāśyapa's smile marked him out as a zhiyin, the sole member of the crowd who could divine the Buddha's intention in raising the flower. Notice, though, that heartmind-to-heartmind communication has to run both ways: registering Kāśyapa's expression, Śākyamuni exhibited his own power as a zhiyin. That faint smile told him all he needed to know about Kāśyapa's awakening and fitness to serve the world as his successor.

Examining this story challenges us, too, to become zhiyin. Unless we do, we'll never get inside what passed between Śākyamuni and Kāśyapa at that moment. What understanding did they come to? How did it occur? Refusal to explain such events became a hallmark of Chan and Zen, honoring the fact that this most vital type of communication, whether wordless or verbally expressed, happens entirely "between the lines." Quiet reigns at the heart of the Great Matter.

In his verse "Riding the Ox Home," sixth of the Ten Oxherding Pictures, the master Kuo'an (or Kuo-an; J., Kakuan) wrote,

Astride an ox, eagerly wending the way home—
note after note of the nomad flute drifts in the evening mist.
One rhythm, just a single song, boundless in its meaning!
For a zhiyin, what need to drum your lips and teeth?[6]

What need, that is, to talk? We'd lapse into literalism if we inter-preted this to mean that, with a zhiyin, one never needs to speak. Nonsense! Kuo'an is evoking the satisfaction of reaching an under-standing that goes beyond words, but a zhiyin knows the tune what-ever medium it comes by—by zither or flute, by silent expression, as in Kāśyapa's case, by a look or touch, by text, or these days maybe by text message.

What would it take for us to become zhiyin? Commenting on the incisive response that won Zhaozhou acclaim as a zhiyin, the emi-nent master Yuanwu offers an observation worth noting: "…when Nanquan raised the head, Zhaozhou immediately understood the tail; when it is brought up, he immediately knows where it comes down."[7] Yuanwu's comment derives, like the zhiyin metaphor, from a non-Buddhist element that Chan incorporated from its culture—a Confucian requirement for disciples to exhibit the ability to intuit a master's intention rather than awaiting an explanation. In the *Analects*, Confucius flatly states, "If I raise one corner, and they don't produce the other three, I don't repeat myself."[8] Boiled down to four words—"Raise one, discern three"—this theme reverber-ates through the Zen tradition. Yuanwu sounds it insistently from the very start of his magisterial *Blue Cliff Record*: "To understand three when one is raised, to judge precisely at a glance—this is the everyday food and drink of a patchrobe monk."[9]

Absent this cultural foundation, Zen teachers in the West prob-ably can't require an equal acuity of their students, but all of us, teachers and students alike, might on our own aspire to meet the old standard. To know the tune of Bodhidharma and Huineng, of Dongshan and Linji, of Yunmen and Pang Lingzhao, of Guishan and Liu Tiemo, of Dōgen and Hakuin, we need to come up with three when they "raise one corner" for us through records of their teaching. If we can't discern whether the tune they're plucking is about the towering peaks or flowing waters, in a real sense it's Game Over. We can't expect them to come back from the dead to reiterate their teachings for our benefit, much less to explain them.

Here's a corner turned up for us in the record of Furong Daokai (or Fu-jung Tao-k'ai; J., Fuyō Dōkai), an important eleventh- and twelfth-century Caodong master:

> After Furong took up residence [i.e., began teaching], a monk asked, "The tune of a nomad flute doesn't descend the five-note scale. Its melody goes beyond the blue sky. Please, Master, play it."
>
> Furong said, "A wooden rooster crows at midnight; an iron phoenix shrieks at dawn."
>
> "If so," the monk continued, "a single phrase of the song contains a thousand ancient melodies. The entire hall of monks—they all know the tune."
>
> The master replied, "A tongueless child can carry the harmony."[10]

Locate the three missing corners, and you can hum at least a few bars of Furong's music.

Important as it may be to "know the tune" of the Dharma ancestors, our interest extends further. For an aspiring zhiyin, the horizon is infinite. Who among us can claim to understand as clearly as we'd like the "tunes" of our partners, children, friends, neighbors, fellow workers—to perceive the nuances of what they say or leave unsaid, their facial expressions, their gestures, their body language, their private interests? The ability to intuit such cues, "to understand three when one is raised," is key to responding to them appropriately and beneficially, and I suspect that may be what persuaded translators many centuries ago to give Avalokiteśvara, bodhisattva of compassion, the Chinese names Guanyin and Guanshiyin (or Kuan-yin and Kuan-shih-yin; J., Kannon and Kanzeon).[11] The yin of those epithets is the same yin in zhiyin. As the bodhisattva who contemplates (guan) the "tunes" of the world (shi), she's the one best suited to locate beings in anguish and to answer their cries.

The zhiyin image corresponds to another story our Chan forebears drew on to illustrate the phenomenon of heartmind-to-heartmind communication and to characterize the challenges of understanding one another fully. This story, from the *Nirvāna Sūtra*, centers on a royal attendant who could unerringly discern what his king wanted when he called for *saindhava*. Since that one word could mean salt, water, a bowl, or a horse, the attendant had to know the king's heartmind intimately, as clearly as if it were his own. Accordingly, Chan adopted *saindhava* as a shorthand for knowing the ineffable fact of buddha-nature and for excellence in a potential successor.[12]

An old, much-loved story demonstrates both these aspects. One day, Yangshan (or Yang-shan; J., Kyōzan) entered the quarters of his master, Guishan (or Kuei-shan; J., Isan), and found him in bed. He'd come to pose a question, but Guishan turned his face to the wall. Undeterred, Yangshan asked why he'd turned away:

> The master got up and said, "I've just had a dream. Locate its source, and look into it for me." Yangshan went and got a basin of water for him to wash his face.
>
> Soon Xiangyan [or Hsiang-yen; J., Kyōgen] also arrived to ask a question. The master said, "I've just had a dream. This honorable fellow traced its source. Now you help look into it for me." Xiangyan came back right away with a cup of tea.
>
> The master said, "Your insight makes you two stand out like cranes among chickens."[13]

The tradition absorbed from Chinese culture a third metaphor for such transparency and mutuality of heartmind: the *fu* or "tally," as the character is commonly translated. Combining the bamboo radical with a word meaning "give to" or "hand over to," it denoted a length of bamboo usually, sometimes another material, that served in days of yore as a means to ensure the validity of an order, contract, or commission. A fu was broken in two and half given to each of the two parties to an agreement. When the fu was later rejoined, the exact matching of its splintered edges gave assurance that the transaction was legitimate. The act of making such a match was also fu, in a verbal sense—the fu "tallied"—and it extended metaphorically to include agreement between people, the "meeting of minds."[14]

Usages of this kind appear in Chinese texts of diverse schools, including the Confucian and Daoist lines,[15] and they occur in Buddhist texts by the early fifth century, if not sooner, already incorporated into a claim of a secret Dharma transmission, independent of words and outside the sūtras.[16] Chan adopted the metaphor and worked it hard, frequently with reference to a disciple's breakthrough to "tally" with a master and with the Dharma itself. Zen continued the image, as in Keizan Jōkin's account of a wordless first meeting between two legendary Indian predecessors:

> The Fifteenth Ancestor, Kānadeva Ārya, paid a formal visit to the *mahāsattva* Nāgārjuna to ask to become a disciple. Perceiving that he was a wise person, Nāgārjuna began by sending his attendant with a bowl brimful of water to place before Kānadeva's seat. When he saw it, Kānadeva immediately took out a needle, cast it into the water, and presented this. Meeting, they joyously tallied and understood.[17]

Of course, not all encounters could have such wondrous, happy results. One of Chan and Zen's foundational tales, about Bodhidharma's meeting with Emperor Wu, registers a consequential flop.[18] The emperor "didn't tally," the story says, so instead of garnering imperial support for his mission to convey the heartmind of the Buddha, the Indian sage retired to a cave and from there, from the bottom up, his message spread throughout the land.

These stories and many others in the tradition use the word 契*qi* (or *ch'i*; J., *kai*) for meetings of mind (and failures of same). Masters also employed it to express the tallying of conceptual opposites, the perfect meshing of dualities or dichotomies that people tend to consider irreconcilable, such as true and false, outside and inside, good and bad. A famous example is the *Cantong qi* (or *Ts'an-t'ung ch'i*; J., *Sandōkai*), "The Tallying of Difference and Sameness," a doctrinal verse attributed to the major eighth-century Chan master Shitou (or Shih-t'ou; J., Sekitō).[19] It joins darkness and light in a seamless tallying that I'll take up in a subsequent chapter.

One more thing: in old China, certain fu were considered evidence of heavenly favor—of one's having "tallied" with celestial powers and thus received the Mandate of Heaven. Some of the holdings in the baozang, the imperial storehouse of treasures, fell under the fu designation, as did talismans that masters in the shamanic stream of Daoism carried as tokens of authority and utilized in rituals to call for divine intervention. This sense of fu, too, had a corresponding aspect in Chan and Zen, where possession of iconic items that had come down through the lineage—a robe, a portrait, a set of bowls— lent masters not just legitimacy but an aura of power, of bearing the mandate of buddhas and ancestors.

Finally, as useful as the metaphors of zhiyin, saindhava, and fu are to convey a sense of the heartmind-to-heartmind transmission so central to the Chan and Zen tradition, unfortunately they also lend themselves to two serious misunderstandings. The lesser of these is the notion that training in the tradition culminates in mental telepathy. Although classical Buddhist texts list an ability to read others' minds among the supranormal powers of a buddha, Chan and Zen downplay such wizardly accomplishments. The "tune" that a master and a successor must know (and recognize that they know in common) is the music of buddha-nature, pure and simple. Evidence of their mutual insight may take many forms, and they may recognize others who "know the tune" as well. In any case, the three metaphors have nothing whatsoever to do with an occult ability to read minds.

The greater misunderstanding concerns our tradition's teachings about heartmind itself. In these metaphors and generally in the stories about its "transmission," heartmind is associated with people, so one readily comes to think of it as exclusive to humans. Nope. But that's a huge subject, best dealt with elsewhere. As a placeholder, here's a gem from the eccentric, eighteenth-century Kyoto personage known in late life as Baisaō, the Old Tea Seller. Formerly a Zen monk, he'd become a sort of wayside sage, eking out a living by pouring tea for passersby. One day, he carried his tea equipment (his "Twelve Teachers") to Rinsen-ji, the riverside temple dedicated to Musō Kokushi, and to commemorate the four-hundredth anniversary of that celebrated teacher's death, he heated some water, brewed a cup of tea, and offered it with a poem, ending:

> You taught seven emperors
> using an ageless tune.
> Here the very river water
> flowing before the hall
> is an understanding friend.[20]

At this point, I suppose it'll come as no surprise that the phrase rendered here as "understanding friend" is zhiyin. Baisaō pops his real surprise by crediting the river water itself with knowing the ageless tune the National Teacher had sung to the emperors. Obviously Baisaō knew it, too—and what about you? It's an awfully bland tune but not too bland for you to hear, not too bland to bring delight.

4 | Cutting and Polishing:
A Matter of Character

In the early 1980s, it became apparent that teachers at several promi-nent American Zen centers had engaged in gross misconduct—covert sexual affairs, lavish personal spending, abuse of authority, heavy drinking—and that a reckoning with ethical issues was overdue. Revelation of the teachers' failings rocked not only the communities directly involved but virtually all of us who felt deeply committed to, and invested in, the tradition. Aitken Rōshi's personal uprightness spared us a crisis in the Diamond Sangha, but spurred on by grief about his colleagues' behavior and the anguish and disruption he witnessed during visits to sanghas at the center of the troubles, he began avidly seeking resources that would help address issues of morality and character in a manner consistent with practice.

Often before the scandals and more often after, Aitken Rōshi quoted a dictum by Yamada Rōshi: "The practice of Zen is the per-fection of character." Following this came a lament that his beloved teacher said little more on the subject, never spelling out what "perfection of character" meant or articulating the way Zen practice affects character—or at least *ought* to affect character. To remedy the perceived deficit, besides seeking out Buddhist precedents Aitken Rōshi explored Christian teachings on character, taking interest par-ticularly in Roman Catholic methods for the "formation" (actually *trans*formation) of character. Discussing this with a Catholic friend, noted Benedictine brother David Steindl-Rast, he said,

Whatever process of formation there is in a Zen monastery is incidental, almost casual. I've heard more than one abbot use the image of a rock tumbler as a metaphor for the beneficial effect that life in a monastery has on a monk's character: in the ordinary life of the monastery, people are thrown together over a long period of time, rubbing against each other, so to speak, and polishing their characters in the process, as stones in a tumbler become smooth by rubbing against one another. That's as far as the tradition of formation goes in Zen.[1]

Imagine my surprise to learn, not long after this statement was published, that the image of "mutual polishing" has an ancient pedigree and represents a coherent system, far from casual, for cultivating good character. It's imparted in Japanese monasteries under the catchphrase *sessa takuma*, which appears in the Confucian *Analects* and ultimately derives from the *Shijing*, or *Classic of Poetry*, a text from the earliest stratum of Chinese literature.[2] Of the precious items in the family treasure house, this is one that we in the West have a truly urgent need to rediscover.

In the *Shijing*, the expression figures in a couplet describing a highly refined youth—"as if carved, as if polished, / as if cut, as if ground."[3] Confucians made this shorthand for personal cultivation across the board, and in much of society, certainly among the educated, it was broadly accepted as an imperative lifelong task. We shouldn't be surprised, then, to find reference to these lines in the earliest surviving regulations for Chan monasteries, compiled in 1103,[4] or in countless other materials from the tradition—masters' records, admonitory letters, poems, calligraphy.

Further study brought home to me as never before the enormous debt Chan and Zen owe to Confucianism. That our traditions arose and matured in Confucian cultures hadn't eluded me, but neither instruction by Japanese and American masters nor my own reading had made plain to me how thoroughly Confucian thought and practices suffused Chan and Zen institutions and how powerfully the Confucian influences, in particular, shaped the tradition's delineation of proper relationships and character. I'd understood Confucianism as having opposed and resisted Buddhism, which indeed it did in certain ways, at times aggressively. But Confucianism so pervaded Chinese society that it also formed a sort of natural or inescapable substrate for Chan and did much the same for Zen in Japan. While Aitken Rōshi recognized that Zen people in Japan took "their moral guidelines" from Confucianism, he understood that as a failure, manifesting a lack of specifically Buddhist attention to ethics.[5]

How Confucian influence actually guided the lives of Chan and Zen practitioners can be seen in the autobiography of the late Master Sheng Yen, a prominent figure in modern Taiwanese and Western Chan. He recalls that his upbringing in a Chinese village "instilled a deep sense of the Confucian values of loyalty and responsibility" by the time he turned fourteen and began his life as a Buddhist novice. In the monastery, rather than diminishing, Confucian impact increased. Assigned a Confucian tutor, he learned "that to become a moral person one had to regulate one's thoughts and behavior and to act with moderation and decorum, to carefully weigh the pros and cons of any action" and not to "live only for oneself." He embraced this principle:

> If you're a layperson you have primary responsibility to your family; if you are a monastic, that responsibility is directed toward your monastery. Confucius urges us to become useful. He teaches a path of interaction with the world that is gentle and subtle and is about cultivating ourselves so that we have beneficent harmonious relations with the people around us. The Confucian sense of responsibility and loyalty would shape my life and fit hand-in-glove with the Buddhism that I absorbed.[6]

When Yamada Rōshi spoke of perfection of character, no doubt he had similar virtues in mind, and evidently it didn't occur to him (or to many other Asian masters) that it was necessary to educate Westerners about them. On the receiving end of his instruction, we had some native understandings of good character that, along with a mainly unconscious universalism—people are essentially the same everywhere, right?—made it easy to suppose that we understood what he meant when he referred to character. But Western understandings of character derive, inevitably, from precedents and influences very different from those that shaped him or Master Sheng Yen. Rather than presuming that Chan and Zen understandings about character had much in common with our own, we might more logically have anticipated significant differences.

Complicating East-West communication on the subject was the way writers presented the tradition's orientation to ethical concerns. All too often in introducing Western readers to Chan and Zen, they dismissed social mores as the products of such dualistic fallacies as good and bad, right and wrong, that any awakened practitioner would have jettisoned. Part of the responsibility for this misconception rests with D. T. Suzuki. In the first volume of his *Essays in Zen Buddhism*, published in 1927 and thus one of the earliest books about Zen in English, Suzuki flatly asserted that for an enlightened person,

> ...propositions will be true—that is, living—because they are in accordance with his spiritual insight; and his actions will permit no external standard of judgment; so long as they are the inevitable outflow of his inner life, they are good, even holy. The direct issue of this interpretation of Enlightenment will be the upholding of absolute spiritual freedom in every way.[7]

What a claim, what an offer—absolute spiritual freedom in every way! As if this weren't bold or definite enough, Suzuki went on to declare that Mahāyāna Buddhists "advocated perfect freedom of spirit, even after the fashions of antinomians. If the spirit were pure, no acts of the body could spoil it."[8] Theravāda Buddhists he considered rule bound, unable "to enter a liquor-shop" or a house of ill repute.

> But to the Mahāyānists all kinds of 'expediency' or 'devices' were granted if they were fully enlightened and had their spirits thor-

oughly purified. They were living in a realm beyond good and evil, and as long as they were there, no acts of theirs could be classified and judged according to the ordinary measure of ethics; they were neither moral nor immoral. These relative terms had no application in a kingdom governed by free spirits which soared above the relative world of differences and oppositions.[9]

Suzuki Sensei borrowed the term *antinomians* from Christianity, where it named a sect preaching that God's grace released the elect from the need to adhere to moral laws, and he later regretted applying it to the freedom that flowed from awakening. Seeing that some of his readers and most ardent fans had taken such statements as justification for transgressing social norms, in 1960 he made a public about-face, writing that "Zen is decidedly not…antinomian" and explaining,

> What Zen emphasizes most strongly in its disciplinary practice is the attainment of spiritual freedom, not the revolt against conventionalism. The freedom may sometimes consist merely in eating when one is hungry and resting when one is tired; at other times, and probably frequently, [it consists] in *not* eating when one is hungry and *not* resting when one is tired. So it is, that Zen may find more of its great followers among the "conformists" than among the rebellious and boisterous nonconformists.[10]

From early on, Suzuki had foreseen a risk of Zen degenerating into what he termed "libertinism," and he'd cautioned against it repeatedly, but evidently he overlooked the possibility that his own trumpeting of spiritual freedom might increase the hazard. He also seems to have overlooked the fact that, during his lifetime and even to this day, Westerners likely to take up Zen could be classed as "nonconformists." Sitting silently for long hours, reciting old Asian texts, studying kōans—these are hardly common behaviors in the West.

At any rate, by the time he issued his clarification, the damage was done. He and fellow enthusiasts had established a lasting image of Zen masters as people exempt from any "external standard of judgment," at liberty to behave however they pleased. It took hold especially in the counterculture of the 1960s and '70s, its grip on American imaginations strengthened by writers who lacked Suzuki's experience with the actualities of Zen practice. Chief among them was Jack Kerouac, whose romantic view of Zen permeates his 1958 bestseller *Dharma Bums*.

All this helped create a climate in which dubious conduct could pass for liberated activity and even for Dharma teaching itself, but contributing to the confusion was a perfectly legitimate, longstanding aspect of Chan and Zen and of prior Buddhist schools: the doctrine of "emptiness" (Ch., *kong* or *k'ung*; J., *kū*). I've put the word in quotation marks not to devalue it, only to mark its canonical status and its nature as metaphor. For centuries, this name for a nameless nonentity has proven helpful to some and extremely problematic for many, and I'm not going to launch an assault on its mysteries here. For now, it'll suffice to say that teachings on this subject destabilize all concepts and, in doing so, open a pathway to "libertinism." Ancient and authentic Buddhist expressions like "*Saṃsāra* is exactly *nirvāṇa*,"[11] which have always been susceptible to misunderstandings and corrupt construals, became more dangerous than ever when they fell on the ears of ethically disoriented young seekers overseas.

Had we known to explore the subject in those early decades of Western Buddhism, we'd have found ample resources on character and conduct, dating back to the emergence of Chan as a distinct school of Buddhism. In the tenth century, for instance, the acclaimed master Fayan (or Fa-yen; J., Hōgen) wrote in dismay about the character failings of fellow Chan teachers and practitioners, making express reference to the terms for personal refinement quoted above from the *Classic of Poetry* and the Confucian *Analects*:

> Those who undertake inquiry and mastery [of dao], when entering a monastery, must select a wise teacher and, secondly, close and bright friends. A teacher is crucial to point out the road;

bright friends are prized for cutting and polishing....[The wor-
thies of old] would admonish an intimate who slipped up, using
the vantage points of human and heavenly beings. Afterward,
they would raise up the family seal and widely disseminate true
methods, detailing the positive and negative points of prior generations and lashing out at misunderstandings of public cases
[kōans].[12]

Besides applying the ancient lapidary metaphor of personal refinement, Fayan links his vision of Chan training to Confucian teachings by emphasizing the necessity of finding good companions and
the crucial role they play in correcting personal flaws. Respectful
remonstration is integral to human cultivation in the Confucian
scheme of human development, and obviously Fayan saw it also as
integral to forming the kind of Chan practitioner who would carry
the tradition reputably into the future.

By Fayan's time, an ascendant Chan discourse of sudden awakening had marginalized discussion of protracted and incremental
personal refinement, yet even masters closely identified with this
"doctrine of suddenness" didn't stop declaring the necessity of long-
term training. Linji, one such master, emphasized the compatibility
of gradual cultivation with abrupt awakening when recalling for
his monks the course of his own career, concluding, "Not that my
mother bore me, and just like that I understood! On the contrary,
there was physically digging into it, refining, polishing, and one
day, all at once, realizing it for myself."[13]

Chan grew to dominate Buddhist institutions in the two centuries
after Fayan called out his colleagues for their shortcomings, and the
problems that had concerned him grew along with it. Perhaps, as
one scholar has summed up the case, its success had "attract[ed]
the wrong kind of people, or rather...too many people [had] come
with the wrong aspirations."[14] Whether that was so or not, rapid
expansion meant that seasoned Chan leaders were in short supply
at a time when increased access to property and power exposed its
masters to temptations as never before.

To combat slippage in ethical standards, two reform-minded twelfth-century masters, Dahui and Zhuan (or Chu-an; J., Chikuan), published a selection of statements they regarded as exemplifying the tradition's norms for personal conduct. This text, *Precious Advice for the Chan Forest*, lends no support to antinomian readings of Chan mores and, quite the contrary, furnishes evidence that sustained refinement of character remained the pattern and the hope:

> Lingyuan said, "When you cut and polish a stone, as you grind and rub you do not see it decreasing, yet with time it will be worn away. When you plant a tree and take care of it, you do not see it growing, but in time it gets big. When you accumulate virtue with continued practice, you do not see the good of it, but in time it will function. If you abandon right and go against truth, you do not see the harm it does, but in time you will come to naught. When students finally think this through and put it into practice, they will develop great capacity and engender fine reputations. This is the way that has not changed, now or ever."[15]

Dahui and Zhuan belonged to the Linji lineage and drew their *Precious Advice* heavily, if not quite exclusively, from masters in that succession, yet their message appealed to Confucian norms common in Chan, irrespective of sectarian affiliations. A century later, when Dōgen Zenji carried the Caodong transmission to Japan, he sang from the same songbook and utilized the same ancient jewel-buffing trope:

> Although each of us inherently possesses dao, personally attaining dao always depends on group conditions. Although individuals may be astute in their own ways, their practice of dao relies on group strength. Accordingly, monastics today should practice and seek dao in unity. Jewels become beautiful through polishing, and people become genuine through training. What jewel is lustrous from the start? What person excels from the beginning? You must always keep polishing and keep training.[16]

In laying such stress on sustained and collaborative training, these masters made it clear that awakening experiences alone won't eradicate our failings or obviate the need for continuing cultivation of character. Notice, though, that Dōgen's statement balances exhortation to practice with acknowledgment that we all "inherently possess" dao. Keizan Jōkin, cofounder of the Sōtō Zen tradition along with Dōgen, underscored this innate aspect of dao in a two-line verse playing on the very terms usually reserved for personal refinement:

> The water is clear all the way to the bottom;
> without cutting or polishing, its own brilliance shines.[17]

Think of this as a Daoist motif in our traditions, in keeping with teachings of the self-so (*ziran*) and no exertion (*wuwei*), yet fully interwoven with the Confucian motif of sustained individual and group training. Superficially, the two seem irreconcilably opposed, but Chan and Zen have embraced them in tandem, treating them as complementary and harmonious themes.

The two occur contrapuntally in an exchange between the illustrious early Chan master Nanquan and a young monk who would go on to become the master Dongshan. Spotting the talent of the newly arrived monk, Nanquan exclaimed, "Though still wet behind the ears, this lad is worthy of cutting and polishing!" whereupon Dongshan replied, "Heshang, don't flatten the good and make it worthless!"[18] Often the two themes converge in a single statement, as when the modern Rinzai master Oda Sessō urged his assembly, "The perfect way is without difficulty. Strive hard!"[19]

In the interest of tailoring instruction to their disciples' needs, as a matter of personality, or to serve sectarian purposes, masters have given the two themes differing degrees of emphasis, but the fine-just-as-we-are position that I've called "Daoist" seldom more than briefly eclipses the "Confucian" promptings toward ongoing refinement of character. Indeed, even canonical Daoist texts give a nod here and there to the project of character change, and Chan latched onto one of those affirmations from the *Daodejing* itself: "A great vessel reaches completion late."[20] Fayan closed his admonishments of errant Chan students by alluding to this line, promising that those who heeded his counsel would become "great vessels,"[21] and down through the centuries, people capable of conveying the tradition to future generations have been hailed as "Dharma vessels."

—

I hope the foregoing examples of the insights and language that Chan incorporated from Confucian and Daoist sources suffice to demonstrate how heavily our tradition drew upon those sources as it developed. Although Chan, Confucian, and Daoist leaders vied to distinguish their teachings when competing for patronage, many of them also endorsed a position shorthanded as "the three teachings united as one" or "three teachings, a single result"[22]—a position, in other words, that the three traditions are completely compatible or at least functionally equivalent. The heavy influence of indigenous Chinese thought is manifest even in masters who rejected it. These include Dōgen, who explicitly condemned the proposition that the three teachings are one yet whose words make it plain, in the words of one scholar, that he "takes for granted…an essentially Confucian moral universe."[23]

It seems indisputable that a double distortion occurred in the transmission of Zen from Asia: both a gross misrepresentation of its historic concern for conduct and character and either ignorance or willful disregard of the way it has addressed that concern. Events have revealed the dangers of overlooking these aspects of the tradition and the folly of buying into the notion that awakening puts a person's behavior beyond question, furnishing a passport to zany, self-serving, transgressive, or abusive behavior.

I'm not proposing that Westerners who choose to take the path of Zen must also study the tenets of Daoism and Confucianism, but I've found it profoundly worthwhile to acquaint myself with the classic teachings of those traditions and certainly recommend that others do likewise. At a minimum, it behooves us to see how deeply they're stitched into the fabric of our tradition and to ponder the consequences of stripping them out. Particularly because Zen destabilizes ideas of right and wrong, good and bad, we need to consider very seriously how we'll orient our conduct without the moral compass those concepts have provided for members of our society.

To answer this need, as I noted earlier, my own teacher turned to standards and practices borrowed from forms of Buddhism predating Chan and largely set aside by Zen, and he frankly acknowledged that his search for and appropriation of these means reflected his Christian youth: "...because I grew up with that [Christian] kind of worldview, I sought it in Buddhism and found it there."[24] In this way, he created a sort of buddho-biblical matrix in which to cultivate issues of ethics and character. Other American teachers have resorted to psychology as a means to plug the gaps left by neglect of traditional "cutting and polishing." A more promising approach, it seems to me, is to address the deficit by framing character and conduct in terms of ordinary traditional values like generosity, kindness, humility, integrity, trustworthiness, obligation, and responsibility. How these can stand up to rampant individualism and materialism, under conditions of distraction and haste, is anybody's guess, but at least they have robust precedents in our tradition as well as in age-old cultures worldwide.

In any event, I suspect a period of study, experimentation, and discussion will be necessary before Zen communities in the West arrive at clarity about the place ethics hold in Zen training, about the way truly "great vessels" actually conduct their lives, and about how to shape such vessels under the fraught circumstances in which we find ourselves. Beyond that will come the challenge of integrating a Western-adapted process of cutting and polishing into the Dharma to produce a synthesis as fitting, though perhaps not as transparent, as the one that our Asian ancestors fashioned. Of course, our situation differs in significant ways from theirs: our task is to retrofit an ancient Eastern tradition to succeed in a modern Western society, whereas theirs was to create a new entity custom-tailored for their society. They also were able to spread that work over a span of several centuries, a luxury of time we're not likely to enjoy.

Still, let's not rush to conclusions. Few of us in the West (again, I include myself) know our tradition intimately, inside and out, and lacking that degree of familiarity with it, how can we assume that we're competent to make major changes? Aitken Rōshi used to say, "Don't monkey with the bandwagon unless you know how to blow the horn!" which seems like a precept to bear in mind as the venerable Dharma vehicle rumbles into the future. We may find solace in hearing or, better yet, realizing that the freight it's designed to transport—the reality too plain to describe or depict or even praise sufficiently—is itself indestructible, but not so the vehicle. A completely contingent thing, subject to decline as much as everything else, its continued viability depends on those of us who love it enough not just to train diligently but also to study it well and to innovate with great care.

5 | A Good, Hard Look in the Mirror

Mirrors were highly prized in days of old. Until production of flat glass was perfected in the nineteenth century, mirrors were rare and expensive, almost always made of metal, and frequently ornate. In Asia and elsewhere, they were owned mainly by elites. This made them objects of interest, if not awe, and surely objects of desire. In premodern societies, mirrors became favorite subjects for painters and seemingly irresistible metaphors for poets, philosophers, storytellers, and others all around the world. Masters of our tradition were definitely among the enthusiasts.[1]

Medieval Chan and Zen teachers and writers gathered such a large and varied collection of mirror metaphors, in fact, that they could be seen as proprietors of a veritable hall of mirrors. Their holdings included the mirror of heaven, taking in everything that happens from its vantage point on high, and the mirror of karma, hanging in the court of Yama, the lord of death, where it reflected a person's lifetime of misdeeds. They also possessed a pair of imperial mirrors—those of the Qin emperor, with x-ray-like powers, and of the Yellow Emperor, which would subdue the mightiest adversary the instant he held it up.[2] Add another four mirrors to these, the ones that our masters spoke about most often: ancient, round, bright, and broken.[3] I'd be remiss not to mention as well the jeweled (or precious or treasure) mirror, mentioned less often but featured in a poem highly esteemed in our tradition.[4]

Of course, there really aren't any mirrors; the metaphors are no more than that. Yet each of them represents the ancestors' attempt to reveal an important attribute of the phenomenon that they thought of as 心鏡 *xinjing* (or *hsin-ching*; J., *shinkyō*), the heartmind mirror or the mirror of heartmind. The underlying concept, of awareness as a form of mirroring, has deep roots in both Indian Buddhism and Daoist thought, and the metaphor continues to find application of this sort even today, in neuroscience. Evidence of neuronal firing that occurs whether a research subject performs an activity or merely *observes* that same activity being performed has led to identification of "mirror neurons" in the brains of humans, other primates, and members of nonprimate species. Intriguing as these discoveries are, and remarkable as it seems that neuroscientists have chosen the same metaphor to describe their findings, it would be a mistake to suppose that Buddhist and Daoist sages "knew all about" brain function thousands of years ago.[5] The convergence in wording does demonstrate, however, the continuing power of the mirror as a metaphor of how our minds work.

I haven't attempted to trace the genesis or evolution of mirror imagery in Buddhism—a very complicated problem that needn't concern us here—but one element in the mix was the doctrine that, with profound awakening, a buddha comes into five kinds of wisdom, among them a Great Perfect Mirror Wisdom.[6] Such wisdom, it was said, enables a buddha to survey the whole world with absolute clarity. A text from Chan's formative period makes a point of characterizing Great Perfect Mirror Wisdom as nondual besides displaying other qualities that came to be associated with xinjing, the mirror of heartmind:

> It is like a clear mirror hung in space. All the myriad images appear in it, but this bright mirror never thinks, "I can make images appear," nor do the images say, "We are born from the mirror." Since there is neither subject nor object, we call this wisdom the Great Mirror Wisdom.[7]

The metaphor of the heartmind mirror naturally gave rise to the secondary metaphor of *cleaning* the mirror. In one of the first Buddhist texts circulated in Chinese, Śākyamuni Buddha teaches a monk that he'll have to work at buffing the mirror if he wants to know "the truth of the Way" and the course of his prior births: "One must maintain the aspiration to practice. It is like polishing a mirror. When the tarnish is gone, the mirror shines, and one sees one's own form."[8] In the sūtra, heartmind loses its innate luminosity due to intrusive elements known as "adventitious afflictions." In Chinese translation, these became "visiting dust irritants,"[9] and early Chan put that image into heavy rotation as it addressed the operation of xinjing in life and practice.

The mirror-cleaning metaphor's assimilation into Chan instruction is apparent from the "Song of Realizing the Way," the foundational poem attributed to Yongjia that I quoted earlier, which unreservedly stresses the necessity of wiping the mirror. Near its beginning comes the exhortation,

> Dust gathers on a mirror that's not cleaned.
> Right now, you must make it completely clear![10]

Returning to the metaphor later, the poem leaves no doubt that the mirror under discussion is that of Great Perfect Mirror Wisdom:

> The mirror of heartmind shines brilliantly, without obstruction,
>   its light limitlessly pervading worlds countless as sands of the
>   Ganges.
> The dense weave of the ten-thousand phenomena is reflected
>   therein,
> each of them fully illumined, no inside, no outside.[11]

When the metaphor turns up a third time, it's to reaffirm both the necessity of cleaning the mirror and the absence from its face of any subject-object dichotomy:

Heartmind as perceiver, things as perceived—
both are like smudges on a mirror.
Once they're completely removed, the light begins
    to show.[12]

It didn't take long, however, for Chan to launch a critique of mirror-cleansing rhetoric. In the vast literature of our tradition, undoubtedly the best-known story concerning mirrors is one in which Huineng, supposedly an illiterate layman, advances this critique in the context of a sort of Dharma poetry contest set up by Chan's Fifth Ancestor. The monastery's head monk, considered the hands-down favorite to win the competition and thus to succeed the Fifth Ancestor, posts this poem:

The body is the bodhi tree,
the heartmind like a bright mirror on a stand.
Time after time, diligently wipe it clean,
never allowing dust to alight.[13]

In the dead of night, Huineng dictates a poem using the same terms but demolishing the rationale for clearing dust from the xinjing:

From the start, bodhi has no tree,
the bright mirror likewise no stand.
With buddha-nature always utterly clear,
where could any dust alight?

Though the Fifth Ancestor publicly praises the head monk's practical approach to the topic, he secretly recognizes Huineng as his rightful successor—a momentous decision outrageous to his community, occasioning Huineng's later dialogue with senior monk Ming, recounted in chapter 2.

Doubts about the historicity of these events abound, but the story starkly, unquestionably marks a turning point in the tradition, emphatically aligning it with awakening to the emptiness of body and mind while denigrating devotion to the project of sustaining spotless mental clarity. Later versions of the story strengthen the accent on emptiness, amending Huineng's third line to read, "Fundamentally, there's not a single thing." From this perspective, the universe is dust-free by nature. Even in Huineng's poem, however, the mirror remains intact, and its metaphorical use continued in Chan and Zen writings, growing in frequency and nuance. What effectively came to an end was uncritical reference to cleaning the mirror. A master three centuries after Huineng put the point succinctly: "One only streaks the mirror by polishing it."[14]

—

A second very well-known story provides a sense of how the tradition downstream from Huineng handled the matter of mirror polishing. Here, Nanyue (or Nan-yueh; J., Nangaku), one of Huineng's Dharma heirs, instructs Mazu Daoyi (or Ma-tsu Tao-I; J., Baso Dōitsu), who would in time become his own great successor:

> There was a diligent monk named Daoyi residing at Quanfa Temple, doing zazen day after day. The master, knowing that he was a Dharma vessel, went and questioned him, saying, "Great worthy, what's your intention in zazen?"
>
> Daoyi said, "I intend to make a buddha." With that, the master picked up a brick and started grinding it on a stone in front of the hermitage.
>
> "Why are you grinding that brick?" Daoyi asked.
>
> "I'm grinding it to make a mirror," the master answered.
>
> Daoyi said, "How can you make a mirror by grinding a brick?"
>
> Nanyue replied, "How can you make a buddha by doing zazen?"[15]

Grinding a brick seems significantly different from wiping a mirror free of dust, but the Huineng story has loud and clear echoes in this exchange. They're audible both in Nanyue's reference to a mirror and in the word I've translated as "grinding," which may also mean "polishing" and often has been translated that way in versions of this story.[16]

It's also the word used in another story illustrating the refinements to the mirror imagery—more specifically, in this instance, to the notion of removing dust from the mirror's face—that developed after Chan embraced Huineng's critique. Somebody asked one of Xuansha's Dharma heirs, Guotai (or K'uo-tai; J., Kokutai),

> "When the ancient mirror hasn't yet been polished, what about that?"
> The master said, "The ancient mirror."
> "What about after polishing?" the student asked.
> The master said, "The ancient mirror."[17]

The mirror in question precedes any "polishing" one may do and in no way depends on it. On the contrary, the antiquity of the xinjing implies that its existence precedes and outlasts you, me, and any other entity that could be imagined to tend or have it. A line from the Zen phrase books hints that we might better say that *it* has *us*, along with the rest of the world: "The myriad-ridged green mountains are stored up in the ancient mirror."[18]

An episode from the record of Xuefeng (or Hsueh-feng; J., Seppō), a leading ninth-century master, exposes a defect in the ancient mirror, yet what appears in the looking glass seems clear as ever. When he and the whole assembly were walking to work in the fields one day, the record tells us, they came upon a troop of macaques. Xuefeng exclaimed,

> "These beasts! Each bears an ancient mirror on its back, and they break off the seedheads of this mountain monk's grain."
> A monk inquired, "Since remotest kalpas, it hasn't had a name. Why designate it an ancient mirror?"
> "A flaw's been created," Xuefeng replied.
> "Why so hasty?" said the monk. "I don't even know what you're talking about."
> "This old monk has transgressed," said the master.[19]

Caught red-handed, Xuefeng cops a plea. But what's his offense, and why is he so hot to confess it? Is it a crime, after all, just to name the mirror? Dōgen takes this story as a focus of his lengthy disquisition on the ancient mirror, loosing upon us an extraordinary shower of questions, starting with what kind of paste the macaques used to secure their mirrors. He goes on:

> Are the backs of the old mirrors the monkeys that they bear on their backs? The backs of the old mirrors are borne on the backs of the old mirrors; the backs of the monkeys are borne on the backs of the monkeys. The words "each bears one" are not an empty contrivance; they are a saying that says it right. Therefore, is it old mirrors? Is it monkeys? In the end, what can we say? Are we monkeys or not monkeys? Whom can we ask? That we are monkeys is not something we know, not something others know. That we are ourselves, our gropings do not reach.[20]

But what marvelous gropings! How resplendently they show up in the ancient mirror! (Sure, *mea culpa, mea maxima culpa*.) I certainly agree that our gropings don't reach, but who ever said they needed to?

Fortunately, the ancient mirror registers our deeds and misdeeds with utter impartiality, in the same manner as that great mirror high overhead: "The mirror of heaven has no self-interest; / it reflects what exists before machinations"[21]—that is, before the wheels of thought begin to crank, judging, correcting, justifying. Hakuin Zenji saw such unmediated, impartial perception as a trait of the very teacher who declared xinjing dust-free: "Are you not aware… that Master Huineng is a timeless old mirror in which the realms of heaven and hell and the lands of purity and impurity are all reflected equally?" Hakuin regarded this as a defining feature not just of a family hero like the Sixth Ancestor but also of any worthy teacher: "See how a clear-sighted Zen master is able to perceive everything at a single glance without the slightest error? Just like the famous mirror of the Qin emperor, which reflected all one's vital organs."[22]

Of the many ways writers of the tradition have extolled the clarity of the heartmind mirror, probably the most often repeated is "A foreigner comes, and a foreigner appears; a native comes, and a native appears." Dōgen quotes the saying that way in his ancient mirror screed but quotes it differently in a presentation before his assembly, reducing it in the latter instance to "A foreigner comes, and a native appears." Some interpreters mistake this for mere abbreviation of a familiar phrase, ignoring the genius that Dōgen exhibits throughout his writings for tampering with stock expressions, upsetting accepted understandings and teasing out fresh implications.[23]

Here, inverting the orthodox reading of the phrase, he brilliantly collapses the foreigner-native opposition and extracts from the xinjing metaphor a second treasure, sparkling and apparently still surprising: in this mirror, there are no strangers. In its crystalline clarity, blinding prejudices—of nation, race, class, gender, age, and so on—disappear, enabling anyone who gets a peek to see both themselves and others beyond labels and categories and ultimately to see through Self and Other per se. With this, the bright mirror's liberative promise and potential become obvious. As Dōgen observes, "The great round mirror is the virtue of the buddhas."[24]

For all the good Chan and Zen masters got out of mirror metaphors, they also made sure to smash the xinjing on their way out the door. A disciple by the name of Changsheng questioned the master Lingyun (or Ling-yun; J., Reiun),

"What about the true and constant stream of awareness?"
"It's like the everlasting luminosity of a mirror," said Lingyun.
Changsheng asked, "Is there even going beyond this matter?"
"There is," the master replied.
"What is that going beyond?" pressed Changsheng.
Lingyun said, "Break the mirror! Then you and I can see one another."[25]

Zen master and poet Jakushitsu composed a poem on this theme, its resonances enhanced by the fact that its recipient was a blind monk named Zesshō, meaning "beyond illumination":

> In daily practice
>   can one who plays with reflections
> Ever attain the Way?
> Smash the worthless old mirror
> And your original face will shine[26]

These and similar texts remind us that, as current custodians of the mirror metaphor, we ought to be on guard against the very human tendency to solidify ideas into things, to reify them. Of course, none of us has a xinjing any more than Xuefeng's macaques did. At most, we're hosts to a complex imaging process that works by means of biochemical and bioelectrical mechanisms that people didn't invent and are only beginning to understand. We can modify the operation of those mechanisms somewhat, with drugs, electrical stimulation, and so forth, but we can't exert full control over the process. I find something wonderful in that. As integral to my writing and your reading as the mental process is, I enjoy the thought that *it* is performing those functions for us, only affording the illusion that "you" and "I" are doing them. Hello! Anybody there?

6 | Putting Integrity
Back into *Integrity*

Guishan ascended the hall to address the assembly, saying, "Wayfarers' minds are upright, without pretense, without front or back, without deceit or delusion either at heart or in behavior."

—*Jingde chuandeng lu* (1004)[1]

An integer, we learn in math class, is a whole number, and a sense of wholeness properly adheres to other words kindred in their etymology. In Latin, *integer* means "entire," "intact," "untouched," and many related phrases carry implications of soundness or coherence, as when we note a building's "structural integrity" after an earthquake or extol the "conceptual integrity" of a proposal. Things with such integrity hang together in an apparent, appreciable way. Other derivatives of *integer* have meanings more akin to "intrinsic to" or "inseparable from": "Spiciness is integral to Szechuan cuisine." These two groups of words maintain the old sense of their Latin root while extending it. As a semantic family, they maintain a certain integrity, you might say, and their meanings are clear.

When it comes to human character, however, the unmodified noun *integrity* becomes at least a little hazy. Ask what distinguishes a person who has integrity from one who doesn't, and you're likely to hear that it's their honesty, forthrightness, dependability. Beyond these generalities, the interpretations diverge, however, clustering in two groups with very different connotations. Though both refer to personal consistency, they point in opposite directions. (Like other categories, the two I'm about to define oversimplify a complex field of experience but are worthwhile, I hope you'll agree, for the instructive juxtaposition they make possible.)

In the first type of integrity, the key criterion is being "true to oneself," a consistency often identified with authenticity, with living authentically. Integrity of this kind turns on alignment of thoughts or feelings on one hand and words and deeds on the other—acting in accord with one's own perceptions and desires, with "my truth," to use a popular expression. In the second type of integrity, what counts is observable fidelity of words and deeds—doing what one has committed to do. The latter sort of integrity, by definition, is public, while the former is private, subject only to self-appraisal and at times altogether indiscernible to others.

These two brands of integrity needn't conflict but often do. Concern for integrity of the private or "internal" kind might, at first thought, seem likely to produce integrity of the public or "external" variety. Thus Shakespeare represented the matter in *Hamlet*: "This above all: to thine own self be true, / and it must follow, as the night the day, / thou canst not then be false to any man." If integrity was all of a piece in the Bard's day, however, with the rise of Romanticism it splintered, as people began to privilege feelings above reason and the personal above the public. Once that shift occurred, being "true to oneself" could serve as a warrant for *in*consistencies of conduct. A self-declared vegan munching a hamburger would appear flagrantly "out of integrity" from the standpoint of public integrity yet could enjoy the burger with a private sense of integrity intact so long as consuming it fulfilled at least a momentary heartfelt desire to eat meat.

This example reveals a problem with integrity of the private variety: since it resembles—and, in some instances, undoubtedly amounts to—living by whim, it may result in conduct others experience as capricious or at least unpredictable. Accordingly, to take private integrity as your guiding principle may earn you a reputation for unreliability or irresponsibility or, at worst, for duplicity—being "two-faced," saying one thing while doing or intending another.

In that case, private integrity will register as the very antithesis of public integrity.

Public integrity has a reciprocal weakness: while it may make for staunch character and dependable behavior, it can also impede changing course when circumstances require. Even very praise-worthy commitments—"I'll never give up!"—shackle us if rigidly maintained. Those who adhere inflexibly to a standard of external integrity frequently earn reputations for stubbornness, obstinacy, intransigence, bullheadedness.

Questions of integrity may become relevant on any social scale—in considering one's own behavior, in negotiating a personal relationship, and in an infinite range of group contexts, from a circle of friends, team, or committee at one end of the spectrum all the way up to national and international levels at the other. Notice that you've been undercharged for a purchase or that a friend's sweetheart is flirting with somebody else or that your company is violating a rule, and you confront a question of integrity. Which version of integrity you subscribe to, perhaps subconsciously, will greatly affect how you resolve it and how you and others *feel* about how you resolved it.

(Lest you start to wonder if pages from another book have got-ten bound into this one by mistake, I hasten to assure you that, as claimants of integrity like to say, "I'm a man of my word" and that how all this relates to Chan and Zen will become clear before long. Bear with me, though, for several more paragraphs that will take this essay into territory likely to seem still farther afield from the topic of Dharma family treasures.)

As important and telling as small-scale issues of integrity may be for us personally or for a group, it's more conspicuous, high-stakes conflicts of integrity that most strikingly illumine the differ-ence between the two types. In the 2016 U.S. presidential race, the opposed understandings of integrity, incarnated by Donald Trump and Hillary Rodham Clinton, came into direct and open conflict. Even before the two candidates secured their party nominations, the contrast was starkly established: Trump identified himself with integrity of the private kind, Clinton with integrity of the public sort.

I don't know if he ever used the word, but Trump made integrity a central theme of his campaign, portraying first his fellow Republican candidates and then Clinton as liars and posers, out to deceive the electorate. Voters couldn't trust a "Lying Ted" or a "Crooked Hillary," said Trump, while demonstrating that he could be counted on to say whatever he pleased, never mind that it might contradict his prior statements, cause offense, fly in the face of well-established facts, or be laced with profanity. Trump enthusiasts love this brash, shoot-from-the-hip oratorical style, the journalist Mark Danner observed: "His 'truth-telling,' so loud-voiced and bold, delights [his base]—and the more it appalls the liberals, the better. It convinces his followers that he, unlike his opponents, says exactly what he's thinking, and what he's thinking is what they're thinking."[2] Some seemed to consider it one of his primary credentials for occupying the Oval Office. Jerry Falwell, Jr., evangelical Christian and then-president of Liberty University, professed on Twitter that Trump had "single-handedly changed the definition of what behavior is 'presidential' from phony, failed & rehearsed to authentic, successful & down to earth."[3]

Don't be quick to dismiss this version of integrity. Its advocates include reputable figures on both sides of the Atlantic, perhaps none more eloquent and fervent in its espousal than Ralph Waldo Emerson. "Nothing is at last sacred but the integrity of your own mind," he asserts in his famous essay "Self-Reliance," and it's evident he has in mind the private, temporary sort I've described. "With consistency a great soul has nothing to do," Emerson goes on to say, promoting the very style of expression Trump used on the stump. "Speak what you think now in hard words and to-morrow speak what to-morrow thinks in hard words again, though it contradict everything you said to-day."[4] Oratory of this nature may even impress people who would seem likely to take offense. When a pollster questioned a focus group about Trump's racist comments, a young man responded, "I don't care. They're all racist. At least he tells me what he is."[5]

Clinton took the reverse approach, appealing to voters on the basis of integrity type two—public and durable. Touting the consistency of her own words and actions over decades in the public eye, she drew a sharp contrast between herself and her opponent, repeating instance after instance in which he said one thing and then said or did something different. Persuasive as these arguments were to her backers, they had no traction with Trump's supporters. To them, Clinton's rhetoric rang utterly false; they mocked it as "focus grouped" and scripted, ergo untrustworthy.

When she told the crowd at a fundraiser that half of Trump's backers belonged to "a basket of deplorables," it provided her detractors damning confirmation not only that she looked down on them but also that she lacked the brand of integrity they saw in Trump: whereas she divulged her real thoughts only to people in her camp, he said whatever he wanted to say, irrespective of who would hear, indeed frequently in the full glare of the news media.[6]

At the same time, some conservatives, including many Republican leaders, voiced grave concern about Trump's lack of public integrity, the mismatch of word and deed. With the party's nominating process nearing its end, Mitt Romney, a presidential hopeful himself just four years earlier, denounced Trump on exactly this basis, publicly declaring, "Here's what I know. Donald Trump is a phony, a fraud. His promises are as worthless as a degree from Trump University. He's playing the American public for suckers...." Whether or not American voters were suckers in 2016, Donald Trump's victory ought to be recognized as a victory for the personal version of integrity. However neatly his rhetoric satisfied Emerson's definition of integrity, I doubt that the gentleman from Concord would have been happy to witness its triumph.

What does this long disquisition on integrity and its role in recent politics have to do with Chan and Zen? What place does integrity hold in their history and teachings, and how does that bear now on our conduct, family lives, sangha relations, and so on? The short answer is twofold. First, the tradition arose in cultures that held integrity to be indivisible, tolerating no discrepancy between public behavior and private inclinations; it carries that sense of integrity in its genes, so to speak, and has promoted it as an element of the Dharma. Second, experientially—that is, as a matter of practice—Zen offers both an alternative to the divided understanding of integrity now afoot in Western societies and an antidote to it that we urgently need.

The very much longer answer begins with the Chinese word most closely equivalent to integrity, 誠 cheng. Formed by combining characters meaning "to speak" and "to complete, fulfill, or consummate," it carries a strong sense of the follow-through that a public integrity demands—living up to your word. Since those who dependably do what they've said they'll do come to be regarded as sincere, "sincerity" often substitutes as a translation of cheng.[7] But whereas we might consider integrity and sincerity personal attributes, cheng has a distinctly social dimension. The Great Learning, a foundational Confucian text, puts it directly: "Integrity inside shapes what's outside."[8] The integrity we can see reflects and depends on an integrity that we can't see. In other words, cheng connotes wholeness, as the Latin integritas did.

Confucian-oriented societies have customarily assigned a very high value to observable integrity, and it's not hard to understand why: socially, integrity has cohesive power. We all can count on cheng people, families, businesses, and officials to carry through on commitments, not to go back on promises or to quit the moment difficulties arise. The Zhongyong, another vintage Confucian text, ascribes to cheng a self-generating quality and an extraordinary potency:

> Integrity fulfills itself and makes its own dao. Integrity informs things from beginning to end; without integrity, nothing happens. For this reason, effective people prize integrity. Integrity doesn't just fulfill itself in us; it also brings things to fulfillment....The virtue of one's nature is a dao joining internal and external, so integrity befits all times and places.[9]

The power of cheng to "bring things to fulfillment" makes it necessary in exerting social influence, according to the Mengzi (or *Mencius*), a third seminal Confucian text: "Never does a person of the utmost integrity fail to move others; never can a person lacking integrity move others."[10] Note that this assertion collapses if one construes integrity to have separable internal and external aspects. Put your mind to it for a second, and I bet you can think of instances in your own society when people of high private integrity have failed to move others and instances when people woefully short in public integrity have succeeded at inspiring others. Such results are unthinkable from a Confucian perspective.

The early Daoist thinkers didn't play up integrity as those of the Confucian school did, but one of the "miscellaneous" chapters of the *Zhuangzi* depicts Confucius humbly taking a lesson from a fisherman-sage who speaks of genuineness and promptly relates it to cheng:

> Genuineness is the ultimate in purity and integrity. Without purity and integrity, you're unable to move others. So forced grieving, even though sad, isn't sorrowful; forced anger, even though impressive, isn't daunting; and forced closeness, even if jovial, is discordant. Genuine grieving is sorrowful without a sound; genuine anger is daunting though not yet expressed; and genuine closeness is harmonious even if not jovial. The internally genuine mystically affects the external. For that reason, we esteem genuineness.[11]

The potency that these writings attribute to cheng extends even to realms that modernity deems magical or supernatural, realms that Chinese thinkers since antiquity have viewed as fully natural, just supra*human*. "Utmost integrity moves the spirits," another Chinese classic declares,[12] and a folk saying takes it one step further: "Accomplish integrity, and green grass will grow on stones."[13] Though its workings may be unintelligible, formidable power is attributed to cheng. So definite is this sense of its generative force that some translators choose to render it as "creativity" rather than "integrity" or "sincerity."[14]

How seriously a breach of integrity was taken in the Chinese court we may judge from an incident that occurred in 1138, when a leading Confucian scholar named Zhang Jiucheng was called to the "classics mat" to deliver a series of lectures to the emperor. Zhang had also studied under Dahui, prominent among Chan masters of the time, earning a reputation as his foremost lay disciple, and that training shows in his incisive checking of the Son of Heaven. When the emperor commented at the conclusion of a lecture, "I have achieved a condition of perfect integrity (*zhicheng*),"

> Zhang Jiucheng said: "I see that you have this [integrity] when you are at court addressing your ministers, but how about when you retire to your private quarters?"
>
> Emperor: "I maintain my integrity there too."
>
> Zhang: "How about when you are with the imperial harem?"
>
> The emperor paused and was thinking about how to reply when Zhang suddenly said: "Right now you have lost your integrity."[15]

Many Chan texts manifest the longstanding Chinese confidence in the uncanny efficacy of cheng, including one of the earliest still extant, attributed to Hongren (or Hung-jen; J., Kōnin or Gunin), the master who came to be regarded as Chan's Fifth Ancestor. Quoting an unidentified sūtra, the text presents cheng as the sine qua non in achieving a turnabout akin to Śākyamuni's: "If beings aren't thoroughly sincere [cheng] in aspiring to awaken, not even all of the buddhas of past, present, and future will be able to help them, though as numerous as sands of the Ganges."[16]

Whether or not they used the word *cheng*, early masters regularly taught the virtue of integrity, establishing that its importance goes beyond a private aspiration to awaken. It was four generations after Hongren, in a presentation to his monastic assembly, that the master Guishan made the statement I placed at the head of this essay, identifying integrity as a signature characteristic of earnest practitioners: "Wayfarers' minds are upright, without pretense, without front or back, without deceit or delusion in either heart-mind or behavior."

The assimilation of cheng into Chan discourse unquestionably reflects its deep roots in Chinese thought yet also remains faithful to Buddhist doctrines received from India. Among the eighteen distinguishing qualities of a buddha enumerated in the Sanskrit sūtras, three combine to delineate unquestionable integrity: a buddha's deeds, thoughts, and words invariably arise out of and conform with wise discernment (*jñāna*).[17] This ideal of integrity encompasses all the so-called "three doors" of karmic action (*tridvāra*), unmistakably marking out a path of consistency that is public as well as private. Other sūtras offer hope that buddhas aren't alone in manifesting such thorough integrity. Defining *kalyāṇamitra*, "good friends" who mentor, goad, encourage, and accompany others on the path,[18] the *Nirvāna Sūtra* declares that they

...preach in accord with the Dharma and act in accord with what they preach. What is meant by "preach in accord with the Dharma and act in accord with what they preach"? It includes everything from not taking life themselves and teaching others not to take life to practicing Right Views and teaching others to practice Right Views.[19]

For a buddha, for a *kalyāṇamitra*, and indeed for any mature student of Chan or Zen, the categories internal and external or private and public are only provisional, of some limited use to designate things but lacking any fundamental basis. Their integrity, accordingly, has no inside or outside. Like these earlier statements, Guishan's teaching undoubtedly represents an ideal of a wayfarer's mind, a demanding standard to live up to, conveying the same quality of boundless integrity—"without pretense, without front or back, without deceit or delusion either at heart or in behavior."

Such integrity lends transparency to one's behavior and provides a stout basis for trust. Recognizing this, the influential twelfth-century Chan master Yuanwu taught that cheng and trust have a crucial, reciprocal relationship in all aspects of our training. He wrote:

> Study of dao proceeds from trust; establishing trust lies in integrity. Maintain integrity throughout, and later you'll enable everyone to shed their delusions; maintain trust yourself, and then you can teach people to avoid duplicity. Only trust and integrity have benefits without fail.[20]

Mark those remarkable words: "Only trust and integrity have benefits without fail."

Yuanwu's words gain heft if you know that the word translated as "trust" is 信 xin (or hsin; J., shin) and that it consists of the common graph for *person* next to the graph representing speech. Chinese characters aren't necessarily decipherable in this figurative or ideographic manner, but xin certainly is: depicting a unity of person and words, it intimates the complete ecosystem of trust. If you give your word, keep your word, are true to your word, people come to trust you. Yuanwu goes on to use these terms to characterize a *kalyānamitra*:

> If we know integrity isn't complete, a person's heartmind can't be assured; if we know trust isn't complete, a person's words won't have any effect. An ancient said we could get by without clothes and food but that trust and integrity are imperative. Truly, *kalyānamitra* will, as a matter of course, teach people through trust and integrity. The moment their heartminds became insincere or their behavior untrustworthy, how could we speak of them as *kalyānamitra*?[21]

Cheng went with Chan as it spread from China to other parts of Asia, embedded in it as a value both implicit and explicit. In

Japan, where Shintō espoused a very similar principle and Confucianism had become established, too, the emerging Zen schools could assume integrity as a cultural value and a basis for practice and realization.[22] Phrasebooks compiled in Japan for use in kōan study contain a vivid Chinese-language couplet bringing the theme home with poetic force:

> Achieve sincerity once, and you've paid your debt to the
>   nation;
> at the frontier, armies will no longer sound the hours of the
>   night.[23]

Without actually employing the word *cheng*, this verse patently advocates it. Where I've written "sincerity," the text would translate literally as "red heartmind" or "naked heartmind," a classical phrase connoting absolute transparency in thought and feeling. To accomplish this even once is a feat deemed so wondrous as to discharge one's obligation to society and bring peace to the whole nation. Dōgen actually borrows from Confucian precedent in advocating such integrity:

> An ancient said [of ministers and high officials], "Their words fill the world without their tongues going astray; their actions fill the world without resentment or offense." This is because what has to be said is said and what has to be done is done. These are words and actions of the highest virtue and the essence of the dao.[24]

As a standard, integrity proved resilient through the transformations ensuing from Japan's opening to the West and subsequent modernization. At the turn of twentieth century, it remained plainly recognizable in the set of commitments that Shaku Sōen Zenji, celebrated abbot of the Rinzai monastery Engaku-ji, enunciated for his own practice: "I will receive guests as if alone," Shaku Sōen vowed, "and live by myself as if in the company of many people."[25]

It stands out even more sharply in a statement my Dharma grand-father Yasutani Haku'un made to one of his students: "If you were completely sincere, you'd be enlightened at this moment."[26] In this formulation, cheng approaches the status of awakening itself. Indeed, one of Yasutani Rōshi's successors, the nun Satomi Myōdō, closed a long account of her circuitous path to realization with this verse:

> Awakening from the dream, I see:
> Sincerity is simply my original nature.
> Where, then, shall I look for it?[27]

As one of the first Japanese priests to settle in the West and teach Zen, Nyogen Senzaki endeavored to carry cheng the difficult next step: communicating this virtue to readers getting a first taste of Zen in English. He placed the Chinese character at the head of a story about the seventeenth-century master Bankei, counting on the anecdote itself to convey the meaning of cheng:

> After Bankei had passed away, a blind man who lived near the temple told a friend: "Since I am blind, I cannot watch a person's face, so I must judge his character by the sound of his voice. Ordinarily when I hear someone congratulate another upon his happiness or success, I also hear a secret tone of envy. When condolence is expressed for the misfortune of another, I hear pleasure and satisfaction, as if the one condoling was really glad there was something left to gain in his own world.
>
> "In all my experience, however, Bankei's voice was always sincere. Whenever he expressed happiness, I heard nothing but happiness, and whenever he expressed sorrow, sorrow was all I heard."[28]

There it is: clear testimony to a wayfarer's transparency of mind, with no pretense, front or back. At least as perceived by one acute listener, Bankei's words conformed completely to his feelings, the ostensibly "external" so congruent with the "internal" as to render the distinction meaningless.

—

It remains to be seen whether Chan and Zen communities outside of Asia will recognize the importance that cheng has had in our tradition. It so permeates our legacy that designating it a Confucian virtue seems too limiting. True, it's a principle championed by the Confucian classics, texts studied in China for many centuries before the advent of Chan, but as I've noted, it also has rough equivalents in Indian Buddhism; to conceive of it as an element our predecessors grafted into the tradition would be incorrect for that reason alone. Even more to the point, as a value fundamental to Chinese culture, it's one that our Chan forebears "brought to the table." It would be remarkable if they'd omitted it from the tradition; in them, it was already present.

Even if it didn't belong to the tradition culturally, it seems likely to me that cheng would have emerged as a feature of Chan and Zen teachings. I wish I could claim that our practice leads inexorably and inevitably to integrity; alas, counterexamples show that's not the case. But I do think it's true that practice reliably *inclines* people to integrity. When one spends hours in zazen, with nowhere to hide, duplicitous words or actions haunt the heartmind, surfacing persistently in various forms—recollection, regret, self-justification, schemes about how to cover them up or apologize. Who wants to sit (or live) with that kind of emotional and mental malaise? The costs are too high to us as well as to our relationships, and no one who tastes the sweetness of integrity will want to give it up. And if conceptual oppositions such as self-other and inner-outer wither and fall away, so do obstacles to integrity.

I certainly won't conceal my hope that the dragons of Western Zen now and in years to come will take the great jewel of cheng in their talons and, enjoying it themselves, ensure that others admire it, too. I hope that integrity will come to be regarded as *integral* to good practice, genuine wisdom, and harmony in our sanghas, families, and other groups to which we belong. I dare to imagine that it might even spread to the institutions that bear so heavily upon our lives, including institutions of government, fantastical as that may seem at present. We can at least keep that possibility alive by actualizing integrity ourselves and looking for it in others.

7 | The Resource of Shame

In the United States, shame's reputation has improved dramatically in recent years. Its sharp and sudden rise in public regard owes a lot to the prominence of a president who behaved shamelessly and, moreover, put shameless behavior on display by speaking about it shamelessly, as if it were something to be proud of. Shame had been trending downward in public discourse, condemned as a burden laid unjustly on people already struggling to hold their heads up—people "overweight" or badly educated, gay or transgender, out of work, formerly incarcerated, or merely poor. However well-founded that critique of shame was and remains, our shameless leader all of a sudden reminded many people that shame may, after all, have a valid and important place in our lives.

I want to make a case here for shame as a constructive force, both in individuals and in a community or populace, and to point out that sense of shame in Chan and Zen as another of the tradition's treasures. Since the word is so loaded and the subject so rife with misunderstandings, I feel obligated to start by specifying what I mean by shame and especially what I don't mean.

Tops among the things I don't mean is the social operation known as "shaming," in which members of our prickly species take it upon themselves to attempt to inflict shame upon a person or group for saying or doing something that they, the shamers, consider worse than simply wrong—offensive, immoral, "unnatural," somehow an affront and danger to what they hold dear. While I can understand shaming as a protective reflex and feel empathy for anyone who succumbs to it, it brings no benefit except to the shamers, who may feel the temporary elation of self-righteousness. Otherwise, it generates animosity, fear, reaction, and heightened polarization, the last thing we need. At any rate, it isn't my subject here.

Secondly, I want to set aside the injurious form of shame I think of as "imposed shame." Many people who've suffered abuse, especially in their childhood, experience shame of this sort, often for the rest of their lives. While their adult experiences of shame may seem internal because they aren't prompted by any overt criticism (indeed, their abuse may not even be known to others), shame of this type truly belongs to somebody else; an innocent party is carrying a shame that their abuser has imposed, a residue of the original shameless conduct.

A related form of shame, likewise distinct from the constructive shame that interests me, derives from widely held, often unconscious social norms rather than from personal abuse. When my father began getting unsteady on his feet, I gave him a pair of trekking poles, thinking that he might be more likely to use them than the handcrafted cane he'd purchased but never took from its place behind the door. To my surprise, I almost had to beg him to try them out, and we hadn't gone far before he made clear the source of his reluctance. "Maybe if someone sees me," he said hopefully, "they'll think I'm doing this for exercise!" By then, my dad had rounded ninety, and I don't know anybody who'd have considered it a failing or in any way unbefitting that he needed a little help in walking about.

But there it was. Through a sort of osmosis, he'd absorbed the prejudice against age, or at least against looking old, that has taken hold in many quarters. Such baseless, harmful prejudices grip us in many arenas besides aging, unfortunately. I've already mentioned some that are now in the public eye; others draw few headlines, if any. Teenagers with acne feel ashamed of their skin. People with hearing problems, young or old, often feel ashamed of wearing hearing aids. People who've lost their jobs through no fault of their own still feel ashamed to pay with food stamps at the grocery store.

People, especially girls and young women, feel ashamed if they can't meet the standards of body image projected in the popular media. These culturally imposed shames seem so baseless that they could be laughed out of existence, and I wish they would be. But again this isn't my subject.

As relational animals enmeshed in cultures—interdependent, to put it in Buddhist terms—we can't claim to have any feelings that are *purely* individual in nature, yet the type of shame I'm going to describe and praise is more personal than overtly social. It doesn't lead to shaming or result from being shamed, nor is it assumed out of private trauma or public prejudice. It arises out of a sense that one has acted, spoken, or perhaps merely entertained a thought in violation of some standard of uprightness that has become one's own. That's as far as I'm going to go toward defining shame for purposes of this discussion. In light of its irregular, inchoate nature, it seems best to treat it as a field of lived experience rather than as a delimitable phenomenon. I'll leave it up to you to formulate your own definition or, probably even better, your own multidimensional *impression* of it. Even to call it "it," after all, makes shame sound like something solid.

Though sidestepping definition, I do want to address a distinction between shame and guilt that's considered real and reputable in some academic quarters. Scholars have gone so far as to group and compare societies using the rubrics "guilt-based" and "shame-based" as if those terms were objective and neutral.[1] Such comparisons, even when grounded in sociological data and phrased in sophisticated fashion, are predicated on distinctions implicit in the comparers' frames of reference. Under their construction, guilt is a product of private conscience and honorable as such, while they consider shame to be driven merely by social concerns, primarily by fear of losing status in one's group. These attributions rest on two underlying premises—an inner-outer dichotomy and a concept of self—that fit some societies better than others and whose ultimate validity Chan and Zen have been questioning and undermining for more than a millennium. Unless we're satisfied to confine ourselves to preconceptions about shame, it seems to me, we need to explore it with reference to specific human contexts.

—

Some societies, including those that produced our tradition, have traditionally held shame up for admiration.[2] Consider an assertion by the Japanese monk Ryōkan (1758–1831), a famously good-natured Zen recluse and poet:

> A sense of shame is the greatest adornment. Shame is like an iron hook: it can restrain a person from misconduct. So one must always preserve a sense of shame and never lose it for even a moment. A person without shame is no different from a beast.[3]

When I chanced upon this statement, twenty-five years into my own Zen training, it struck me as odd, verging on bizarre. I saw no connection between shame and the Dharma I'd come to know and appreciate. Shame, as I conceived it, was a form of emotional distress. What could possibly make it beneficial rather than a *kleśa*, a factor complicating the process of liberation?

Twenty more years of practice shifted my sense of shame unwittingly toward Ryōkan's. Since shame has received scant discussion in American Zen circles, I don't know if many other long-term Western practitioners have arrived at a similarly altered appraisal of its meaning to our predecessors or of its potential value now. Perhaps not. But however common or uncommon this constructive sense of shame may be, it clearly belongs to our heritage, and I see it as intelligible and valuable, whether or not one has devoted any time to Zen study.

The relevant contexts for the passage by Ryōkan are readily identifiable. Chinese culture and Mahāyāna Buddhism both taught the virtue of shame, and this understanding flowed directly into Chan and thence into Zen. In the *Analects*, which remains a foundational text even today in Chinese society, Confucius presents shame as a vital contributor to both personal uprightness and social harmony. A few specimens:[4]

- Noble people feel shame if their words surpass their actions.
- Smooth talk, flattering looks, and excessive courtesy—Zuoqiu Ming considered them shameful, and so do I. Concealing distain and acting friendly toward someone—Zuoqiu Ming considered that shameful, and so do I.
- When the world sustains the tao, show up; when it doesn't, step back. When the tao is sustained, to live in poverty and obscurity [instead of serving in public office] is shameful; when it's not sustained, to live in wealth and prominence is shameful.
- Yuansi inquired about shame. The master said, "When the nation keeps to the tao, you receive a salary; if the nation abandons the tao and you receive a salary, that's shameful."
- In your actions, have a sense of shame. If dispatched to the four quarters on a mission, don't disgrace your lord's directives.
- Guide people with edicts, order them through laws, and they'll try to avoid punishment but will have no shame. Guide people with virtue, order them through ritual, and they'll have shame and exercise restraint.

Don't let unfamiliar or archaic elements in these statements obscure from you the evidence they offer of the beneficial function that shame has in Confucian doctrine. It probably understates the matter to say that shame serves as a pillar of Confucian ethics.

Building upon the foundation that Confucius laid down, Mengzi taught, "One can't do without shame. The shame of lacking shame—that's shamelessness indeed!" More explicitly, he proclaimed, "Shame is great for us. Cunning opportunists have no use for shame. Unashamed of being inhuman, what humanity do they have?"[5] All these pronouncements emphasize staying true to one another, not promising more than we can deliver, following through on what we do promise, and maintaining the respect of others as well as self-respect. Thus they square with and buttress the virtue of cheng, integrity, outlined in the preceding chapter. One of the Zen capping phrases makes the relationship crystal clear:

> A heartmind that doesn't betray others,
> a face that won't wear the blush of shame.[6]

The same relationship underlies the shared etymology in English of *sham* and *shame*: taking part in a sham, one incurs shame.

The *Zhongyong*, that third classical Confucian text I've been citing, draws a connection between having a sense of shame and having the fortitude to act under difficult circumstances: "Knowing shame is tantamount to courage."[7] In the Confucian scheme of things, that is, instead of exerting repressive force, shame emboldens us to rise to the needs of an occasion and thus to live shamelessly in the very best sense of the word: doing, saying, maybe even thinking nothing shameworthy.

In support of this lofty paradigm of personal conduct, the *Zhongyong* cites the urtext of Chinese literature, the *Book of Songs*: "Observed living in your own home, / be unashamed even in the most private corner."[8] In other words, live in such a way that you have nothing to conceal, nothing to be ashamed of. This is a principled refusal to maintain a double standard, but it's also a way of freedom, so it's somewhat less than surprising that the indigenous Chinese orientation to shame aligned closely with the Mahāyāna teachings that arrived from India.

Considered a basic mental factor of all wholesome actions, shame turns up on various lists of the attributes considered to signal advancement on the buddha-way and as one of seven Dharma riches or assets. In the *Vimalakīrti Sūtra*, the eponymous layman sage names it expressly in his description of bodhisattvas:

> Their form displays all the auspicious marks;
> every good feature adorns them.
> They're clothed in garments of shame and remorse,
> with a deeply searching mind their garland.[9]

According to the *Lotus Sūtra*, shame separates those who'll be able to receive Buddha's message of the *ekayāna*, the single vehicle of buddhahood, from those who won't:

> When corrupt people in ages to come
> hear Buddha's preaching of the single vehicle,
> they will be confused, will not believe or accept it,
> will reject the Dharma and fall into the ruinous paths.
> But when there are those with a sense of shame,
> people of purity determined to seek the buddha-way,
> then for the sake of such people as these,
> you should widely extol the single vehicle.[10]

Conversely, the people most wanting for wisdom and virtue, the *icchantikas*, or incorrigibles, set themselves apart by their shamelessness, forfeiting all hope of reaching buddhahood according to the *Nirvāna Sūtra*. The message could hardly be clearer: shame—don't leave home without it.

The passage from Ryōkan I quoted earlier evidences the migration of these Mahāyāna doctrines into Chan and Zen. It derives from the *Sūtra of Bequeathed Teachings*, long regarded as a record of the Buddha's final instructions but in fact, scholars now reckon, probably Chinese in origin.[11] It was one of three sūtras (or pseudo sūtras) bundled in the ninth or tenth century into a handbook for Chan monastics, a convenient anthology subsequently carried to Japan and widely utilized in Zen circles. Presumably Ryōkan copied out these words because he deemed a sense of shame essential to his own and others' comportment.

When Chan and Zen gave shame a place in texts of their own, they typically treated the subject in a manner virtually indistinguishable from that in Confucian and Mahāyāna writings. In the last sections of Fayan's "Treatise on Ten Admonishments for the Ancestral Gate," for instance, he evoked the shame bound to ensue when teachers and practitioners failed to live up to the school's historic standards and to guard its reputation. "With their mouths, people talk about the causes of liberation," lamented this famed tenth-century master, "while in their minds they do the business of ghosts and spirits. Since they lack shame, how can they avoid committing offenses?"[12] Fully in keeping with Confucian and Mahāyāna precedent, we find Fayan relying on shame to provide a bulwark, maybe even the chief bulwark, against wrongdoing.

Evidence of such efficacy appears in *Precious Advice for the Chan Forests*, the twelfth-century miscellany focusing on principles and practices of leadership in Chan communities (the "forests" of its title). It quotes a remarkable reflection by a master named Gaoan Shanwu (or Kao-an Shan-wu; J., Kōan Zengo) on the trust that his disciples had in his teaching: "My study of dao is no greater than that of others. It is just that I have never done anything to be ashamed of in my heart."[13] Apart from affirming the link Confucian teachers had made between trustworthiness and one's sense of shame, Gaoan implies that excellence in Chan study doesn't, in itself, foster upright behavior. Other masters, past and present, might dispute that conclusion, but it surely deserves consideration in light of the ethical problems documented in Zen communities both East and West in recent decades.

Gaoan's contemporary, the prominent master Dahui, regarded shame as a prerequisite for carrying Chan training to true fruition. "This matter is extremely difficult," he wrote one of his many lay followers, "not easily completed. You have to generate shame to begin to attain it. Frequently, intelligent people with superior knowledge"—a respectful, elliptical reference to his correspondent—"attain it without much effort, consequently engender mental laxity, and fail to continue practicing. Many get wrapped up in visualizing past circumstances or grasping after the future and don't acquire any discipline."[14]

—

I've drawn heavily on ancient precedents in this account of shame, but it's not because masters have ceased teaching or exemplifying it. One of China's most highly regarded modern masters, Xuyun (or Hsu-yun), began a lecture on this humble note:

All of you come to ask me for guidance. This makes me feel ashamed. Everyone works so hard—splitting firewood, hoeing the fields, carrying soil, moving bricks—and yet from morning to night you have not forgotten the thought of cultivating the Way. Such determination for the Path is touching. I, Xuyun, am ashamed for my inadequacy on the Way and my lack of virtue.[15]

Besides treating the topic in this expository manner so patently faithful to Confucian and Mahāyāna precedents, Chan occasionally engaged the issue in the snappy repartee that became a hallmark of the tradition, as in this exchange from Zhaozhou's record:

Someone asked, "What place do you accord an individual entirely without shame?"

"Not among us," the master replied.

The questioner persisted, "How about if one suddenly appeared?"

"Throw him out!" said Zhaozhou.[16]

In a different context, the later master Wumen cheekily criticized Zhaozhou's teacher: "It must be said, Nanquan in his dotage didn't know shame. Cracking his stinky mouth, he revealed the family disgrace."[17]

Discussion of shame consistent with the Confucian and Mahāyāna teachings continued as Chan took hold in Japan and morphed into Zen. According to the *Shōbōgenzō Zuimonki*, Dōgen resorted to now-familiar language in urging members of his thirteenth-century assembly to set their sights high:

...even if one wants name and fame, rather than be well thought of by the inferior people of the present time, one should only have shame before the sages of antiquity and the good people of later ages. And even if one thinks of equaling someone, rather than the people of Japan, we should be ashamed before the past masters and eminent monks of India and China and think of being equal to such as them.[18]

Keizan Zenji, Dōgen's successor three generations later, inherited this spirit. Having risen to monastic leadership at just thirty-six, Keizan acknowledged that he'd accepted teaching duties prematurely and held himself accountable to both his predecessors in the Sōtō lineage and future descendants:

> Throughout the day, my conduct isn't good enough to serve as a sign for those who come after me. As I stand, sit, walk, and lie down, my attention is utterly unfocused. How can I face three or five monks and come up with a Dharma phrase or even half of one? What a shame and disgrace! How fearsome, how dreadful to be like this under the scrutiny of the ancestors and founders, the invisible eyes of former sages![19]

The discourse of shame stayed in play in Rinzai training, too. In a very unusual instance, instead of impressing on his monks the difficulty and necessity of speaking a true phrase and of living up to the standards set by Dharma ancestors, the irrepressible eighteenth-century master Hakuin raised the example of a common river porter—a man who eked out a living for himself and his family by literally renting out his back at a dangerous ford, carrying travelers through its raging current on his shoulders. Finding a money pouch lost by a man who earlier had dickered with him over his fee and eventually chose to wade the river unassisted, the porter gives chase, catches up to the man, returns his money, and stoutly refuses a reward, saying he'd be ashamed to accept it. "If I act against what I feel to be right, my heart would never feel at ease," he tells the pouch's weeping owner, "it is not made of stone." By the story's end, the porter's wife and aged father both have exhibited the same unshakable integrity, and Hakuin Zenji seems, for once, at a loss for words, closing his account with little more than a sigh of admiration.[20]

Still more recently, shame became a necessary topic as major Zen institutions in Japan responded to criticism for having provided tangible support to the country's military campaigns of the 1930s and 1940s. At a large anniversary commemoration staged by the

Myōshin-ji branch of Rinzai in 1995, its chief abbot, Kōno Taitsū, raised a saying attributed to the celebrated tenth-century master Wuzu Fayan (or Wu-tsu Fa-yen; J., Goso Hōen): "I have practiced for twenty years, and now I truly know shame." Expanding on this line, Kōno Rōshi said,

> The shame of which Wu-tsu speaks is not, of course, the shame of failing to understand the Dharma. It is the shame of realizing the Dharma and yet not being able to manifest it freely in the activities of one's everyday life. Wu-tsu had come to awakening and attained peace of mind, yet had not fully integrated his experience into the everyday practice of the Buddha Way.[21]

That same shortcoming, he suggested, accounted not only for Myōshin-ji's support of militarism during World War II but also for its half-century-long failure to acknowledge its complicity, much less to atone for it.

We may applaud Kōno Rōshi for holding Myōshin-ji's feet to the fire and wag our heads sorrowfully about the extent of Zen teachers' and institutions' participation in the war effort, but much more important now is considering whether we ourselves "truly know shame" and what relevance that could have for us. Wuzu's statement implies an increasing sensitivity to shame as he continued his training; it's not that he grew less *able* to integrate his realization and daily practice but rather that he grew more *aware* of his shortcomings. I suspect he might equally well have said, "I have practiced for twenty years, and now I truly know joy." That, at least, is my experience: after five decades of Zen training, I can honestly say that I've come to "truly know" grief, gratitude, trust, satisfaction, love, and a host of other emotions in addition to shame, emotions that earlier in my life I knew poorly—dimly or unreliably, often only in retrospect. I'd place candid perception of our own thoughts and feelings among the many fringe benefits of Zen practice.

Having now claimed a true knowledge of shame, I can fairly be expected to describe it—to say how it *feels* even while continuing to decline any attempt to define what it *is*. I'll do so but with the double caveat that I have only my own experience to go by and that how I answer today is very different from how I'd have answered, if I could answer at all, as a boy. Boyhood shame I remember as a head-hanging misery, feeling constricted and estranged, immured from others and from everything pleasant, dejected, foreign even to myself. Shame today feels almost the reverse. Of course it begins with a realization that I've screwed up, which is never joyful, but my regret doesn't lock me in or plunge me into despondency. On the contrary, it shows me something encouraging: the discrepancy between what I've done or not done and the more honorable way that I, perhaps unconsciously but genuinely, *want* to think, speak, and behave.

When it operates this way, shame turns from burden to blessing. Recognition that you've erred becomes an indicator of which way your ethical compass actually points, lending shame an ennobling aspect. To feel it is honorable, a mark of good character, which is what our Buddhist predecessors had in mind in designating it an adornment.

So much for description. More illuminating may be a set of examples—shame in action, so to speak—recorded by a diverse set of writers. I don't claim that it's a comprehensive or even representative sample of the word's usage; it's just culled from instances when it jumped out at me from my reading. I omit specimens pertaining to the former president, preferring not to skew the selection by dwelling on its application to him. I offer this set according to no particular logic and without comment, as a thicket of uses, not a coherent mosaic:

- Playwright and performer Noel Coward, from a letter to his mother at the beginning of World War II: "...if I ran away and refused to have anything to do with the war and lived comfortably in Hollywood, as so many of my actor friends have done, I should be ashamed to the end of my days."[22]
- In an essay published after his death in 1949, Aldo Leopold lamented the proliferation of cheat grass he'd observed in the

western United States. Commenting on public lack of determination to combat this invasive weed, he wrote, "There is, as yet, no sense of pride in the husbandry of wild plants and animals, no sense of shame in the proprietorship of a sick landscape."[23]

- *The Autobiography of Malcolm X* records for posterity Malcolm X's regret about an early girlfriend's turn to drugs and prostitution after he ditched her in favor of a white lover: "One of the shames I have carried for years is that I have blamed myself for all of this. To have treated her as I did for a white woman made the blow doubly heavy."[24]
- W. S. Merwin, a poet foremost but also a superb writer in other genres, published "Avoiding the News by the River" in his 1967 book *The Lice*. He wakes from a bad dream of "the heavens... eating the earth" to the bad news he was avoiding—news of the U.S. war in Indochina. While the predations of wren and badger don't ashame him, the war's destruction is another matter: "If I were not human I would not be ashamed of anything."[25]
- When his next book won him the Pulitzer Prize, Merwin declined it, explaining to the public:

  ...after years of the news from Southeast Asia, and the commentary from Washington, I am too conscious of being an American to accept public congratulation with good grace, or to welcome it except as an occasion for expressing openly a shame which many Americans feel, day after day, helplessly and in silence.[26]

- Writing in 1975, journalist James Fallows recalled starving himself as a means, six years before, of avoiding the draft: when his ploy paid off, "I was overcome by a wave of relief, which for the first time revealed to me how great my terror had been, and by the beginning of the sense of shame which remains with me to this day."[27]
- From Vietnam in June 1975, the daring journalist Martha Gellhorn wrote a friend about the war that had just ended, "I felt it as a personal guilt and shame and horror."[28]
- During his enslavement as a boy, Frederick Douglass found that

in urban circumstances, "There is a vestige of decency, a sense of shame, that does much to curb and check those outbreaks of atrocious cruelty so commonly enacted on the plantation."[29]

• To the critic Susan Sontag, the photographs of torture inflicted at Abu Ghraib prison told a tale of a much wider and deeper failure: Soldiers now pose, thumbs up, before the atrocities they commit, and send the pictures to their buddies. Secrets of private life that, formerly, you would have given anything to conceal, you now clamor to be invited on a television show to reveal. What is illustrated by these photographs is as much the culture of shamelessness as the reigning admiration for unapologetic brutality.[30]

• In a 2018 article about musicians playing for the down-and-out in Los Angeles, music critic Alex Ross wrote: "To walk through the streets of Skid Row to the Midnight Mission is to feel shame for the state of the city and the state of the country. Block after block, the sidewalks are crammed with tents, boxes, broken furniture, and shopping carts full of possessions."[31]

• Journalist George Packer, reporting in 2007 on the U.S. failure to furnish adequate protection to Iraqis employed during the occupation, recalled the 130,000 Vietnamese refugees admitted to this country in the mid-1970s. He quotes then-president Gerald Ford: "To do less would have added moral shame to humiliation." [32]

• Scholar, critic, and activist David Shulman reflecting in 2017 on Israeli society as he'd come to know it fifty years before: "Shame, sincere or not, had not yet disappeared from public life."[33]

• That same year, the *New Yorker* correspondent in France, Jane Kramer, informed her readers that some of his compatriots considered Nicolas Sarkozy, who soon became the French president, "shameless, 'like an American.'"[34]

• Bob Dylan put to music his feelings about the boxer Rubin "Hurricane" Carter being "obviously framed" and imprisoned for a murder he didn't commit: "Couldn't help but make me feel ashamed to live in a land / Where justice is a game."[35]

- For her book about Sylvia Plath, *The Silent Woman*, the investigative journalist Janet Malcolm tracked Ted Hughes to his home. Plath's husband when she committed suicide, Hughes often has been blamed for her death, and as she observed his house, Malcolm "felt shame at my complicity in the chase that has made his life a torment; I had joined the pack of his pursuers."[36]
- In researching an article on *yakuza*, powerful mafia-like gangs that operate in Japan, journalist Peter Hessler learned from a police expert on underworld crime that yakuza behavior changed when the Japanese economy hit the skids in the 1990s: "It used to be that they didn't do theft or robbery," the detective told him. "It was considered shameful."[37]
- Atul Gawande, physician and author, delineates three models for doctors' relationships to their patients—paternalistic, informative, and interpretive—and remembers a terminally sick patient he bewildered with a description of potential treatments: "The options overwhelmed her. They all sounded terrifying. She didn't know what to do. I realized, with shame, that I'd reverted to being Dr. Informative—here are the facts and figures; what do you want to do?"[38]
- Canadian philosopher Charles Taylor takes the long view: "Civilization is in a sense a matter of feeling shame in the appropriate places."[39]

I hope this miscellany demonstrates, if nothing else, shame's continuing usefulness as a resource in thinking about how we conduct our lives, each and together. Constructive awareness of shame can serve as a means to take one's bearings and to change course, to rectify errors and live up to our intentions. An unheroic personal example: over the span of two decades, my wife and I saw our local bank swallowed up by a regional bank, then the regional bank absorbed by a nationwide bank whose business practices drew criticism and later a federal lawsuit and a large settlement. Our accounts were small, but we felt increasingly ashamed to support this corporate malefactor at all, and eventually, when shame overcame the inconvenience of making a change, we closed the accounts, telling the management why, and moved our money into a local credit union. Did the big bank alter its behavior? Apparently not. But we weren't so naïve as to believe it would, and the years since have furnished more reasons to feel glad we pulled out. (Meantime, the credit-union movement has grown—and the megabanks certainly notice that.)

Besides serving in this way, as a corrective for past actions or an existing situation, shame may function as an early-warning system to prevent malfeasance. Notice a thought or feeling that you're ashamed of, and it drastically reduces the likelihood that you'll actually do or say something to be ashamed of. This is the "iron hook" of restraint that Ryōkan praised, and its use makes shame-free personal conduct at least conceivable. Robert Bringhurst has passed on a proverb of the Haida people that shows the hook functioning at a very high level:

> In its simplest form it is this: *Asi tlagaay xhan dii qinggasang*: "The ground might see me" or "the earth might see me." You could say, in Haida, I won't do this or I mustn't do that *because the ground might see me.* Or you could say, If I did this or that, *taajaay xhan dii qingghayaagasang*, "the beach sand would be able to see me."

Bringhurst hammers the point home, commenting, "If that's what you say and you mean what you say," if you practice integrity in other words, "the earth is more than just a place to go hunting and fishing and drilling for oil. It's a moral and ethical benchmark. A benchmark with eyes. Other people may be good ethical reference points as well, but the basic moral reference is the ground beneath your feet."[40]

Shame-free conduct at the largest scales is hard to imagine. Elias Canetti, Bulgarian-born author and Nobel laureate for literature in 1981, spoke for me and surely many others in saying, "It is a mark of fundamental human decency to feel ashamed of living in the twentieth century."[41] He was referring to the genocides, wars, atomic bombings, and other sorrows of his lifetime—and would say the same thing, no doubt, of the twenty-first century if he'd lived to witness its horrors. This is a sense of shame we can't truly avoid, it seems to me. We needn't minimize the accomplishments of our species or the upsides of modernity to acknowledge that we've disgraced ourselves by the harm we've done. I "truly know" this as a shame that's mine through simple membership in the offending species but mine also to the degree that I participate, willingly or even unwillingly (as a taxpayer, for instance, funding terrible things), in the mechanisms of destruction. It motivates me to minimize all such participation and to respond to ongoing griefs as creatively as I can.

—

Canetti's words and the preceding grab bag of specimens remind us that Buddhist and Confucian societies hold no monopoly on understanding shame as virtuous. After I took up this topic in a Dharma assembly, a sangha member sent me the 74th of 147 maxims inscribed on the walls of the temple at Delphi, attributed to the temple's famous oracle: Αἰσχύνην σέβου, "Revere a sense of shame."[42] Subsequent centuries may have diminished its status, but a positive sense of shame has survived, and I'd like to think it has sufficient strength to rebound and help us today to feel "shame in the appropriate places," as Charles Taylor puts it.

None of this means that we have to stagger through our remaining years feeling horrible—not if we truly know shame, truly realize the honor inherent in it, and truly do our best to live accordingly. For inspiration, we can look to Bo Juyi (also Bai Juyi or Po Chü-i), one of the great Chan poets of all time. In 813, at the age of forty-one, he was a rising government official and literary figure who had gone home to observe a customary three-year period of mourning for his mother, when an exceptionally heavy snowfall prompted him to wonder how residents in the nearby village might be faring. In a poem written at the time, he noted that, "of ten houses, eight or nine

[were] poor" and imagined ill-clothed families around meager fires, "huddled all night, waiting for dawn." He, on the other hand, was

> snug in a thatched hall, gate shut,
> in woolens and furs, under silk coverlets,
> sitting, lying down, warmth overflowing....

He ended the poem, "Thinking of those others, I'm filled with shame, / ask myself what kind of man I am."[43]

It's a good question, and those of us living in circumstances even more comfortable than his should surely ask it of ourselves. For him, the poem answers: the kind of person who would write such a verse and make it public, the kind concerned for the welfare of people less well-off than himself, the kind who knew shame—in short, an honorable person. It follows that his sense of shame didn't end with that blizzard or that poem. Returning to office the next year, he took it upon himself to criticize imperial policy toward the peasantry and did so frankly and forcefully enough to draw a demotion and, in 815, exile to the hinterlands.

Bo Juyi offers an uplifting example but no template for our own answers to the question of what kind of people we are or our own responses to shameworthy situations. I thought of him as I read a *New York Times* article describing affluent Manhattanites' furtive attempts to conceal from their domestic help how much they paid for gourmet bread or high-end furnishings.[44] Clearly, they'd felt the honorable prick of shame, as Bo did, and just as clearly, their response—to tear off price tags and otherwise dissemble—is grossly inadequate. It can't work more than momentarily to assuage the discomfort they feel and won't work at all to remedy the staggering disparities in wealth that underlie their discomfort. Many of those well-heeled and well-meaning New Yorkers probably contribute large sums to good causes as another way to relieve the shame they feel, and I imagine that isn't wholly satisfactory to them either.

From a global perspective, of course, most of us citizens of the First World are in more or less the same boat: the high standard of living we enjoy presents us our own, less acute versions of the dilemma of wealth. And this just inaugurates a long list of shames we may feel, mounting in the direction of the all-inclusive shame Canetti voiced. For me, shame peaks when I reflect on the injuries we've inflicted and continue to inflict in nonhuman contexts. As terribly as people sometimes treat one another, nothing seems worse to me than the damage that we've wreaked on blameless life forms other than our own and on the natural wonders generally seen as inanimate—mountains, rivers, forests, deserts, the glorious seas, the very skies. We can't retract all of this devastation, but some we can remediate, and it's never too late to bow in shame and to salvage a few shreds of dignity. Nor is it too late to decide to do less harm in the days and years ahead.

All of the forgoing hinges on "truly knowing shame" in the way that I've characterized it, freeing it from now-usual pejorative connotations. Zen training has been my way, my inadvertent and lucky way, of doing that, and I recommend it to you, with one important caveat: to take it up specifically for the purpose of coming to terms with shame or other feelings is to defeat yourself before you start. Earlier, I called this a fringe benefit of Zen practice, and that's what it has to be. If you go hunting for such effects, your greedy looking will always get in the way. Ultimately, to know shame we need to know heartmind and self, to realize truly their deliciously empty nature. Realize this profoundly, integrate it well, and shame will have no lasting purchase. It'll come and go in accord with conditions, evoking responses. It's shame, yes, yet shameless in the best sense—an adornment, if you will, instead of a kleśa or a burden to other beings.

8 | Studying with the Water Buffalo

It's widely assumed that Chan and Zen go hand in hand with eco-logical understanding and behavior. That conclusion seems correct, but so far, the evidence offered to support it has been thin and often drawn less from Chan and Zen than from texts and metaphors that developed in other Buddhist traditions, especially the Huayan and Tiantai schools, or even from non-Buddhist sources such as Shintō. The Huayan image of an infinitely vast net of mutually reflecting jewels, the Indrajāla or Net of Indra, is a particular favorite, though seldom invoked in classical Chan and Zen literature.

To the extent that proponents of green Zen make reference to his-torical precedents, they typically draw upon two vigorous debates that took place during the tradition's formative period, debates as to whether nonhumans—dogs? stones?—have buddha-nature and whether inanimate things can preach the Dharma. With these important controversies long ago decided securely in the affirma-tive, it's been easy to consider the whole tradition to have earned a seal of ecological approval. But this leaves intriguing questions undiscussed and a vast amount of source material unexamined. One scholar has made a persuasive case that "ecoBuddhism" at present owes more to American transcendentalism than to buddhadharma.[1] This suggests, if nothing else, a need to pay more attention to the tradition's own teachings on the subject.

Curiously, one of the most arresting and provocative manifesta-tions of Zen's ecological affinities—a lively discourse concerning 異 類 *yilei* (or *i-lei*; J., *irui*), other kinds or species—has received little, if any, attention from advocates of green Buddhism. Part of the problem surely lies in the fact that few of us in the West have firsthand acquaintance with the Chan and Zen canon or with its original languages. Like so much else, *yilei* easily gets lost in translation, commonly reduced to "animals" or "beasts." Yet texts available in English yield evidence of the yilei theme, and even these have gone unexamined, as far as I can tell, not only by Chan and Zen students and environmentalists but also by scholars. Perhaps the foregone conclusion that our tradition is certifiably green has stifled inquiry, as a foregone conclusion so often does.

The yilei motif surfaces conspicuously in the great thirteenth-century kōan collection the *Congrong lu*. Commenting on a statement by the much-revered Nanquan, the book's author, the master Wansong, traces the lofty pedigree of what he calls "this discourse of other species," beginning with Nanquan and continuing through four equally eminent masters—Guishan, Daowu, Yunyan, and Caoshan. He also cites a string of stories in which these teachers and two other Chan luminaries, Zhaozhou and Yaoshan, address the subject of other kinds.

I'll return to some of those stories, but I want to begin with the bare bones of the matter in the form of a kōan from the *Shūmon kattōshū*, a Japanese compilation of mostly Chinese Zen texts. In its entirety the kōan reads,

> Nantang's "Ten Admonitions" says, "Walk among hitherto different species."[2]

This is the tenth of ten injunctions set forth by Nantang (or Nan-t'ang; J., Nandō), an important twelfth-century master in the Linji succession. In this instance, I've translated *yilei* as "different species" rather than "other species," hoping to clarify the sense of the kōan: Nantang is advising us to walk (or to *practice*, another valid translation of the verb) among species we've previously regarded as different from us humans—as Others. Whatever else one may derive from this dictum, it unmistakably points away from anthropocentrism, implicitly aligning Chan with modern ecological critiques.

Nanquan and others play freely with this theme in the stories gathered in the *Congrong lu*. Before recounting them, I owe it to you and to the masters involved to acknowledge that they'll seem enigmatic to many readers. Writers sometimes attach the label "Zen antics" to such accounts, as if the words and actions of Chan and Zen masters weren't serious or at least that we shouldn't take them seriously. Hooey. I used the word *play* in the first sentence of this paragraph, and I love the shining evidence of levity and friskiness found in the records left by the masters of old, but it hardly outweighs the evidence that their game was the big one of birth-and-death. The stories that follow may remind us that the game doesn't have to be played grimly, but they aim in all seriousness at its nature, at our nature. If nothing else, their repeated references to our animal kin alert us to the field we're playing in. In recapitulating their exchanges, I'll interject my own comments on the repartee, and these, too, will have a playful aspect, but I hope they'll serve the serious purpose of identifying important features of the yilei dharma.

—

One of the stories depicts Nanquan, as his life neared its end, asked by his seniormost monk where he would go when he died.[3] "To the foot of the mountain," Nanquan answers, "to serve as a water buffalo." He's already hitched to the plow. But what's that look in his eye?

The monk follows up: "Can somebody still accompany you?" A faithful follower! He doesn't give up easily.

"If you accompany me," replies the master, "you'll have to come with a stalk of grass in your teeth." An exclusive invitation. I wonder if he found a taker.

In another story, Nanquan questions a monk-lecturer about the central principle of the *Nirvāna Sūtra*. When the lecturer tells him it's "thusness," Nanquan retorts, "As soon as you call it 'thus,' it's already gone. Monks today ought to walk among other species."

A third story begins with a question from Nanquan's illustrious successor Zhaozhou: "I don't ask about differences. How about species?"[4] Thereupon, without a word, Nanquan drops to all fours. Watch out! He might charge!

No, he doesn't have a chance. On this occasion, as in the woeful case of the cat, Zhaozhou knew Nanquan's tune, and this time he responded by immediately kicking the old fellow over. Just deserts indeed.

The yilei theme gets its fullest treatment in the last of the stories repeated in the *Congrong lu*, involving the brothers and fellow monks Daowu (or Tao-wu; J., Dōgo) and Yunyan (or Yun-yen; J., Ungan).[5] Upon meeting Daowu, Nanquan asked his ordination name. "Zongzhi," Daowu responded—an impressive moniker, meaning Ancestral Wisdom.[6] How could anyone live up to it?

Sensing a soft target, Nanquan posed a question premised on the name: "Where wisdom doesn't reach, how do you realize *that*?" Uh-oh, looks like trouble! Which of them knows more about the blessed province that wisdom doesn't reach?

"We mustn't speak of it," said Daowu. Damn! We're dying to know. Why keep mum? "If you speak of it," Nanquan teased, "clearly horns will grow on your head." Maybe so, but aren't you the guy who wants to wind up a water buffalo? We should talk further.

Sure enough, three days later, as Daowu and Yunyan were doing some mending, Nanquan came upon them and said, "The other day, we commented, 'Where wisdom doesn't reach, don't speak of it' and 'If you do, horns will grow on your head.' Now, how do you practice that?" Not bad! Three days to find his tongue, five more and he might locate his nose!

Daowu immediately got up and went into the monks' hall. Pretty nimble for such a big fellow! Nanquan left, too. Well matched. Hitch them to the same cart.

But that still wasn't the end of it. Later, Yunyan asked Daowu why he hadn't answered the master's question. Wasn't it rude to leave without speaking a word? Daowu replied, "You're brilliant!" His manners haven't improved. A sibling knows how to hit you where it hurts.

Yunyan still didn't get it, so he went to ask Nanquan why his brother hadn't answered the question. Nanquan replied, "He's practicing among the other kinds." Well, that explains everything! I wish you were, too!

Flummoxed, Yunyan begged, "What is practicing among the other kinds?" Nanquan replied, "Didn't you hear me say, 'Where wisdom doesn't reach, don't speak of it; if you do, horns will grow on your head?' You should go practice among the other kinds." I say, Don't bother! Your horns are already magnificent.

According to the story, Yunyan still didn't understand, and it continues, elaborating on the point, but this much should suffice to illustrate the uses to which Chan put the other-species discourse as well as the strong connection between that discourse and the Great Matter that "wisdom doesn't reach." The issue of wisdom's nature and its limits stands at the center of the kōan in the *Congrong lu* that all these other dialogues are intended to elucidate:

> Nanquan addressed his assembly, saying, "All the buddhas past, present, and future don't know existence. Raccoon-dogs and oxen, though—they know existence."[7]

I ask you, where does true wisdom lie? With the buddhas' not knowing? Or with other species' knowing? Watch out for the horns! You don't want to wear them or get skewered on them either. The pointer introducing the kōan hones them to a terrifying sharpness:

> Becoming a buddha or serving as an ancestor is deplored as taking on a mucky name; bearing horns and fur is esteemed as occupying a superior position. Hence "True light doesn't shine" and "Great wisdom seems foolish." Still, there's one who's deaf by way of convenience and pretends not to come with an endowment. Know who that is?

Ratcheting the ambiguity up even further is the prediction that earned the ninth-century master Guishan a place of honor among the advocates for yilei listed in the *Congrong lu*. He informed his students that, like Nanquan, after his death he'd return as a water buffalo to the home of a monastery supporter at the base of the mountain. On his left flank, he added, would be the words "Guishan Monk So-and-So," and he asked his listeners what they should call him at that time, a water buffalo or a Guishan monk? Yangshan, who went on to become his greatest successor, thereupon stepped forth, made a deep bow, and left. What do you call *that*?

The other-species discourse seems to have brought a porous quality to monks' identities. When the future teacher Changqing Da'an (or Ch'ang-ch'ing Ta-an; J., Chōkei Daian) began to train under the noted master Baizhang (or Pai-chang; J., Hyakujō), he said he was seeking to know buddha and asked what it is. Baizhang replied, "This greatly resembles seeking the ox while riding the ox." Accepting that, Changqing asked what to do in the future and received a straightforward, deceptively simple instruction: "Just the same as a man riding an ox home."[8] Changqing later moved to the monastery at Guishan, the site of the preceding story, and decades afterward, when the abbotship passed to him, he chastised the assembly for making the same mistake that he'd made—seeking what they already had. He pointed their way home:

> For this purpose, I've dwelled for thirty years at Guishan, eating Guishan rice, shitting Guishan shit, not studying Guishan Chan, just looking after a water buffalo. If it plunged into the roadside grasses, I tugged it back. If it trampled someone's budding grain, I got out the whip and trained it. For a long time, how sorry I felt about its life, putting up with a human's talk! But now it's changed into a white bull on open ground, always before me, clearly evident all day long. Try to chase it off, and it still doesn't go away. You fellows all have a great, priceless treasure.[9]

In the parlance of our culture, many would call this a story of a man making peace with his inner water buffalo, but the vivid physicality of the description communicates a confusion of self and other, a Changqing who's as much water buffalo as human. The animal he speaks of training has evidently completely outgrown his control, becoming an indomitable presence and disposing him to teach what seems to have unavoidably become water-buffalo Dharma.

One of Changqing's most influential contemporaries, the master

Xuefeng, is said to have embraced water-buffalo nature even more explicitly. One day, he asked a monk, "This water buffalo—how old is it?" When the monk didn't respond, Xuefeng answered for him, giving his own age, seventy-seven.

"But master," the monk objected, "why should you take the part of a water buffalo?" We can't blame him, I suppose; he probably thought Xuefeng's stature placed him far beyond the state of a mere animal. Xuefeng himself had no such idea: "What would that violate?" he demanded.[10]

While some masters concentrated on blurring the species boundaries, others worked to clarify the relationship of human and nonhuman in other ways. Meeting a monk who recently had arrived from southern China, Zhaozhou questioned him, using a word that in Chan dialogue often signified the body:

> "Who's been your companion?"
> "A water buffalo," the monk answered.
> "Such a splendid monk!" Zhaozhou exclaimed. "Why do you keep company with an animal?"

The monk should turn tail and flee! How many are there, after all? Instead, he plodded straight ahead, alleging,

> "It doesn't differ."
> Zhaozhou replied, "What a beast!"[11]

—

I hope the preceding makes it clear that the instruction to practice among other species became an important element of classical Chan teaching and that it doesn't reduce to simplistic notions about the goodness of animals, the importance of remembering that people are animals, too, or anything of that sort. Intimately addressing the nature of heartmind as it does, this discourse eluded easy understanding. Indeed, when Zhaozhou wanted to impress upon his monks how far they had to go to equal their predecessors, he selected this phrase as a litmus test of maturity in the Dharma and readiness to teach:

> For instance, Nanquan very commonly said, "You must practice among other kinds." Now, how would you understand that? These days, nurslings and pipsqueaks head for the crossroads. They prattle about tangling vines in exchange for sustenance and go looking for respect. Gathering a crowd of three or five hundred, they say, "I'm a *kalyānamitra*. You are students."[12]

Don't let it happen to you!

The theme of practicing among other kinds crossed to Japan at an early date, turning up repeatedly in the writings of Dōgen.[13] It also got some new twists, perhaps none better than one inspired by an ox and delivered by the freethinking fifteenth-century master Ikkyū. Noticing the massive creature at the home of a lay supporter, Ikkyū brushed a poem and impaled it on one of its horns:

> Practicing among the different species—I've done that.
> Capacities depend on sense fields, sense fields on capacities.
> Entering life, we forget the time and route we've come by,
> not conscious these days of which monk family I'm from.[14]

Please tell me, who's speaking here, the man or the ox? We all know which one wrote the poem, but can you extricate one voice from the other? Moo!

This essay is no more than a curtain raiser on our tradition's other-species discourse, a first peek at a subject that I hope others will examine more thoroughly and expertly. Preliminary though it is, it's not too soon to observe the extraordinarily prominent part that water buffalo and oxen play in it. Their role as engines of Asian farm work since time immemorial probably goes a long way to explaining this; few animals would be as familiar and even fewer as highly valued or attractive to exemplify the placidity, power, and reliability of our original nature. It's certainly no coincidence that the famous Oxherding Pictures presents its visual and poetic paradigm of Chan and Zen training in terms of a monk who seeks, tracks, sights, ropes, tames, "rides the ox home," and then forgets both the ox and himself at the moment of awakening.[15] The ox and water buffalo also had good precedents in Mahāyāna texts such as the *Lotus Sūtra*.[16]

As the raccoon-dogs of Nanquan's dictum remind us, affinity with the ox and water buffalo didn't blind masters of old to the usefulness of other "other species" in pointing the way. Dongshan borrowed another image from classical Indian Buddhist texts, calling on disciples to "follow the bird path."[17] When the noted master Changsha (or Ch'ang-sha; J., Chōsha) was asked about different species, he replied laconically, "A foot short, an inch long,"[18] propping the door to further inquiry wide open. Ants, fish, crabs, sheep, frogs, monkeys, deer, dogs, foxes—many other kinds of creature surface in the literature of Chan and Zen and deserve attention for what they suggest about the nature of heartmind and the relationship of humans to members of other species. It would be a shame to overlook sayings like this one, from the Zen phrase book: "A whale drinks water from a clean bowl; / a rhinoceros's touch lights an oil lamp."[19]

Finally, we'll have to ask ourselves what these teachings and our own training imply for the way we see nonhumans and the way we meet our responsibilities in the world we share with them. It doesn't seem overhasty to judge the tradition profoundly respectful of what other species have to teach us or to conclude that it beckons us toward a less managerial, more humble attitude to Earth and its nonhuman members than our reputedly advanced civilizations presently take.

This preliminary look at our tradition's other-species discourse also seems sufficient to give pause to any ecology-minded Western Buddhists who assume that transcendentalism and buddhadharma go hand in hand. The foregoing stories scarcely comport with this mainstream transcendentalist view:

> He is blessed who is assured that the animal is dying out in him day by day, and the divine being established. Perhaps there is

none but has cause for shame on account of the inferior and brutish nature to which he is allied. I fear that we are such gods or demigods only as fauns and satyrs, the divine allied to beasts, the creatures of appetite, and that, to some extent, our very life is our disgrace. [20]

So wrote Thoreau in *Walden*. As fond as I am of him and of that book, as fond as *he* was of the scraps of Asian wisdom he encountered in his reading, and as observant and knowledgeable as he was about species (especially the plant life) of his place, Thoreau evidently saw animals through bifurcating lenses of purity and impurity and would have rejected instruction to "practice among the other kinds."

I urge everyone, Buddhist or not, to take up that practice. If we can go beyond the conceit of a species hierarchy with *Homo sapiens* at its pinnacle, it will be an excellent first step toward rectifying our relationship with other beings. For those of us who inherit the traditions of Chan and Zen, embracing this practice and realizing its implications might launch a fresh exploration of what its teachings could contribute to ecological understanding and living.

9 | Apples and Oranges, Fruits of the Incomparable

My late teacher often cited the adage "Comparisons are odious," a slice of wisdom that dates from at least the middle of the fifteenth century and mirrors an even earlier French saying, *Comparaisons sont hayneuses,* "Comparisons are heinous, hateful." A Chinese maxim takes an even stronger stance: "Comparing people leads to death; comparing produce leads to waste."[1] We seem to have a consensus across cultures on the unpleasantness and the potential destructiveness of comparisons. Yet they keep coming, as though innate to human thought. Wherever they come from, it seems important to sensitize ourselves to them and their dangers and to learn to respond to them wisely. Chan and Zen offer a critique of comparison that could be of help.

A verse by the semi-legendary Chan poet-recluse known as Han-shan, Cold Mountain, encapsulates the conundrums of comparison in four short lines. After opening with an attractive comparison, he pivots to the impossibility of comparison before handing the whole problem over to his reader:

> My mind resembles the autumn moon,
> pristine, glittering in a moss-green pool.
> Nothing in the world bears comparison.
> Advise me: how shall I express it?[2]

That concluding line poses what literary people call, often disparagingly, a rhetorical question. Rhetorical it may be, but I read it as a serious question, too. How could I ever convey to anyone else the actual quality of my own mind? Or how could I truly convey the sight of that luminous moon, shimmering in that particular pool, that night? I can't adequately express such experiences or their impression, their sensory or supersensory impact on me.

Hanshan's "Advise me" has the impish aspect of a challenge, a dare almost. Can you do it? Can you do it better than he just did it? If not, we have to admit language's inadequacy, and the step just beyond that is admitting the utter incommunicability of any experience. And yet…somehow Hanshan *has* done it, even in translation. He's brought us along. We see what he was pointing to, never mind the flaws of comparison. "The failure," as the master Wumen observed in a different context, "is an elegant performance!"[3]

I suspect my teacher's fondness for "Comparisons are odious" derived in large measure from the man who introduced him to Zen, R. H. Blyth. It's an expression Blyth loved, and in his book *Zen in English Literature and Oriental Classics*, he went so far as to opine that "All Zen is contained in this proverb. Zen is the comparison-less life."[4] While that pronouncement claims too much for the proverb and too little for Zen, it's true that Chan and Zen teachers have criticized comparison from an early date, usually attacking it sternly and frontally, without the humor and indirection of Hanshan's poem.

The *Xinxin ming*, or the "Trusting Heartmind Inscription," the early doctrinal verse whose authorship is customarily credited to the Third Chan Ancestor, flatly declares comparisons fundamentally baseless: "Lacking grounds and criteria, / things can't be judged or compared."[5] In his record, the great Tang-dynasty master Baizhang is found emphatically seconding the point, saying, "The Dharma has no comparisons because there's nothing it can be likened to; the Dharma-body is unconditioned and doesn't fall within the scope of classification."[6] The acclaimed later master Dahui took a more practical tack, reminiscent of the Hanshan poem. He quotes Śākyamuni—"One may wish to reveal it with comparisons, but in the end, there's no comparison that can explain"—and comments,

"Saying it is 'broad' and 'vast' has already limited it, to say nothing of wanting to enter this broad and vast realm with the limited mind."[7] From the perspective of these masters, comparisons simply don't work; they can't.

I don't know if many contemporary teachers besides my own have explicitly cautioned their students about comparison, but Peter Matthiessen recalls an instance of the late Nakagawa Sōen Rōshi doing so as he was conducting *sesshin*, a multiday period of intensive Zen training. In his colorful, somewhat broken English, Sōen Rōshi exhorted the attendees,

> "Do not compare to anybody else: do your own zazen. Some young, some old: just do your best! Do not compare elephant and flea! The elephant walks...—but the flea can *spring*!" He made a springing motion. "Both flea and elephant are best in world!"[8]

None of us have the option of approaching Zen practice, or life as a whole, the way someone else does. Identical twins share most circumstances—genetic, familial, economic, historical, cultural, geographic—but not even they have exactly the same formative experiences or lead lives in lockstep. Our differences, however small, make everyone's practice unique and all comparisons faulty.

Sōen Rōshi's speech exemplifies a central theme of Zen teaching on this subject: not to deny differences, simply to respect things as they are. The Zen phrase books abound with sayings that appear comparative if read with comparative eyes but, taken at face value, acknowledge and celebrate specificities by simply placing them in juxtaposition:

> Willows green, flowers red.
> A jackal yelps; a lion roars.
> Mountains have hazelnuts; marshes have lotus seeds.
> Birds fly into the ungovernable heavens; fish frolic in
>   unfathomable pools.
> Cold fowl go up into the trees; cold waterbirds go down into
>   the water.[9]

On one occasion, the famously eloquent Zhaozhou presented such a contrast as the epitome of his teaching:

> Question: "Elsewhere, if somebody abruptly asks, 'What Dharma does Zhaozhou expound?' how should I reply?"
> Zhaozhou said, "Salt costs a bundle; rice comes cheap."[10]

Often when someone these days exclaims, "No comparison," it's actually to underscore a comparison: "That's the best pickup on the road, no comparison!" But when a Zen teacher says, "No comparison," it ought to genuinely mean no comparison. Aitken Rōshi called this the teaching of perfect differences, offering as his own favorite example, "The crow goes caw-caw; the sparrow goes cheep-cheep."

—

In espousing this way of noncomparative seeing, as on many other subjects, Chan and Zen undoubtedly drew upon the indigenous Chinese wisdom traditions, Confucian and Daoist, as well as upon Buddhist sources. The *Analects* state the principle in no uncertain terms, though in a manner that seems oddly self-canceling: "Noble people include and don't compare; petty people compare and don't include."[11] Just saying, huh? This formulation advocates inclusion better than it models it, and compilers of Zen phrase books have chosen to select only the first clause, omitting the second and thus eliminating the comparison that otherwise muddies the vital message.

The evenhanded acceptance of things evident in Chan sayings such as "Willows green, flowers red" had stronger precedents, parallels, and inspirations in Daoist texts. Assimilated into the corpus of Chan and Zen more or less directly, for instance, was a passage from *Zhuangzi*:

> Something long doesn't constitute a surplus; something short doesn't constitute a deficit. Accordingly, although a duck's legs are short, stretch them, and it would feel distress; although a crane's legs are long, cut them off, and it would grieve. So what's

by nature long needs no trimming, and what's by nature short needs no extension.[12]

We find this expression reverberating through a number of texts, including the teaching record of the influential twelfth-century teacher Yuanwu, where it appears in one of his instructions to the monastic assembly:

> The heat of a fire can't compare with the heat of the sun; the cold of wind can't compare with the cold of the moon. Crane legs are naturally long; duck legs are naturally short. A pine is naturally tall and straight, while brambles loop and bend. Geese are white, crows black. Everything is manifest in this manner. When you completely comprehend this,... everything you meet will be the teaching.[13]

This argument for incomparability goes far beyond the frequently heard complaint about comparing apples and oranges. That's an objection only to the *terms* of a comparison, not to the enterprise of comparison itself; it stops at asserting that a comparison is unfair because the items being compared aren't sufficiently alike. In contrast, the Chan and Zen examples I've cited, like the *Zhuangzi* text, turn similar pairings into expressions of inherent completeness, and Yuanwu has taken it a step further, teaching that each thing just as it is—if viewed noncomparatively—presents the Dharma.

Elsewhere, commenting on a Chan poem, Yuanwu says,

> If you pass through at these lines, then and there above, below, and in the four directions, there's no comparison. The myriad forms and multitude of appearances—plants, animals, and people—everything everywhere completely manifests the way of your own house.[14]

From this vantage point, the whole of life and death, no matter whose, defies comparison—each moment incomparable, all beings unique, every set of circumstances unprecedented in its details and unrepeatable. Whether or not one awakens to this "comparison-less life," by no means does it begin or end with Zen. Should you decide to practice and succeed in realizing it, though, it will affirm "the way of your own house"—the dao of everyday affairs and, at the same time, the very dao of the Chan and Zen tradition.

A verse in the *Congrong lu* drives home the point in a manner at once firm and graceful:

> In beehives, the pollen of cliff-face flowers becomes honey;
> in musk deer, the nourishment of wild grass becomes
>   perfume.
> In keeping with its kind, whether three feet long or sixteen,
> brilliantly apparent, wherever you go it looms magnificent.[15]

The "it" of the poem, whether you call it dao or buddha-nature, proceeds to fruition along diverse pathways and reveals itself in unique, infinitely various forms, each of them "in keeping with its kind."

Still, comparisons and implied comparisons persist in our thoughts and language, so we might do well to consider the dangers they pose. Look back at that Chinese proverb, "Comparing people leads to death; comparing produce leads to waste." The second clause makes good sense: fruit with blemishes, repeatedly rejected in favor of perfect specimens, will eventually get tossed out. The first clause seems grossly exaggerated, though, since we and others compare people every day without lethal consequences. But this literal reading misses the point: comparisons lie behind the us-them thinking that produces prejudices, divisions, and conflicts among us of all kinds, thus leading to death figuratively and, alas, all too actually.

Between the World and Me, Ta-Nehisi Coates's justly praised book about growing up Black in contemporary America, provides an illuminating example of this process—the distress he felt upon reading a snide question posed by Saul Bellow, one of the last century's most highly regarded American novelists: "Who is the Tolstoy of the Zulus?"[16] The implication, of course, was that the Zulus have never produced an author who could compare with Tolstoy, that their culture was inferior. Looking into the context of Bellow's question, I saw that it flowed from his despair about the multi-culturalist trend in literary studies, which he considered faddish and unwarranted. Asking, "Who is the Tolstoy of the Zulus? The Proust of the Papuans?" he was out to defend his cultural heritage against the idea that the peoples of Africa, the Pacific islands, and other nations distant from the metropole had produced literatures deserving equal attention and appreciation. He may have meant no harm, but it was, all the same, a deadly comparison.

As an African American student attending Howard University in the mid-1990s, Coates reacted to this putdown by scouring the library in search of African novelists who *could* measure up to Tolstoy, who could defeat Bellow's invidious comparison for him. He describes the eureka moment that occurred when, instead, he happened upon the response the author Ralph Wiley had made to Bellow's question: "'Tolstoy is the Tolstoy of the Zulus,' wrote Wiley. 'Unless you find a profit in fencing off universal proper-ties of mankind into exclusive tribal membership.'"[17] These words brought home to Coates that he'd fallen for Bellow's premise, the "fencing off" that gives rise to "racecraft." Bellow spoke out of a sense of a privileged Us, whose literary standards could stand as a global yardstick of literary accomplishment, thereby legitimizing denigration of Them.

The "insects of comparison," to borrow a phrase from poet and Zen student W. S. Merwin,[18] typically work in this manner, out of sight and unnoticed but doing terrible damage. Those on the receiving end of injurious comparisons suffer the worst of the harm, but anyone who makes such a comparison is injured, too. Bellow's comparative thinking blinded him to the merit of what the "Zulus" have to offer and accounts, I suspect, for a mean-spirited, super-cilious tone that sometimes intruded on the work of his late years.

Even positive comparisons may be injurious. In the case Sōen Rōshi spoke of, the "flea" diminished itself by comparison to an "elephant," in the process overlooking its own strength, its extraordinary capacity to "spring." Less obvious, probably, is how flattering comparisons also do harm to their objects by trapping them in others' expectations. Though supposedly superior Zen students may never *know* that people have projected elephantine qualities upon them—strength, toughness, placidity, majesty, leadership, memory, whatever—those notions can't help but subtly or not so subtly distort interactions, often resulting in disappointment when an "elephant" proves fallible. Of course, this dynamic plays out in groups of all kinds, not just in Zen communities; we see it most blatantly when celebrities, divine in the fantasies of their fans, publicly stumble and find themselves suddenly demoted to idiots or villains.

This isn't to suggest that we ought to dispense with comparison altogether, especially if it's turned to a benign or positive use. "Shall I compare thee to a summer's day? / Thou art more lovely and more temperate."[19] A Chinese adage reminds us, "Without lofty mountains, you don't see the plains."[20] To avoid habitual comparison seems wise, however, and the wisdom of "perfect differences" offers a way to enjoy the merits of comparison while, at the same time, savoring the "comparison-less life" that Mr. Blyth advertised.

The shift required—from judging phenomena against one another to seeing them neutrally juxtaposed—is challenging, though. We've worn the lenses of Better and Worse so long that we forget we're wearing them or how powerful they are. It may not be difficult to appreciate perfect differences in nature, to enjoy the luminous fact that "Cold fowl go up into the trees; cold waterbirds go down into the water," but sustaining that perspective in a charged social interaction is a mighty test for the best of us. Of course, it's in arenas of that sort, politics for one, where the wisdom of perfect differences also stands to have its biggest payoffs.

By way of inspiration, I recommend an approach to societal differences advocated by the trailblazing cultural anthropologist Clifford Geertz, a method he called "comparing incomparables," apologizing, as he did so, "for this Zen koan...way of putting the matter."[21] Geertz demonstrated his method with an account of the remarkably different definitions that three societies have historically given "fact" and have practiced law. His fascinating essay lays out each of those three systems of thought and practice with respect, even admiration, as an ingenious means that its people developed to deliver justice in their culture and thus to enable their members to live together compatibly for the long haul.

By treating these systems of fact and law descriptively, each as an order complete unto itself, Geertz avoids the pitfalls of comparison. We see profound differences among the systems, alright, but arraying them sympathetically side by side illuminates their differences instructively, with an enlivening rather than deadening effect. Geertz describes this as a procedure of

> ... bringing incommensurable perspectives on things, dissimilar ways of registering experiences and phrasing lives, into conceptual proximity such that, though our sense of their distinctiveness is not reduced (normally it is deepened), they seem somehow less enigmatical than they do when they are looked at apart.[22]

That seems right but doesn't capture the aesthetic quality of his accomplishment. I'm reminded of a Dutch Renaissance still life: a cluster of purple grapes, a juicy slice of cantaloupe, a couple of blushing pears, some apples, each fruit glowing with its own peculiar brilliance, improved by proximity to its companions. Contrast, yes, and truly no comparison.

10 | Crossing Over:
From Saving to Liberation

A few years ago, I collected fourteen translations of the Four Infinite Vows, a brief verse of commitment typically recited every day in Zen centers, temples, sitting groups, and homes as well as in other Mahāyāna Buddhist settings. Of these translations, ten used the word *save* in the first line, including the one that I'd chanted with slight variations for more than forty years: "The many beings are numberless; I vow to save them."[1] I drew my sample from diverse sources, and though far from complete, it probably represents usage in Zen communities in the United States reasonably well. It certainly demonstrates how hard translators have leaned on the verb *to save*.

It's an old, compact, and powerful word, with several clusters of meaning and numerous applications. That makes it at the same time very useful and often nebulous, with some part of its usefulness derived, no doubt, from that very vagueness. One can save time by performing a task efficiently, save money by finding a bargain price, save leftover food by storing it properly, and save someone from bleeding to death by applying a tourniquet. But what does it mean to save a species? Is it enough to maintain a small population reproducing in a zoo, aquarium, or botanical garden? Can a language be saved in a meaningful sense by compiling a dictionary, working out its grammar, and archiving recordings of its last native speakers? In 1860, when a federal "Indian schools" program was established in the United States, how did its founders suppose they could, as they said, "kill the Indian, save the man"? What did Mary Pipher imagine the subtitle *Saving the Selves of Adolescent Girls* would mean to buyers of her bestseller, *Reviving Ophelia*? What hope was it that pioneering forest ecologist Suzanne Simard meant to offer us when she wrote, "This is not a book about how we can save the trees. This is a book about how the trees might save us"?[2]

No doubt some of the appeal and power of the verb *to save* stems from the importance of salvation in Christian doctrine, preaching, rite, and symbol, and even when the word appears in a decidedly nontheological context like "Save the whales!" it has at least a muted messianic tone. First-time visitors to a Zen temple reading the vow to "save" others might intuit that it has a different import than in common parlance, but they'd have to have superhuman insight to guess what "save" actually denotes in the context of that vow.

Since translators have employed *save* to interpret the meaning of several Chinese words, confusion about it goes well beyond the first of the Four Infinite Vows, but let's begin with the character used in this instance, *du*. It may be written with the water radical, like *dan*, or without, but it typically refers to making a crossing of some kind, very often crossing a body of water.[3] In medieval China or Japan, one could du by means of a boat or a bridge or by wading. (No one seems to swim.) People could du under their own power or be carried across through the efforts of others, and the crossing could be literal or, as in the first vow, figurative. Ordination came to be known as 得度 *dedu* (or *te-tu*; J., *tokudo*)—to attain crossing. Buddhas and teachers were sometimes given the epithet Master of the Great Crossing,[4] other times called upon to serve people by functioning as a Great Bridge.[5]

Once we recognize that the vow to "save" others entails this sense of traversing a body of water, we find ourselves in a frame of reference that "saving" in itself doesn't convey. It derives from an image, established in early Buddhism, of using a raft to cross the perilous river dividing "this shore" from "the other shore," samsāra from nirvāna.[6] The Four Infinite Vows originated in another school of Buddhism, and the dualistic nature of the image made it a somewhat awkward fit for Chan, as a tradition insistent on the *identity* of saṃsāra and nirvāṇa,[7] but the metaphor of the two shores and of liberation as a crossing from one to the other was cemented into Buddhist heritage so firmly that Chan and Zen masters inevitably retained it, albeit often subtly modified to suit their own purposes.

Sometimes in our texts, the word *du* alone conveys the idea, without explicit mention of the two shores, and in such instances, its translation as "saving" masks it totally. For example, in the classic account of the monk Huike begging the Indian sage Bodhidharma to instruct him, he frames his plea as an entreaty to "ferry over all kinds." Even in highly reputable translations, this becomes a request to "save all sentient beings."[8] Similarly, though the recluse and poet Hanshan wrote, "With skillful means, I carry over all beings," English readers have instead received, "I use what remedy is at hand to save the world."[9]

Seldom do Chan texts make ostentatious reference to the theme of crossing, but in a late account of the Sixth Ancestor Huineng's awakening, an unlikely, almost slapstick scene overtly dramatizes the idea. To help Huineng escape pursuit by angry monks, Hongren, the elderly Fifth Ancestor, accompanies him to a river crossing in the middle of the night, directs him onto a small boat, and takes up the oar. Huineng objects:

> "Your Reverence, please sit. Your disciple should row."
> Hongren said, "I should take you over."
> Huineng said, "When one is deluded, one thinks teachers take [you], but when one has awakened, one realizes that one crosses over by oneself. Although 'cross over' is only a single term, its uses are varied....I have received transmission of the Dharma from you, master, and I have now become awakened. Can it be anything other than that self-natures have crossed themselves over?"[10]

This heavy-handed enlargement of the Huineng legend exploits the metaphor to showcase Huineng's brilliance, to exemplify the relationship of master and disciple, to shed light on how such a crossing occurs, and to advertise its transformative impact.

More often, the tradition has called on the image of crossing simply to promote the ethic of helping others to liberation, as in guidance that Yuanwu gave one of his students:

> When you yourself have crossed over, you mustn't abandon your bodhisattva vows. You must be mindful of carrying all beings across, steadfastly enduring the attendant hardship and toil that comes from serving as a boat to the realm of thoroughgoing wisdom.[11]

In a political context, the much-admired Zen abbot Shaku Sōen resorted to this imagery during the Russo-Japanese War of 1904, in an effort to assure American audiences of his nation's noble motivations:

> ...every follower of the Buddha builds a great boat of compassion, launches it on the great ocean of birth and death, steers it with the rudder of great faith, and sails forth through the whirling tempest of egotistic desires and passions. No Buddhist will ever relax his energy, until every one of his fellow creatures be safely carried over to the other shore of perfect bliss.[12]

Notwithstanding these examples, members of the tradition have preferred to soft-pedal the crossing metaphor, especially its going-from-here-to-there aspect. The concept gets trashed in a text customarily attributed to Bodhidharma but probably from a later hand:

> When deluded, this shore exists; when you awaken, it doesn't. Accordingly, ordinary people stay completely on this [shore]. But those who wake up to the supreme vehicle, their heartminds dwell neither on this [shore] nor on the other, so they can leave behind this shore and that. If people view that shore as differing from this one, their heartminds utterly lack dhyāna.[13]

Masters also found ways to turn the imagery of boat and bridge in directions compatible with the tradition's primary teachings. One approach has been to direct attention to the means and manner by which the great crossing is made. For instance, a dialogue in the record of Zhaozhou (later a well-known kōan) alludes to a beautifully engineered bridge, still standing, in the city that gave the master his name:

> A monk said to Zhaozhou, "For a long time, I've looked forward to seeing the stone bridge of Zhaozhou. Now I've arrived and see just a rude wooden bridge."
>
> Zhaozhou said, "You just see a rude wooden bridge. You don't see the stone bridge."
>
> The monk asked, "What is the stone bridge?"
>
> Zhaozhou said, "It carries donkeys over. It carries horses over."[14]

Some translators alter the grammar of Zhaozhou's response, making the animals the subject of his dictum—"Horses cross, donkeys cross"—and thereby mistaking his emphasis.[15] The animals cross, alright, but Zhaozhou was pointing to the bridge that enables their transit, the beautifully *un*-engineered bridge that accepts and carries over all comers everywhere, regardless of status, weight, time of day, species, or any such factor.

Another tale depicts Zhaozhou viewing the bridge with his head monk and asking who built it. The head monk gave the historically correct answer—an official of old named Li Ying—only to have the master press him further: "When he built it, where did he set his hand?" In other words, where did he start his work? The head monk couldn't reply. "People *talk* about the stone bridge all the time," comments Zhaozhou. "When asked where to set a hand, they don't know."[16] This oblique but stinging rebuke, if it struck home, showed the head monk where to start work. Zhaozhou's graceful span almost begs to be crossed.

These tales of the stone bridge have echoed through the Zen

world for centuries, inspiring untold private insights as well as many public responses. Their influence is evident in a poem by the multitalented thirteenth-century master Musō, honoring a Kyoto landmark, the Togetsu-kyō, or Moon-Crossing Bridge:

> It arches like a rainbow
>   dividing the stream
>   joining the shores
>   one line
>   a road bringing life
>   crossing the quiet waves
>   It has carried
>   donkeys across horses across
>   but there is more to come
>   In the middle of the night
>   the moon is crossing it
>   pushing a cart[17]

How strange! With this unexpected closing, Musō shifts attention from the bridge, how it works, and what it carries to the still greater mystery of who makes the sort of crossing that our tradition regards as its reason for being and how such a crossing occurs.

The later master Hakuin, another person of extravagant gifts, liked to take bridges as a subject for his ink paintings. A number of them depict blind travelers on their hands and knees, in grave peril as they crawl across precipitous gorges on narrow bridges built of jointed planks. The cautionary message of these paintings reveals itself at a single glance. A related set of his works conveys a complementary ideal: a solitary monk standing at ease, midway across a bridge of the same kind, gazing into the distance. A painting in the latter group, representing a historic bridge northeast of Tokyo, bears an inscription in which Hakuin restates the first vow in fitting terms: "Let's erect a bridge like this for all the people of this world, too."[18]

Boat imagery has offered equally rich possibilities for evoking the crossing to nirvāna. In passages already quoted, Yuanwu and

Shaku Sōen conjured ships "carrying all beings across," piloted by captains (read "teachers") deeply committed to the cause. Expressions like "great boat of compassion" invite us to imagine vast, oceangoing vessels, but ships capable of doing the job might be of extremely modest dimensions, as Yuanwu playfully observed elsewhere, applauding a succinct presentation of the Dharma: "A one-leaf ship containing the whole empire!"[19]

Teachers down through the centuries have given assurance that vessels bound for the other shore are readily available and have furnished tips on where to get aboard. The twelfth-century master Hongzhi ended one of his finely crafted verse commentaries, "Today's rivers and lakes—what obstructs or impedes you? / Everywhere are fords and crossings with boats and carts!"[20] An earlier master, Danyuan (or Tan-yuan; J., Tangen), pointed out a ferry "beneath a shadowless tree."[21] Anyone who succeeds in locating such a tree, one that flourishes outside the realm of light and dark, will find a very peculiar vessel waiting there—"bottomless," to quote Chan master and literary virtuoso Wansong, with "a single place to cross."[22] As such a boat rides the currents, Dōgen notes, a passenger "looks at the shore and mistakenly thinks that the shore is moving," not the ferry.[23] Altogether, it amounts to a pretty strange trip.

The image of boats gliding along on the current is one of several metaphorical options that the mobility of boats opened up, options that bridges couldn't offer. Hanshan exploited this possibility in a poem that celebrates his seclusion on Cold Mountain for enabling him to escape confining notions, including the idea of getting anywhere at all, even to the other shore:

> Settling at Cold Mountain, many concerns ceased right off;
> instead, I don't have mixed-up thoughts fixed in my head.
> In my leisure, I daub impromptu poems on the cliff face
> and yield, turning this way and that like an unmoored boat.[24]

The maverick Zen monk who dubbed himself Baisaō, the Old Tea Seller, found similar freedom in busy eighteenth-century Kyoto. Dispensing tea by the cup at scenic sites, he eked out a meager subsistence from donations he received and left poems registering the liberty he found amidst all the commotion and delusion:

> ...seated squarely in the city streets
> red dust far as the eye can see,
> an empty boat drifting freely
> among the troubled urban waves.[25]

Nine centuries earlier, Bo Juyi had used the same image but in reverse. This government official and Chan layman who recorded his shame at the winter sufferings of poor villagers, lamented the degree to which he himself was tied down and tossed around by illness and concerns: "I'm a boat bouncing on the waves, / moored to this, tugged away by that."[26]

So slip the moorings we must, whether dwelling in the capital or in the boondocks, but a boat drifting on the current is much more likely to wash downstream than to make it to the other shore. It's best to not worry about that, these writers hint; preoccupation with crossing may only impede your crossing. Indeed, Wansong mooted a prospect actually superior to crossing:

> This matter is like someone riding in a boat, not landing at either shore, not staying in midstream. ... But tell me, how about when turning the rudder, turning the boat around? Deep in the night, resting in the reedy shoals, going far beyond the middle and two sides.[27]

Suffering such disorientation, it's not easy to find the crossing point, the 津 jin (or chin; J., shin). It appears on various Zen maps, a narrows usually specified as a ford or a ferry crossing or sometimes a bridge. Recapping his career as a monk and later a lay tea seller, Baisaō says that he sought the yaojin, the necessary or crucial crossing point, in a hundred places before finding it at last, and he grieves that many jabber about it but few "know the tune."[28] An early Chan text, known as "Treatise on Contemplating the Heart-mind" or "The Treatise on Breaking Through Form," equates the elusive crossing point with the heartmind, *xin*: "Heartmind is the entrance to the whole world. Heartmind is the critical ford [*guanjin*] to liberation. Those who know the entrance—why fret the hardship of passing through? Those who know the critical ford—why worry about not getting past?"[29]

A verse preface to the *Record of Linji* portrays that master as governor of a ford near his temple, at once its stern guardian and a beneficent ferryman enabling wayfarers not only to get across but even to become Dharma prodigies:

> His temple overlooking the old crossing [du],
> he ferried across those who came and went,
> decisively controlling the vital crossing point [yaojin]—
> a sheer cliff eighty thousand feet high.
> Tearing away person, snatching away circumstances,
> he molded and shaped saindhava.[30]

Though you may not have made the crossing yourself or possess the exquisitely sensitive ear of a zhiyin, now that you're keyed in to these crossing-point metaphors, the story of a diligent monk's crossing will read more clearly than it previously would have:

> Qingshou Xiang went all-out from daybreak to night. One day, on an errand to the town of Huiyang, he bypassed the Zhao crossing [du]. His questioning lucid and unbroken, he didn't notice that he'd reached the crossing point [jin]. A fellow traveler brought him to, saying, "This is the river-crossing!" Suddenly compassion and joy came together.[31]

This tale illustrates what experience repeatedly confirms: the crossing point is right at hand, but we only reach it when, thoroughly absorbed in what we're doing—"questioning lucid and unbroken, he didn't notice"—we're *oblivious* to reaching it. Thus, making the keenly hoped-for crossing occurs as a sort of accident, usually precipitated by something mundane, in this case by a perfectly resonant phrase. A subsequent passage reports another exemplary detail: Qingshou's teacher dismissed this breakthrough, prodding him toward greater awakening.

Okay, if one gets lost enough to find the elusive crossing point, then what? In the sūtras, Śākyamuni teaches that, upon reaching the other shore, you should abandon the raft that carried you there, but in Chan and Zen refinements of the metaphor, successful seekers often steer their boats back to the shore they've left, bringing home the treasure they've received—"a boatload of moonlight," in one interpretation of the gift.[32] Other traditional sayings situate the return poetically both in the landscape and in the process of Zen training. One emphasizes its beauty and serenity: "White sea grasses in a light breeze, autumn river dusk, / By the old bank, a boat returns swathed in mist." Another saying lays the accent on the messiness of returning to samsāra: "The old ferry landing— mixing with mud, drenched in water."[33] Willingness to jump into that muck, to get down and dirty, defines the bodhisattva.

—

Translators have also applied the language of saving to standard Zen terms other than *du* and to metaphors other than boats, bridges, and fords. I won't attempt to inventory and evaluate them all, but a couple of them deserve notice, starting with the one that seems closest to ordinary conceptions of saving, 救 *jiu* (or *chiu*; J., *ku* or *gu*). This character, denoting rescue or deliverance from hardship, occurs in many epithets for the bodhisattva of compassion, Guanyin, and some traditions of East Asian Buddhism do imagine Guanyin interceding to save people in the literal sense, swooping in to catch a person who's fallen off a cliff, for instance. As a rule, however, Chan and Zen give narratives of that sort little space and less credence.[34]

When *jiu* occurs in a Chan or Zen text, it rarely refers to saving someone physically—from fire, say, or drowning[35]—more often to delivering them from delusion. A case in point:

> One day, at Nanquan's temple, Zhaozhou went up into the well house to draw some water. Seeing Nanquan passing by,

he grabbed a post, let one of his legs hang into the well, and shouted, "Rescue [jiu] me, rescue me!"

Nanquan hit the well-house ladder and said, "One, two, three, four, five."

Zhaozhou thereupon came down from the tower, put on his robes, went up to Nanquan's quarters, and said, "Thank you for rescuing me a while ago."[36]

This, too, exemplifies the sort of "direct pointing" and "saving" that our tradition has taken as its core business. At the close of the *Platform Sūtra*, Huineng actually combines *jiu* with *du* in exhorting his audience to perpetuate the way of awakening: "Direct teaching of the Dharma has flowed [to China] from the west; / in order to rescue and ferry worldly people across, you must train yourselves."[37] In a similar vein, Dōgen Zenji chose *jiu* to characterize his own aspirations: "to spread the Dharma and rescue beings."[38]

Wei, a second verb that translators have repeatedly rendered in terms of saving, is the *wei* of *wuwei*, a broad, multipurpose word roughly equivalent to the English *to do*.[39] Joined with the character for person, it means something like "to work for people" or "conduct as a person" but has received strangely salvationist translations such as "to save people according to their type, he mixes with mud and water" and "how did the old-time sages save men?"[40] Once, after Zhaozhou informed his assembly that he didn't like to hear the word *Buddha*, one of the monks asked him, "All the same, do you wei people or not?" At this, the master leapt straight into the slime, crying out, "Buddha, Buddha!"[41] How many crossed over at those words the record doesn't say.

Translators and teachers have applied the idiom of saving to several more words that play a prominent part in Chan and Zen texts, but further examples would add little to the point of this essay thus far—that recourse to the rhetoric of "saving" has obscured our tradition's primary and unambiguous commitment to awakening people and, in the process, has allowed or suggested to Western readers a range of interpretations never intended. Though this overview hardly exhausts the creative ways that teachers in our tradition have applied metaphors of "crossing over," I hope it makes plain that they didn't intend the vow to du all beings to denote saving others by feeding them, freeing them from prison, protecting them from violence, and the like, worthy as such actions may be.

For quite a few years, I myself spun the vow to "save beings" that way, assuming (and arguing in print and in person) that it demands engagement in political activism or at least public service as an aspect of our practice. One piece of evidence I often marshaled in making my case was the last of the Ten Oxherding Pictures, which I initially encountered under the title "Entering the Marketplace with Helping Hands."[42] In that tenth frame, having awakened, the oxherd transforms into the jovial, big-bellied, gift-giving figure known as Hotei, often mistakenly called the Laughing Buddha.[43] I understood, or thought I understood, that realization relieved a person of selfish concerns, spontaneously remaking each of us, sooner or later, into a universal helper and benefactor. When I later read D. T. Suzuki's translation of the title, "Entering the City with Bliss-bestowing Hands,"[44] it confirmed and strengthened that impression, and years passed before I saw the incongruousness of such interpretations. Hotei wasn't giving free massages or handing out checks to pay the rent.

Once again, inspection of the original text made it clear that these pictures don't imply "saving" or "helping" others in a practical sense. Jolly old Hotei exemplifies the bodhisattvic turnabout; he's made the fabled crossing and returned to offer the townspeople the chance of awakening, nothing more, nothing less. The title for the tenth frame actually makes no mention of either helping or bliss; it reads, "Entering the Town with Dangling Hands."[45] This is an image open to several interpretations, but its uses in canonical Chan and Zen literature are consistent with the project of carrying other beings over to nirvāna. It connotes complete liberation and availability: having one's hands free, unconstrained by social convention or even priestly ideals. At the same time, it also indicates a refusal to tamper in the process of awakening—Chan and Zen masters' longstanding commitment to take a hands-off approach to teaching, "directly pointing" rather than explaining. Reflecting on the term *dangling hands*, my Dharma grandfather, Yamada Kōun Rōshi, said, "When a Zen master leads the student in practice, he pulls the student along although his hands are at his sides."[46]

The texts accompanying the tenth picture make Hotei's purpose plain. The introduction concludes, "At the wine shop and fishmonger's, changing people's course to become buddhas," and the verse confirms, "With his direct teaching, dry snags burst into bloom." This image of a dead tree suddenly blossoming is a classic metaphor of awakening and leaves no room for doubt about what Hotei has up his sleeve or in his sack.[47] Modern explications of the Oxherding Pictures tamp down expectations that a master or accomplished practitioner can pull up to a gas station or enter a grocery store and cause "dead trees" to flower (not so fast!),[48] but that doesn't alter the fact that the course of training depicted in the oxherding sequence is consistent with the imagery of du, of ferrying others to liberation, and has nothing to do with offering other forms of salvation, however beneficial.

—

So far, I've focused on specimens of crossing imagery from Chan and Zen texts, but our tradition was hardly alone; such imagery not only abounds in writings of other Buddhist schools but also passed into popular works. Among the latter, the most famous and in many respects the most outrageous and influential is *Journey to the West*. Published under a pseudonym toward the end of sixteenth century, it fictionalizes the epic journey to India that the monk Xuanzang made nine hundred years earlier. At a climactic moment, the pilgrim and his companions reach "a torrent of water eight or nine miles wide" spanned only by a narrow log. Some log! They're spared the terror of a crossing on this grossly inadequate bridge by the appearance of, you guessed it, a bottomless boat. As the boatman (a buddha in disguise) poles them across, the corpse of the Xuanzang character floats by. With this, at last the surviving Xuanzang has made the crucial crossing of the river of birth-and-death and soon goes on to meet Śākyamuni himself![49]

Study of the literature of crossing, fanciful or not, has left me no choice—leaves none of us any choice, I think—but to concede that there's negligible support for broad interpretations of du, jiu, wei, or other words commonly translated as "saving." What our predecessors intended by the vow to carry others to liberation can be fairly summed up under three headings. First, it expresses an orientation to one's own training: a wish that it redound to the benefit others, not serve narrow self-interest. American Zen pathfinder Ruth Fuller Sasaki called it a "vow to share with all fellow sentient beings the fruits of the practice, whether they be few or many." She saw it, functionally, as the true point of departure for the whole of Zen training: "Only when the first vow has been fully taken," she wrote, "is the Zen follower ready to begin the practice."[50] Although medieval Asian masters may have couched the point differently, they unquestionably considered that intention normative to Mahāyāna tradition.

Second, the vow encapsulates the teaching that one person's awakening inherently entails all beings' awakening. This understanding is epitomized in the pronouncement that, according to Chan texts, Śākyamuni issued after his great liberation beneath the bodhi tree: "I and sentient beings of the great earth have in the same moment accomplished the Way."[51] So functions the boat metaphorically empty and bottomless that our ancestors imagined. Accommodating all beings, it ferries its vast cargo across somehow, all at once. One of the few masters to hazard an attempt at saying how this happens was Huineng. At least that's what the Platform Sūtra tells us:

> Wise friends, "All beings without limit I vow to du" doesn't indicate that Huineng carries you across. Within heartmind, all beings, each with its own body and own nature, cross themselves over.[52]

You got that? It sounds like he's telling us that we all make the crossing *ourselves*, as we are, yet that we do so *within* a heartmind that has no possessor. If I tried to explain what Huineng might have meant by this, I'd only add proof that such explanations are utterly fruitless.

A third sense of the vow complicates the subject even further. To fulfill the vow in this sense requires that you, once you've carried all beings over with your own awakening, also help others find the crossing point and awaken. Don't let the contradiction bother you; it's only an artifact of logic. This mirrors the tenth Oxherding Picture, and Chan and Zen texts have historically called it the "downward turn" in the arc of training, with the paradigmatic example being Śākyamuni's post-awakening descent from the mountains to preach the Dharma in the dusty world below. Masters have used several colorful phrases to call those who've had the heady experience of awakening to make this figurative descent: to "lower their clouds," "fall into the weeds," or even "go down into the blue dragon's cave."[53] Chan adopted a concise statement of this principle from another school of Buddhism: "Above, seeking awakening; below, affecting all beings."[54] Like the motif of carrying all beings from one shore to another, this above-and-below formulation meshes poorly with the tradition's condemnation of dualistic thinking, and masters made sure to note that—while using it anyway.

—

The strong textual record that the vow to du all beings didn't mean saving others from poverty, violence, and the like doesn't mean that our predecessors in the tradition turned a blind eye to suffering or completely rejected helpful activities. When it came to "affecting all beings" in samsāra, the bodhisattva ideal furnished a rationale for charitable actions, one that Eisai Zenji called up when challenged on his decision to donate some metal, intended for a new figure of the Buddha, to a man whose family was starving. Admitting that doing so violated the monastic rule against private use of sangha property, he told his questioners,

But consider the will of the Buddha. He cut off his own flesh, his limbs, for the sake of living beings. For people about to die of starvation, wouldn't it accord with his will to have given them the whole figure? Even if I had to suffer rebirth in a hell realm for the offense, I would still save people from starvation.[55]

The evidence Eisai cites comes from the *jātaka* tales, which recount Śākyamuni's previous lives in which he again and again sacrificed himself for others' welfare. Each of these instances is seen as a step on the immeasurably long path to buddhahood for him and also for the beneficiaries of his kindness.

Inhibiting use of this rationale (and probably the reason that it seldom appears in Chan and Zen texts) is the fact that longstanding Buddhist doctrine placed charitable activity under the rubric of accumulating merit and that, starting early in its development, our tradition denigrated merit-making as an inferior path at best. Teaching that all beings are innately buddhas and that we can, and should, realize this now by making the vital crossing, Chan and Zen masters have typically considered generation of merit an approach fit only for people who lack the aspiration to awaken in their current circumstances and who only seek future blessings (such as a salutary rebirth) for themselves or someone else.[56]

That said, like the other schools of Buddhism, ours depended for support on the merit-making of patrons, and its annals give evidence that our predecessors themselves engaged in the sort of public service said to generate great merit. I don't think it can simply be coincidental that they often directed such efforts to providing safe means of crossing bodies of water or that these ranked high among ways to acquire merit listed in texts such as the *Sūtra on the Fields of Virtue and Merit*. Translated early in China's encounter with Buddhism, the sūtra depicts Śākyamuni ticking off seven particularly worthy forms of donation, of which two involve water crossing:

The first is to construct stupas, monastic quarters, halls and buildings. The second is to provide gardens, orchards, pools, woods and cool places. The third is to donate medicine and treat the infirm. The fourth is to maintain boats to help the people cross rivers. The fifth is to establish bridges so that the ill and weak can cross rivers. The sixth is to dig wells close to roads so that the thirsty may drink. And the seventh is to make latrines and places of convenience.[57]

Providing boats at river crossings may have generated merit, but it didn't leave physical traces as bridge building did, and for that reason, if for no other, we have little more than scattered stories about Buddhist ferry services.[58] Erecting bridges, on the other hand, captured the sustained interest of both patrons and chroniclers, producing ample documentation of Chinese monks' involvement in bridge construction. Acting as fundraisers, project managers, and engineering specialists, they were called on so regularly that a count of bridges built with monastic assistance in one province during the Song dynasty comes to nearly a hundred.[59] One Chan master of that period, venerated for his civic contributions, left a "Sermon on Repairing Bridges" in which he declares that "building bridges is a Buddha act that brings peace to people and causes heaven to rejoice."[60]

Sangha involvement in bridge building seems to have been less common in Japan than in China, but it continued at least intermittently. The records of Hakuin Zenji contain his appeal for funds to span the Yahata River at a point prone to flooding, where people were frequently swept away, sometimes drowning. Initiating the campaign to erect a bridge at the site, he engaged in an ingenious bit of wordplay:

> Putting up a bridge here is of vital importance and would be a deed of the greatest virtue as well.... An undertaking such as this, which would provide great relief to people, can also be seen as a kind of skillful means, promoting crossing over.[61]

Hakuin's voluminous writings leave no doubt whatsoever that carrying people to liberation in the classical sense—inspiring, guiding, urging, goading, enticing, browbeating them to cross over to realization—was his lifelong mission, but his record also manifests his willingness to respond in energetic fashion when impressed by public need. For him, as for other masters before and after, the two senses of *du* chimed.

Given the long, rich history that the imagery and rhetoric of river crossing has in our tradition and teachers' creativity in deploying them, it seems a shame to let it continue to be subsumed under, and obscured by, the idiom of saving. Admittedly, the language of crossing has lost some of the salience it possessed in medieval times, when even relatively small bodies of water sometimes posed a risk to life and when boats, bridges, and fords held correspondingly great importance, but surely "crossing" hasn't exhausted its relevance or its usefulness in communicating the Dharma. Indeed, current events lend it fresh potency. The news brings regular images and reports of desperate people crossing rivers and seas to escape violence, deprivation, and persecution, reminding us of other urgent forms of crossing: crossing national borders without authorization, "crossing the aisle" in an epoch of ruinous partisanship, crossing boundaries of race, gender, class, and belief, and crossing the divide between people and "other kinds."

The language of saving is obviously attractive to translators; it's so common in everyday parlance that it can be taken for granted, used without explanation in translating a wide variety of positive terms. I hope no one comes to the close of this essay imagining that I consider it inferior to the language of crossing over. It does, however, have a long, complex history of its own, with strongly theological overtones that make it a dubious choice for Chan and Zen texts. Our school has always held Śākyamuni up as a model of wisdom and virtue, a guide and inspiration, not as a redeemer or a source of salvation. The future buddha, Amitābha, is viewed as a sort of savior by Pure Land Buddhists but has scarcely any place in Zen tradition.[62]

Let's be clear when reciting that first of the Four Infinite Vows! All beings, without limit, I vow to carry over to liberation. I really do, and this boundless commitment aligns me—and all those who join in the vow—with our Dharma predecessors through the centuries. An impractical vow at the best of times, it seems especially far-fetched in the disastrous conditions we face now, demanding a completely unreasonable trust in the Dharma's potency. Yet somehow I share in the wild, inordinate trust that the eminent tenth-century Chan master Fengxue (or Feng-hsüeh; J., Fuketsu) expressed in a verse presented to his students on the morning of his death:

> The dao, borne by time, must necessarily carry beings over;
> those far off now, longing for it, will themselves rise and soar.
> Ages to come will have old coots with sentiments like mine;
> every day incense will burn, every night the lamp will glow.[63]

Having read this far, you won't be surprised to learn that the language of salvation clouded this text, too, when it was initially published in English: "Truth, availing itself of the flow of time," wrote the well-meaning translator, "must of necessity save all beings."[64] But never mind! The lamp, whether you understand it as the flickering altar light of a wizened master or the lamp of the Dharma transmitted through the generations—it still shines. That much I can promise you.

11 | Walking in the Dark

A spring night in 1989 found me, my wife, and two fellow sangha members on a beat-up jeep road in Death Valley, walking in the dark. Owing to an accident, we needed to make the hike at night to join the rest of our party, which had walked into the canyon by day and established a campsite. We had flashlights in our backpacks but left them there, knowing that if we used them they'd go dead before we reached camp. A new moon low in the sky cast a wan light, lighting the old two-track just enough so that we could negotiate it reasonably well, without stumbling on its stone-studded surface or straying into the brush. Our eyes opened to the darkness. It seemed oddly substantial, varied, rich.

We walked more or less shoulder to shoulder and, by agreement, in silence. The road ran generally due west, giving us moonlit stretches where we could stay on course with ease. Often, though, came spells of perfect blackness, as canyon walls forced the road south or north and cut off the moonlight completely. Then we had only foot sense to go by, literally feeling our way, differentiating the hard-packed, rutted road from the loose gravel and rock of the roadside. The first couple of times we entered that total shadow, we inched along, but the more we walked, the less tentative our steps became in even the darkest patches.

Maybe we sank into a sort of group samadhi; I don't know. Whatever happened, it felt good. The walk probably lasted three hours but, as we walked, seemed to go on forever, forever in the best sense—as if it had always been like this and, owing to our mishap on the road, we'd received the privilege of entering it. We stopped a couple of times to ask for one another, laugh, and sip some water, then went on. The moon set before we reached the slumbering camp, alert, tired, happy.

Unusual as our trip into the canyon seemed, it felt familiar, too. I'd done some walking of a similar sort during my years as a school-teacher on Maui, limbering up after long nights grading papers, pacing unlit, thinly trafficked upcountry roads. I'd become accustomed, too, to stepping out of my new home in the Sierra Nevada foothills to relieve myself under its wonderfully dark, starry skies. But the peculiar sense of familiarity I experienced as we hiked into the canyon that night had a second source, which revealed itself the next morning as our group settled into a two-hour period of zazen before daybreak.

For seventeen years, I realized, Zen practice had been teaching me to walk in the dark—to leave behind all that I knew, or thought I knew, to enter a terrain at least as unknown to me, as winding and unforeseen, as that canyon road in Death Valley. It wasn't only the trackless terrain of Zen practice. Just as murky, I had to admit, were the realms of work, romance, the economy, politics, the state of the Earth—in short, of all but the most immediate, tangible things. Zazen had been teaching me, I now saw, how to step into the future.

That experience inspired a poem titled, inevitably, "Walking in the Dark," which I gave to one of the friends who'd made the hike. He showed it to other friends, who teased him, taking the poem as a not-so-subtle suggestion that he knew nothing about Zen, that I considered him "in the dark," benighted. Here was another discovery: not that they'd misconstrued what I wrote but *how* they'd misconstrued it. Their negative interpretation brought home the bias our society held, and still holds, against darkness. Three years later, I revised and expanded the poem, dedicating it to a sangha friend in Hawai'i dying of cancer. He understood well. He too was feeling his way, forgoing steroids in order to read the road ahead as clearly as possible, walking soberly hand in hand with his wife and four-year-old son.

It seems unremarkable that previous generations felt a fear of the dark or that we moderns inherited it from them. When the night world was lit only by the stars and moon, then by torches, candles, gas lamps, and the like, fearsome things commonly transpired under cover of darkness, and even now, in cities whose glow can be seen from space, many awful things still do. But since prehistoric times, cultures have fortified the association of darkness with danger, equating it with skullduggery, death, and spooky, malevolent forces—"dark powers," as they're known. It seems almost a matter of necessity that God's inaugural act in the Judaic and Christian creation story is to drive out darkness and that Satan be crowned the prince of darkness, sovereign of a dismal hell.

The ancient Greeks envisioned Hades, fierce ruler of the underworld, wearing a helmet of darkness and invisibility, driving a team of black horses, and maintaining a jealous reign over the population of the dead, so the dire imagery of darkness predates the Abrahamic traditions, and it has thrived ever since. Do you see any sign that it's weakening? I don't. The modern social imaginary often seems not much more than a many-chambered underworld thronged by "shady" characters whose prevailing language is violence.[1] Dr. Freud, of course, authorized such an understanding of ourselves, postulating the presence of a lively id in each of us, "the dark, inaccessible part of our personality" perceptible only in small degree through dreams and neurotic symptoms and largely "of a negative character."[2]

The association of darkness with mental illness is especially strong in characterizations of depression. While the medieval belief that "black bile" causes melancholy seems naïve and absurd in light of modern neuroscience, we moderns still seem unable to avoid representing this particular type of anguish as an enveloping, abyssal darkness. His skills as a novelist enabled William Styron to describe depression, his own and others', in creative and wonderfully diverse ways, but when he picked a title for his trailblazing book on the subject, it was *Darkness Visible: A Memoir of Madness*. Since then, the disease model of depression has gained strength and may someday weaken the rhetorical hold that darkness has maintained. In 2022, however, the author of *A Cure for Darkness: The Story of Depression and How We Treat It* tightened that hold with his patently ironical title, reminding us that medicine still has no more a cure for depression than geophysics has a cure for night.[3]

In public discourse, the staying power of darkness as a negative trope was demonstrated when the *Washington Post*, soon after Donald Trump's inauguration in 2017, adopted the slogan "Democracy Dies in Darkness." Representatives of the paper downplayed the timing, saying that the phrase had been a newsroom favorite for years and that it simply expressed the importance of "certain institutions" in ensuring that there's light. Three years later, speechwriters for Joe Biden felt no such compunction about deploying the trope, using it relentlessly as Biden accepted his party's nomination. Trump had "cloaked America in darkness," declared the president-to-be, and had authored a "chapter of American darkness," while he himself pledged to be "an ally of the light, not the darkness."[4]

An orientation toward light as the medium of knowledge and truth, foe and dispeller of darkness, is as deeply rooted in culture as equating darkness with things dangerous and demonic. Here again, though not without precedent or parallel, biblical imagery has contributed heavily to popular use. The gospels transfer Yahweh's function as the great illuminator to Jesus, the savior, whose unequivocal pronouncement "I am the light of the world" and promise that his followers "shall not walk in darkness, but shall have the light of life" continue to echo in popular song and story as well as in sermons and prayers.[5]

Its ecclesiastic heritage hasn't prevented light's association with truth and goodness from radiating into secular realms of endeavor. Indeed, in the eighteenth century, with the ascendancy of empiricism, science, and technology, light became emblematic of dispassionate thought—the freeing of reason from the constrictions of faith. The thinkers driving this development in France thought of themselves as *les lumières*, and in the English-speaking world, the movement came to be known as the Enlightenment. It was seen as casting its clarifying light into every field of study and serving the cause of human progress as a whole, materially and otherwise.

It's unsurprising, then, that people today of very different persuasions reach for light as a metaphor when they describe their efforts to drive out a darkness of some sort. Biologist, avowed atheist, and author Richard Dawkins, as ardent a rationalist as ever strode the earth, chose to title his autobiography *Brief Candle in the Dark: My Life in Science*. Congresswoman Marjorie Taylor Greene, whose ultraright-wing views have made her something of a news totem, thinks of herself as a bringer of light, too. Defending her decision to speak at a conference of white nationalists, she piously declared, "We must tutor our youth in the ways of righteousness so they do not stray into darkness."[6]

I don't mean to suggest that metaphors of light and dark are unidirectional. For either of them, countervailing expressions aren't hard to find. Light may be glaring or blinding, darkness a refuge from heat, guarantor of privacy, ambience for romance.[7] There's no question, however, about the value usually assigned to them: darkness is negative, light positive. It's utterly normal to assimilate darkness to something feared or unwanted and thus expectable that, for example, Dylan Thomas would bid his dying father not to "go gentle into that good night" but instead urge him, "Rage, rage against the dying of the light."[8]

Of course, there's nothing incorrect about these light-dark metaphors in themselves, and their organic relationship to human experience of day and night has made them commonplace in cultures worldwide, including those of India and China. In Chinese, 明 *ming* (J., *myō*) couples the characters for sun and moon, with a span of meanings rich and familiar: light, brightness, clarity, perception, perceptive, intelligent, wise, and so forth. It's the standard translation of the Sanskrit *vidyā*, which is usually brought into English as *knowledge* but shares its root with *view, vision, evident, wit,* and *wisdom*. Its opposite, *avidyā*, became 無明 *wuming* in Chinese (or *wu-ming*; J., *mumyō*), without light, and has typically been translated as *ignorance*—referring not to an educational deficiency but to the delusions that cause and perpetuate suffering.

The oppositional construct underlying both the usage of light and dark in contemporary English and the formation of these Sanskrit and Chinese terms didn't survive in Chan and Zen. Undoubtedly reflecting Daoist influences, early Chan masters destigmatized darkness, depicting it as equal and reciprocal to light, with its own virtues and its natural place in the great scheme of things. The *Platform Sūtra* depicts Huineng stressing the inseparability of the two:

> Darkness is not darkness by itself; because there is light there is darkness. That darkness is not darkness by itself is because light changes, becoming darkness, and with darkness light is revealed. They originate each from the other.[9]

"The Tallying of Difference and Sameness," a Dharma poem credited to the esteemed eighth-century master Shitou, at once seconds and complicates the relationship:

> In the very midst of light, there's darkness,
> but don't take darkness as its equivalent.
> In the very midst of darkness, there's light,
> but don't take light as enhancing vision.
> Light and dark respond to one another,
> cooperating like front and back legs, walking.[10]

Light and dark co-respond, you might say, in every respect. Without darkness, how could light even be conceived? Without light, what meaning would darkness have? Endlessly entailing one another, they exemplify the mutuality of Shitou's title and of all being.

In the following century, another master who looms large in early Chan history, Huangbo (or Huang-po; J., Ōbaku), borrowed the language of light and dark for a discourse on buddha-nature. Read in literal fashion, it says,

Our root substance, from the start, is buddha. It doesn't rely on practice and realization, doesn't depend on gradual progression. It's neither light nor dark. It's not light and thus dark, not dark and thus lacking darkness. Hence, "There is no darkness and also no end of darkness." To enter our family gate, you must perceive it this way.[11]

Translated more figuratively, it becomes,

Our root substance, from the start, is buddha. It doesn't rely on practice and realization, doesn't depend on gradual progression. It's neither wise nor ignorant. It's not wise and thus not ignorant, not ignorant and thus lacking ignorance. Hence, "There's no ignorance and also no end of ignorance." To enter our family gate, you must perceive it this way.

The embedded quotation, from the *Heart Sūtra*, cements this discourse of light-and-dark into a fundamental doctrine of Mahāyāna Buddhism. For Huangbo and teachers after him, to "perceive it this way" became a sine qua non for membership in the Chan school and, later, in that of Zen.

Freedom from the conventional, oppositional view gave masters scope to put the imagery of light and darkness to work with great abandon, as inspiration struck. Case 86 of *The Blue Cliff Record* offers a particularly lovely and potent example:

Yunmen gave instruction, saying, "Each of us, without exception, has a brilliant light. If you look for it, you can't see it. The darkness is dark, dark. What generates this brilliant light of all humankind?" On behalf of the assembly, he himself answered, "The storeroom, the gate."[12]

Zhaozhou struck a very different note, describing in almost rhapsodic terms the darkness that he experienced doing zazen as dusk deepened into night:

> Sitting in solitude, the one empty room dark,
> without a flicker of candlelight the whole time:
> before my eyes the purity of perfectly black lacquer.[13]

In a contrasting, unpoetical vein, Yuanwu simply affirmed both light and dark as dao: "As for brightness, it fits; as for darkness, it fits."[14] A century later, his fellow commentator, Wansong, got playful with the old metaphors, relieving buddhas and other illustrious predecessors of the "stink of Zen" and lauding the perfection of nonhuman animals:

> Becoming a buddha, serving as an ancestor—dubious badges, foul names! Wearing horns, being cloaked in fur—esteemed positions, superior status! Thus true light doesn't dazzle; great wisdom resembles ignorance.[15]

I could easily proliferate examples of Chan and Zen masters' deployment of metaphors of light and dark, but I trust the preceding will suffice to indicate that our tradition has given darkness its due, appreciating its virtues no less than those of light.

To close this discussion and bring it full circle to walking in the dark, consider a capping phrase in the record of Daitō Kokushi, fourteenth-century teacher of Japan's emperor: "Though the Jiange Road is perilous, / nighttime travelers are more numerous."[16] To appreciate this little gem, you need to know that the *ge* of Jiange, 劍閣, refers to a plank walkway chained to the face of a cliff, an expedient but extremely perilous means of traversing sheer heights. *Jian* means a double-edged sword but here names the set of sharp natural spires that surround a pass entering the Chinese region now known as Sichuan (or Szechuan). As for "nighttime travelers," shorthand for thieves, we can be sure that Daitō had a particular sort of robber in mind—someone intent on breeching the walls of self and other and making off with the prize of bodhi.

Why would such a thief take this dangerous route under cover of night? In the daylight, others can see where you're headed, and even the idea of others will make this pass impassible. Worse yet, in the daylight, *you* can see where you're headed, in which case there'll be near and far, high and low, concerns about safety, and fantasies of arrival. In the dao of Chan and Zen, walking in the dark is sometimes the only way—walking in a darkness of wu wuming.

Yet any attempt to remain in the dark, to avoid light in its turn, masters of our tradition wouldn't tolerate. This is exemplified by a dialogue between Zhaozhou, on pilgrimage, calling on the established master Touzi (or T'ou-tzu; J., Tōsu). Zhaozhou posed the question, "When someone undergoes Great Death and revives, what about that?" Touzi replied, "Night travel prohibited! Presentation by daylight required!"[17] Nighttime is the right time for release from all constricting notions of self—for Great Death—but afterward, no, "Presentation by daylight required!"

Three decades and more since our night walk in Death Valley, I continue to feel grateful for the accident of circumstances that brought darkness home to me as native habitat, a vast and abundant territory I'd largely overlooked till then. Our hike opened up for me, too, the interplay of light and dark—the light in the dark, the darkness in the light—and sensitized me to darkness as a vital aspect of our tradition, revealing its place among the family treasures. I love sunshine, the dance of flames in a campfire or a woodstove, the lamp's beam on my book at night, and all the possibilities light presents for expressing the otherwise inexpressible, but it seems to me now that, in Zen practice and in the uncharted transit from birth to death, darkness may teach us what we most need to learn.

12 | How the World Works

I know—a preposterous chapter title, a subject impossible to cover adequately at any length, certainly in an essay, and a topic, moreover, that I'm absolutely unqualified to address. I'm foolish enough to take it on only because the set of observations I'm going to offer here is, like the rest of the book, focused on what Chan and Zen tradition have had to say over the course of many centuries, not on personal theories recently hatched. The grandiosity of its title notwithstanding, this essay won't attempt an explanation even remotely comprehensive. Leave that particular version of the Big Picture to seers and philosophers, physicists and biologists.

For our purposes, we can start where Chan starts, with its First Ancestor, Bodhidharma, and a statement in verse that he's said to have made in recognizing Huike as his Dharma heir:

> I've come as rootstock to this land,
> to convey the Dharma, settle delusions.
> A single flower opens five petals,
> setting fruit that matures on its own.[1]

This seems an undistinguished bit of poetry, judged either by literary criteria or as a presentation of the Dharma, and its bearing on the question of how the world works is, I imagine, somewhat less than apparent. But consider: this is the verse chosen by compilers of the massive, imperially sanctioned *Transmission of the Lamp* to mark an occasion that, from their perspective, was truly momentous: the Dharma's transfer from Indian to Chinese hands. It would be peculiar, given the consequential nature of that event, if Bodhidharma's quatrain *didn't* somehow encode their understanding of the world's dynamics.

Indeed, inspection of the text turns up a conspicuously Chinese philosophical element in an utterance supposedly from the lips of an Indian master. Its fourth line contains a two-character phrase I've translated as "on its own"—自然 *ziran* (or *tzu-jan*; J., *jinen* or *shizen*)—literally "self-so," so of itself. Etymologically, this seems to mean self-igniting, and translators typically interpret it with the words *natural* or *spontaneous*. It's how things effortlessly take place: the sun brings light and heat, stars rotate through the night sky, rain falls, streams flow, glaciers advance and recede, hawks pounce on rabbits, flowers open, and fruit forms—a process occurring universally and without guidance, independently. Ziran is a fundamental concept in the tradition known in Western thought as Daoism, the basic organizing principle of the cosmos as presented in the *Daodejing*:

> People take after the earth,
> earth takes after the heavens,
> the heavens take after dao,
> and dao takes after ziran.[2]

My very recognition of ziran, I see in retrospect, may be put down to ziran: it began with an accident—on its own, without my intention—and has since grown in the ten directions, with no terminus in sight. That process conforms with almost eerie precision to the promise that Dōgen makes in concluding his primer on zazen, the *Fukanzazengi* (and that I chose as the epigraph for the introduction to this book): "The storehouse of treasures will open of itself"—there it is—"and you may use them as you please."[3]

Dōgen gives an especially exuberant exposition of such functioning in a text titled "Plum Blossoms," conspicuously alluding to the Bodhidharma poem and to ziran in particular:

This old plum tree blossoms all at once, and of itself fruit is born. It brings forth spring; it brings forth winter. Sometimes it brings forth gusty winds; sometimes it brings forth torrential rains. Sometimes it's simply the head of a patch-robed monk; sometimes it's the eye of an ancient buddha. Sometimes it becomes grass and trees; sometimes it suddenly becomes a pure fragrance. Its sudden uncanny transformations and wondrous ways are inexhaustible....

When the old plum tree suddenly comes into bloom, the world of blossoming flowers appears. Whenever the world of blossoming flowers appears, that's what we call "spring arriving." On that occasion, there's a single flower that opens five petals. At the time of this single flower, there are three, four, or five blossoms, or a hundred, thousand, or ten thousand blossoms, innumerable blossoms....

All blossomings everywhere are offerings from the old plum tree. There is the old plum tree of the human world and the old plum tree of the heavenly world. Owing to its tree-merit, the old plum tree manifests both ordinary human realms and heavenly realms. Accordingly we call the hundreds and thousands of blossoms both ordinary and heavenly. Thousands and millions of flowers are the blossoming of the buddhas and ancestors. At that instant, "Buddha has appeared in the world!" is exclaimed; "I've come as rootstock to this land!" is exclaimed.[4]

In light of modern science, this paean to self-so blooming and fruiting may seem naïve and ziran a paltry concept, but it frames the crucial question of how humans fit—individually, as societies, and as a species—into the spontaneous processes, the wild dynamics of the cosmos. From the broadest perspective, we clearly participate in the mix as much as anything else. Unless you reject the evidence of evolution, it's apparent that our bodies, faculties, traits, and behaviors have developed ziran, in the same way other creatures have, and our history has unspooled in that manner, too— not randomly but not "according to plan" either, driven by complex forces that remain debatable centuries afterward. From another standpoint, though, humankind has intruded mightily upon the self-so, rearranging the world (and, lately, sending missions into space) to suit its interests rather than allowing the ten thousand things to develop unmolested.

This difference not being lost on Laozi, Zhuangzi, and kindred thinkers, they drew a distinction between two types of activity—what happens on its own, which they termed *wuwei*, literally "without doing," and its opposite, what happens because people actively make it happen, *youwei* (or *yu-wei*; J., *yūi*). Wuwei includes bodily functions like digestion, respiration, and circulation that typically proceed without our intervention, ziran, so this isn't a distinction that excludes humanity, nor is it as clear-cut as it may seem at first blush. Isn't a rabbit *doing* something as it nibbles the grass? Doesn't a hawk dive on that rabbit as purposefully as you or I prepare a meal? The line between wuwei and youwei gets still blurrier if we admit that the thought processes enabling us even to entertain concepts like wuwei occur beyond our control, the product of neuronal excitation in circuits of the brain that takes place without our conscious direction.

Blurry though it is, the wuwei/youwei distinction is serviceable enough for the purpose of discussing human habits and their impact on us and on the world we belong to and depend upon. Beyond any point Laozi might have imagined, ingenuity has magnified our power to intervene in the self-so and to modify things to suit our needs and wishes. Other creatures modify things, too, of course, but to a relatively modest extent and, as far as we can tell, with very limited intentions, if you classify them as intentions at all. A beaver dams a stream to make a pond that serves its needs within its immediate circumstances; it doesn't construct a hydroelectric dam to generate power to light distant cities. Our youwei capacity has swollen vastly beyond our requirements for survival and the perpetuation of our species, yet we—especially people of so-called advanced societies—have pursued knowledge and put it to work for us as if there were no tomorrow and as if there were no others warranting consideration. We behave as though we hold a mandate to control the rest of the self-so and to indulge at a grand scale in because-we-say-so.

Underlying and enabling this exercise of power is a conception of how the world works that contrasts starkly with ziran and makes it seem quaint: efficient causality. "Felix qui potuit rerum cognoscure causas," wrote Virgil in the first century B.C.E. "Happy is one who's able to know the causes of things."[5] By his time, Indo-European civilizations already had established a pattern of dis-integrating the world into units of matter and forces and had begun the continuing endeavor to determine basic elements (still often referred to as "the building blocks of life" but now reaching infinitesimally small size) and to establish laws governing interactions among these elements. Efficient causality is a sort of billiard-ball paradigm in which units of matter or energy exert specific forces upon one another with quantifiable and generally predictable results.

Explanations generated under this paradigm, particularly in the biological and physical sciences, have proven immensely powerful in extending our capacity to understand and control the self-so—to light up the dark, to raise crops and livestock, to fly, to split atoms, to transplant organs, to forecast weather, to explore the sea depths and outer space. These extraordinary feats have led its most ardent practitioners and proponents to pooh-pooh any perspective on life, death, and the cosmos that can't be corroborated in strictly scientific terms. A much-decorated member of that tribe, the late entomologist and conservationist E. O. Wilson, went so far as to predict that someday knowledge will be integrated in "a skein of cause-and-effect explanations from brain to mind to culture, connecting the natural sciences with the social sciences and humanities."[6] In this vision, the scientific project will culminate in a full, triumphant accounting for causes not just of wondrous phenomena like color vision but also of Picasso and perhaps, beyond that, of his breakthrough painting "Les Demoiselles d'Avignon."

As far-fetched as Professor Wilson's forecast seems to me, I imagine all of us can feel the momentum that the paradigm of efficient causality has gained and recognize the degree to which it has penetrated societies around the world. It isn't just trade, finance, and communications that have "globalized" in the past half century; the successes of this paradigm and of its instrumental, exploitive relation to so-called resources have made it irresistibly attractive, at least to business and government elites, even in cultures where it has little or no historic standing. As costs of the resulting plunder come clear, however, the crush of events—ecological and social destruction, if not outright collapse—is forcing reconsideration of our extravagant doings.

—

That the medieval Chinese were no slouches at understanding what makes things tick is indisputable in view of their achievements prior to 1500, which included the magnetic compass, ball bearings, smallpox vaccination, lacquer, printing, metallic amalgams for dental fillings, and dendrochronology (tree-ring dating).[7] The practical knowledge of cause and effect demonstrated by these inventions, however, was nested within a worldview that granted considerable power to influences of a kind that many today would class as superstitious or spiritual. Joseph Needham, an English biochemist and the first Westerner to make a close study of Chinese science and technology, called this worldview "organismic" and recognized its organizing principles as "correlative."[8] At not too great a risk of oversimplification, it can be said that, under this conception, nothing solid exists. The whole shebang is in process: a person, the weather, a mountain, an idea, a nation—each is an unfolding event, not a fixed entity, and develops in keeping with a system of influences. Governing the process is a patterning force known as *ganying*, literally evoking-responding, which is famously exemplified in the *Zhuangzi* by the fact that a note plucked on an instrument in one place will call forth an answering note from an instrument lying untouched nearby.[9]

Affinities between such similar or otherwise correlated "events" create these resonances. A famous, early commentary on the *Yijing* (or I-*ching*), the *Classic of Changes*, explains:

Like tones resonate together, like energies seek one another.
Water flows toward moisture, fire moves toward dryness.
Clouds follow the dragon, winds follow the tiger.
Sages arise, and the ten thousand things take note.
The heaven-rooted feel kin to above, the earth-rooted feel kin
    to beneath.
Like this, each follows its own kind.[10]

While the more physical of these paired "kinds" seem obvious, the assertions that clouds follow the dragon and winds follow the tiger rest on ancient Chinese beliefs in the dragon as the maker of weather and ruler of the waters and the tiger as master of the mountains and forests.

You don't have to accept those correspondences or others endemic to Chinese cultures in order to appreciate the core premise of the paradigm: that the world is intricately networked and responsive in keeping with natural affinities. Chances are, you've experienced resonances of this sort yourself—feeling inexplicably simpatico with someone you've just met, drawn to a certain place or an activity you've never tried, struck with an unaccountable force by something you've just heard or read or tasted. What's going on here? Ganying seems, at the least, a plausible way of construing such dynamics, and I think we can acknowledge without indulging in a narrative of preternatural Asian wisdom that it bears a resemblance to a dynamic that physicists have found in the behavior of subatomic particles, which they call "spooky action at a distance."

Notice that the *Yijing* commentary includes an apparent exception to the rule that like tones resonate together and that like energies attract: when sages appear, they engage the attention of the entire world, not just of phenomena with specifically sagely aspects. This too reflects a belief, deep-seated in Chinese cultures, that virtue orders our existence. The emperor is cast as the polestar; if he takes his proper position, facing south, then the stars, so to speak, will rotate around him properly—the seasons passing in familiar fashion, the people well-fed and at peace, the culture humming, everything proceeding along time-honored courses. Other classical

Chinese texts affirm that this pattern holds at all levels of society, the influence of virtue reliably radiating from even the humblest home. In the *Analects*, when Confucius expresses his desire to live among a people regarded as barbarian, a skeptic asks, "Their crudeness— what about that?" The master replies, "If a noble person went there to dwell, what crudeness would there be?"[11]

To square this faith in the impact of wisdom and virtue with the like-attracts-like pattern of ganying takes just one step: recognizing a capacity for sagehood in all things. That premise meshes with the expansion of Mahāyāna doctrine that occurred in Chan and some other schools of Chinese Buddhism, extending buddha-nature to include all beings, even the inanimate. In the realm of metaphor, the universal evoking and responding of ganying are epitomized by a mirror, instantly reflecting what appears without favor or prejudice; by a valley, answering every sound with a faithful echo; and by a bell, resounding immediately at the slightest touch. This sense that the world functions in an exquisitely responsive manner was broadly held in old China, as can be seen from the report of a third-century geographical treatise that, on Mt. Feng, "When frost falls, the bells ring."[12]

To further this inadequate sketch of how the world works—of the understandings, that is, that our predecessors absorbed from their culture and carried with them into the tradition—we need to have a look at another word and concept used extensively in this connection: 機 *ji* (or *chi*; J., *ki*), defined in the earliest surviving dictionary of Chinese as "that which controls activation." Originally referring to the trigger of a crossbow, its scope widened over the centuries to include devices of many other kinds, even *feiji*, the "flying machine" known to English speakers as an airplane. Construed more broadly, it may encompass a wide range of things that "trigger" events or unleash the energies inherent in a situation. In that sense, *ji* may also translate as "incipient" or "opportunity," indicating potential yet to be realized.[13]

The ability to recognize such potential and to "activate" it was seen as the mark of a sage, since a sage, in longstanding Chinese conception, has the ability to read conditions that aren't yet apparent to others and to make small gestures that determine what ensues. The master image here is of influence exerted far upstream from results—diversion of a trickle that will become a raging torrent capable of moving heavy boulders far below. The importance of such early actions underlies another culture-wide understanding: the reverence due to founders. Those considered initiators of a state, family, lineage, field of learning, art, or enterprise of another sort are held in the highest possible esteem. The story of Bodhidharma's coming from the West fits this narrative perfectly, his arrival seen as having released a latent energy that burgeoned into Chan and went on growing, bringing forth in time the tradition's Korean, Vietnamese, and Japanese branches.

But the Bodhidharma story is just one instance of how thoroughly the ancient Sinitic understanding of how the world works permeates Chan and Zen. To whatever degree that fact has escaped the appreciation of practitioners outside Asia, it's high time to review the evidence, beginning with ziran, self-so. It turns up in many Chan texts besides the Bodhidharma poem, including the "Trusting Heartmind Inscription," the early doctrinal verse I referred to in chapter 9. It occurs twice in the text's terse, four-word lines, on each occasion evoking an ease discoverable through Chan practice.

> Grasping, you forsake crossing over,
> and inevitably enter mistaken ways.
> Releasing, you are self-so,
> a body free of leaving or staying.

And later:

> Doubts and qualms fully cleared,
> perfectly trusting, harmonious,
> not a single thing constrains you—
> nothing to fix in words or retain,
> vacant, luminous, self-so,
> you don't tax the power of heartmind.[14]

In one of the three hundred–plus poems put down to the authorship of the fabled Hanshan, ziran characterizes how fully and readily the world reveals itself once the heartmind is unburdened:

Water pure, crystal-clear, shining,
right to the bottom—visible self-so!
In a heartmind with not one concern,
the myriad conditions can't divert you.
Once heartmind doesn't falsify or formulate,
endless kalpas pass without disruption.
If you can know the world like this,
it's knowing without obstruction.[15]

And in a presentation to his monks, Zhaozhou called upon ziran to describe awakened action, citing a famous story from the *Lotus Sūtra* about an eight-year-old *nāga* princess:

"The dragon-girl made an offering [to the Buddha] with a heart-mind of intimacy. It was a matter utterly self-so."
    Someone asked, "If it was self-so, when she was making the offering, why was she doing it?"
    The master said, "If she didn't make the offering, how would we ever know the self-so?"[16]

This exchange illustrates the relationship of ziran to wuwei. The question presupposes that the princess, in making an offering, must have been purposefully doing (wei) something. Zhaozhou sees it otherwise: hers is an action totally consistent with the self-so, demonstrating that it's possible for us to act yet not *do* in the relevant sense, that we can maintain wuwei the same way wind does as it whisks through the pines. The "Song of Realizing the Way," another early Chan poem I've referred to previously, opens with lines that affirm the wuwei ideal, depicting a Chan adept as someone who's "cut off study, wuwei, at ease in the tao / neither rejecting false thoughts nor seeking truth."[17]
    Perhaps to clarify the point that wuwei precludes only the sort of

doing that imposes our designs willfully on others, some members of our tradition chose to draw upon another phrase with roots in Daoist tradition: 無事 wushi, meaning "without concern(s)." Among instances of its use in the Daodejing is the injunction, "Do without doing (wei wuwei), have concerns without concern (shi wushi), and taste what has no taste."[18] The Hanshan poem I've just cited contains the phrase in emphatic form—"without a single concern"—and it became a common feature of Chan rhetoric. Lack of concerns was a theme in Linji's instructions, sometimes stated in graphic terms:

> Followers of the dao, buddhadharma doesn't involve exertion. Just be ordinary, without concerns. Shit and piss. Wear clothes and eat food. If you tire, lie down. Foolish people may laugh at me; the wise know the point.[19]

Don't let the bluntness of his words fool you; as Linji saw it, "Having no concerns—that's a noble person."[20] His dictum made its way into the Zen anthologies of capping phrases, as did this more poetic evocation of wushi and its impact: "Motionless, you sit without concerns; / spring comes, and the grass grows by itself."[21]

Right along with ziran, wuwei, and wushi, ganying lodged deep in Chan and Zen discourse. A respected eleventh-century teacher, Langye (or Lang-yeh; J., Rōya), applied two favorite metaphors of responsiveness in presenting buddha-nature itself: "...it's like a huge bell waiting to be struck and resounding in response throughout the emptiness or like a bright mirror reflecting everything that appears from the moment it's set on its stand."[22] The authors of the Transmission of the Lamp paired echoes with shadows, another image of infallible correlation, to expound the inerrancy of karma: those who question the truth of karma "don't know that shadows and echoes follow [our deeds] absolutely, without the most minute error, straight through hundreds, thousands, millions of kalpas and are ineradicable."[23]

Most often, however, it seems that luminaries of the tradition resorted to ganying with reference to the enterprise of teaching. The teacher Fayan characterized virtuous Chan masters as those who "don't scheme to excite interest or spread their names, don't lust after or covet gain and patronage. Like great temple bells, they wait to be struck."[24] In the same vein, Yuanwu urged his ambitious heir Dahui to forgo teaching until thoroughly ready: "Wait until you are like a bell sounding when struck or a valley returning an echo."[25] Such perfect responsiveness develops self-so, according to the eminent scholar-monk Zongmi, a master himself and a chronicler of early Chan. He employs ziran four times, italicized in the following translation, to explain how Chan training, specifically the experience of freedom from compulsive thought, underlies the responsiveness of a buddha:

> Just achieve a mind of no-thought, and desires and aversions inconspicuously diminish *on their own*; compassion and wisdom grow brighter *on their own*. Binding karma drops away and ends *of itself*; meritorious activity bursts forth *of itself*. In terms of liberation, it's seeing that all marks have no marks; in terms of practice, it's called training without training. When afflictions have come to an end, birth-and-death is cut off; production and extinction having ceased, serene radiance becomes manifest. Boundless responsive [ying] functioning—this we call buddhahood.[26]

Of all the applications of ganying, perhaps the most common in the Mahāyāna schools generally identifies gan, the evoking, with cries of suffering to which buddhas and bodhisattvas ying, respond. In China, the Nirmāṇakāya or "transformation body," the body a buddha takes on when entering the world, came to be known as the ying body, the response body. In this view, the historical Buddha wasn't just a solitary seeker whose awakening and subsequent teaching proved to benefit others; on the contrary, his appearance reflected an ongoing, inseparable partnership with him. Without the world's need for awakening, buddhas wouldn't emerge, nor would Buddhist teachers.

Chan and Zen attribute this responsiveness to an inscrutable 感應

道交 *ganying daojiao* (or *kan-ying tao-chiao*; J., *kannō dōkō*) between buddhas and beings and likewise between masters and close disciples—an evoking and responding of, through, and in the dao, with *jiao* connoting a level of interchange subtler, more fine-tuned than ordinary communication.[27] Dōgen reports that his teacher, Rujing (or Ju-ching), impressed upon him the ineffability of such profound rapport and the great importance of developing it. "Ganying daojiao is impossible to conceptualize," Rujing told his Japanese disciple on one occasion and on another admonished him, saying, "You must know what creates ganying daojiao. If not for ganying daojiao, buddhas wouldn't enter the world, and our Founding Master [Bodhidharma] wouldn't have come from the West....You must know and without fail establish ganying daojiao."[28]

In his own teaching, Dōgen took pains to link ganying daojiao to the workings of karma, rejecting the belief held in some quarters that bodhi, awakening, appears spontaneously—self-so in that mistaken sense, as if somehow it were independent of karma. He wrote, "...where there is ganying daojiao, the heartmind of bodhi is brought forth. It is not something bestowed on us by buddhas and bodhisattvas, not something we bring about by ourselves. Because heartmind is brought forth through ganying daojiao, it is not self-so."[29]

Indeed, to achieve such intimate mutuality in interacting with their students, masters had to be ready to offer guidance flexibly, often in novel ways. *Precious Advice for the Chan Forest*, the twelfth-century advice manual compiled for masters of the school, counsels them:

> For wayfarers of all times, proper strategy for skillfully spreading dao essentially lies in adapting to communicate. Those who don't know how to adapt stick to the letter and cling to doctrines, get stuck on forms and mired in sentiments. None of them succeed in strategically adapting. An ancient sage said, "The dark valley has no preferences; any call will be echoed. The huge bell, struck with the tolling beam, resounds every time." So we know

that experienced people…don't fail to change responsively by sticking to one thing.[30]

Promoting this ideal of versatility in responding to students, Yuanwu insistently reminded readers of *The Blue Cliff Record* that "Great function appears without respect to conventions."[31]

On the disciple's part, ganying daojiao requires keen response to a master's "evoking" words or actions. It's what makes the zhiyin a zhiyin, as exemplified by the story behind that term and by the Chan tale of Yangshan and Xiangyan wordlessly "interpreting" their teacher's dream. More adroit illustrations of responsive functioning would be hard to conceive. Of course, the events reported may not have actually transpired, but that's beside the point: this is the *model* of mutual understanding and interaction that the tradition established, to be lived up to as best we can.

As for *ji*, our predecessors relied on the word heavily, using it in a slew of phrases. The assortment that follows, culled from a glossary of Zen terms,[32] is far from comprehensive, and since *ji* and many of the words joined to it have very flexible connotations, the definitions I've supplied do little more than hint at their meanings, with the best translation in a specific instance dependent on context.

大機 *daji* (or *ta-chi*; J., *daiki*): great potential or capacity
機緣 *jiyuan* (or *chi-yuan*; J., *kien*): opportunity and condition
機巧 *jiqiao* (or *chi-ch'iao*; J., *kigyō*): dynamic skill
全機 *quanji* (or *ch'uan-chi*; J., *zenki*): total activation/
    dynamism
機關 *jiguan* (or *chi-kuan*; J., *kikan*): activating barriers/
    junctures
機境 *jijing* (or *chi-ching*; J., *kikyō*): realm of potential
當機直截 *dangji zhijie* (or *tang-chi chih-chieh*; J., *tōki jikisetsu*):
    presented an opportunity and directly cutting through

As this assortment of phrases may suggest, Chan teachers often applied *ji*, like *ganying*, in the context of working with students.

Victor Hori actually defines *jiyuan* as meaning "disciple and master" rather than "opportunity and condition," interpreting a disciple as pent-up potential and a master as the trigger that releases the potential.[33] If a master's 機語, activating words, occasioned such a freeing up, it then became traditional for the fortunate student to compose and present a 投機偈, literally "a mutual ji verse," expressing the gist of that realization, that "activation."[34]

Besides putting ji to manifold uses of this sort, Chan authors and teachers also took a leaf from Daoist writings, where ji serves in the larger critique of youwei—of doing, attempting to manipulate and control.[35] Entanglement in "devices" corrupts the heartmind, the Daoists taught, whether the ji in question be physical contrivances or standards of character and comportment. Chan embraced this critique, cautioning practitioners not to obsess over practice methodology, not to think in terms of gain or progress, and not to attempt to "put another head on top of your own." Chan and Zen proverbs emphasize that ceasing such "machinations" is imperative in the journey to liberation: "A single word stems the flow, and ten thousand ji come to an end," says one, while another promises, "One moment of forgetting ji—the grand void without flaw!"[36]

The tradition also manifests the importance that Chinese thinkers ascribed to beginnings. Yuanwu states it as an aphorism in *The Blue Cliff Record*: "Gathering up the causes, wrapping up the results—complete at the start, complete at the end."[37] His younger colleague Yingan (or Ying-an; J., Ōan) spelled it out more fully, drawing on an oft-quoted formulation of the principle in the *Daodejing*:

> The beginning of self-cultivation rests right with you; on a thousand-mile journey, the first step is most important. If you accomplish both of these well, the infinite sublime import of hundreds of thousands of teachings will be fulfilled.[38]

The reverse case also was noted, as exemplified by lines from Yong-jia's "Song of Realizing the Way," where practitioners' inability to reach sudden awakening is chalked up to the inferiority of their original karmic endowment: "A bad disposition (種性, literally 'seed nature') warps understanding, / denying success in the Tathāgata's perfect, sudden discipline."[39]

Chan and Zen texts are peppered with expressions concerning the consequential nature of initiation, of actions and attitudes that open, start, or occur first. The continuation of this deep-seated discourse in contemporary Zen teaching is vividly revealed in a twentieth-century Rinzai abbot's comments in his conversation with a Japanese business magnate:

> I feel you succeeded because your point of departure was right. You were able to come hellbent up to today, the same as [a] track athlete who races on, full of determination. If his start is good, he can meet the challenge. That's why I feel that the highest appraisal lies not so much in the success you enjoy today but in the fact that you made a good start.... [The company's extraordinary growth] wasn't because you planned it that way. It came as a natural result because you contained the source of a natural growth and because the point of departure was correct.[40]

Needless to say, perhaps, belief in the profound influence of sages found a secure place in Chan and Zen historiography and teachings. Besides Bodhidharma, numerous masters after him have been honored as founders in some capacity—Baizhang as the originator of the Chan monastic code, Linji as the fountainhead of the lineage bearing his name, Dōgen and Keizan as the progenitors of Sōtō Zen—including many enshrined as founders of particular monasteries and temples. Often these individuals are said to have exerted beneficent influence extending beyond the usual bounds of causality. *Precious Advice for the Chan Forest* testifies to the inexplicable power of such virtue:

> I have never seen [a master] who was personally upright whose community was not orderly. Truly in this lies the meaning of the saying "Looking upon the countenance of a virtuous person clears people's minds."[41]

With that, I'll quit this show of evidence that Chan and Zen incorporate age-old Chinese understandings of how the world works. What to a devoted practitioner may have seemed a long and pedantic exercise would seem cursory, I'm sure, and perhaps naïve to a specialist in Chinese thought or Buddhist studies, an attempt to convey matters better left to book-length investigation.[42] I've risked falling short on both sides for the same reasons I've dusted off other family treasures: because these long-held understandings are an important, underappreciated part of our heritage, yes, but also because they're valuable in a variety of ways—beautiful, encouraging, appealing in their own right, and potentially useful to us, whether we're participants in the tradition or not.

I'll hold off, for now, on their possible usefulness, in favor of returning for a second look at Bodhidharma's verse:

> I've come as rootstock to this land,
> to convey the Dharma, settle delusions.
> A single flower opens five petals,
> setting fruit that matures on its own.

This is the story of the Chan founder in a nutshell, as members of the tradition set it down for us who've come after. The first couplet heralds Bodhidharma's high purpose and could be mistaken for the beginning of a heroic narrative on a par with "I came, I saw, I conquered." But the second couplet undercuts that reading altogether, with the great master representing himself as a simple flower opening like any other, initiating a process of fruition that will conclude explicitly ziran, wholly without his involvement. He intervenes intentionally but lightly by traveling to China and doing little more than sit facing a wall, yet his arrival triggers a cascade of consequences that are still spilling forth today. Later masters recognized this explicitly. One of them, Wuzu, quoted Bodhidharma's verse and commented,

> This great teacher Bodhidharma went where his feet took him
> and said what came out of his mouth; descendants of later

generations mostly made theories and arguments. Do you want to know where the flower blooms and the fruit forms? The pears of Zheng province; the dates of Qing province; in all things nothing surpasses a good origin."[43]

Nothing about the Bodhidharma verse is incidental. It balances the importance of natural initiation—the images of "rootstock" and the petals "opening"—with the perfect confidence that fruition happens ziran, of itself. Bodhidharma came to be known as *kaizu* (or *k'ai-tsu*; J., *kaiso*) or opening ancestor, using the same word as in the verse.[44] Likewise, the character I've translated as "fruit" is the one adopted for the Sanskrit *phala*, denoting the effect or result of words or actions.[45] Encapsulated in this tiny poem, then, is a Chan teaching on how the world works and how a master works in and with the world. It invites us to imagine treading the path in the same manner and to do so, if we dare.

13 | To Know Enough, to Know Contentment[1]

One afternoon in April 2000, in the hip Humboldt County town of Garberville, I sat down with Zen friends for a celebratory meal after a week on the trail. We'd been getting our news through the soles of our boots as we hiked from one watershed to another along a stretch of the California shoreline known—because cars can't get there—as the Lost Coast. Having ordered our lunch, we picked up the local newspaper to learn what, by its account, we'd missed as we sojourned among the redwoods, ferns, and purple irises. Eleven years earlier, at the close of a similar outing in the stony uplands of Death Valley, a local newspaper had brought us word of Edward Abbey's death, and the news seemed perfectly fitting. Surely Abbey would have smiled on the fact that, the day he died, a small band of us were in the desert, sitting in silence, walking, delighting in the sort of place he loved and did his utmost to defend. The conjunction definitely pleased *us*.

This time, the news felt utterly wrong: a front-page story on the latest success in cloning, jubilantly predicting a day when human body parts would be "replaced as easily as brake shoes." It's hard to imagine a report more completely at odds with the message of the Lost Coast, of its glowworms and gray whales, Roosevelt elk and brown pelicans. The dense mists of that week, the stinging nettles so tasty in a night's soup, the labor of carrying our gear up a thousand feet each day and down to a new seaside campsite, quick dips in the chilly waves, the seals eying us as they bobbed in the surf—all that threw this biomedical achievement into sharp relief.

My fellow Americans, now we can have it all: fresh fruit out of season, telephones in our pockets, disposable diapers, jumbo houses, movies on demand, news tailored to our preferences, erections to die for, babies by design, pills to make us "better than well," robots to keep grandma company, refrigerators that tell us when to buy eggs, instantaneous worldwide communication, personal computers that take dictation and translate, and now not only all that but new knees, lungs, and livers if we want them (and have the money to buy them). Pain-free existence could be around the corner, maybe immortality. Hey, why not?

That afternoon's collision of news from the trail with news from the medical frontier stunned me. People's seemingly insatiable appetite for things, conveniences, comfort, novelty, fun, longevity, and the rest had impressed and concerned me for years, but probably because I was so fresh from the Lost Coast, so strongly under its influence and opened up by our practice there, suddenly the absurdity of these habits came startlingly clear. Never before had modernity seemed such a bubble dance to me, so obvious and so crass.

If I'd been better versed in the Chan and Zen tradition at the time, I might have seen this revelation coming or at least might have recognized that my predecessors long before had faced the issue and taught to it directly. Chinese texts, including Chan texts, frame the problem as one of 知足 zhizu (or chih-tsu; J. chisoku), literally "knowing enough." In her translation of the Daodejing, Ellen Chen calls it the "keynote of the Taoist state."[2] Zhizu doesn't refer to having adequate knowledge but rather to knowing how much—how little—is enough. Since zu also means "sufficient," "satisfactory," and "contentment," the implication is always that people need to cultivate an acceptance of life within limits. The Daodejing spells out the point in a passage that repeats zu four times:

> No offense exceeds that of greediness,
> no disaster exceeds that of not knowing enough [zhizu],

and no fault brings on grief like covetousness.
So the satisfaction [zu] of knowing enough [zhizu]—
how perpetually satisfying [zu]![3]

Satisfaction has everything to do with knowing enough, etymologically and otherwise: the Latin root *satis*, too, means "enough."

Zhuangzi seconds the teaching of the *Daodejing*, describing noble-minded people as epitomes of contentment. Such individuals

> ...leave gold safe in the mountains and pearls safe in the depths; don't use money or property to get advantage; aren't drawn in by status or riches; don't delight in longevity or bemoan early death; don't glory in succeeding or feel shame in coming up short; don't lay claim to the proceeds of an entire age and make them their personal share; don't take ruling the world as an occasion for personal renown. Their renown resides in elucidating the ten thousand things as a single treasure house, living and dying as similar situations.[4]

Classical Daoist teachings frequently conflict with those of the Confucian masters, but on this point, they agree. Confucius extolled his prize student Yan Hui as a paragon of contentment: "How worthy that Hui! One caddy of rice, a single gourd of water, living on a back alley—others couldn't endure his travails, but it didn't disrupt Hui's joy. How worthy that Hui!"[5] Elsewhere the master explicitly affirms contentment as his own standard, too: "Eating poor food, drinking just water, using a folded arm for a pillow: happiness may surely be found in these. Ill-gotten wealth and status: to me, these are like fleeting clouds."[6]

In naturalizing Buddhism to China, translators and teachers drew upon these precedents. Though Indian texts espoused a middle way between rigorous asceticism and indulgence in sense pleasures, in tenor they run more to escaping suffering through renunciation and austerity than to singing the pleasure of life under lean circumstances. Early in the process of converting Buddhist texts to Chinese, some unknown genius hit on zhizu as a way to render an expression common in the Sanskrit materials, saṃtuṣṭi, meaning "satisfaction" or "gratification." Besides indigenizing it, this had the effect of marrying the Buddhist teachings into those of Chinese origin and occluding their differences.

A particularly eventful application of zhizu proved to be in the *Sūtra of Bequeathed Teachings*, a Chinese text masquerading as an authentic Sanskrit scripture. Ostensibly a speech the Buddha delivered on his deathbed, it includes this admonition:

> You monks, if you want release from the various impediments [kleśa], you must contemplate knowing enough. The dharma of knowing enough is precisely the abode of plenty, joy, peace, and seclusion. People who know enough experience joy and peace even if they sleep on the ground; people who don't know enough still complain if they dwell in the heavens. Those who don't know enough feel poor even when rich; people who know enough feel rich even when poor. The five desires constantly drag around those who don't know enough, provoking sympathy and dismay in those who know it. We call this "knowing enough."[7]

Another noteworthy use of zhizu occurs in the *Vimalakīrti Sūtra*, translated by the acclaimed Kumārajīva in 406. There it's joined with the term 小欲 *xiaoyu* (or *hsiao-yu*; J. *shōyoku*), reducing desires, a pairing that has echoed through the ages.[8]

Very early in its development, Chan aligned itself with this dharma of reducing desires and knowing enough, folding them into one of its foundational texts, the *Platform Sūtra*. There, preaching to a large assembly, Huineng instructs,

> Wise friends, take refuge in and rely on the three treasures of self-nature: the Buddha's awakening, the Dharma's rightness, and the Sangha's purity. In your own heartminds, take refuge in awakening and rely on it. Then biases and confusion won't arise. Reducing desires and knowing enough, you leave behind wealth and appearances. This we call "honor among the two-legged."[9]

Subsequent masters haven't maintained this standard evenly, but in their ritual and lore, Chan and Zen consistently have praised the virtue of living in humble fashion and have deplored waste or excess. A number of figures revered in the tradition—Zhaozhou, Fenyang, Xuansha, Wumen, Hanshan, Layman Pang, and Daitō Kokushi, among others—gained reputations for their small wants and plain habits.

The most outstanding example must be the cave-dweller known to posterity as Lazy Zan or Unambitious Zan,[10] whom Yuanwu praises lavishly in *The Blue Cliff Record* for his perfect indifference to a messenger bearing an invitation to the imperial court. Without rising or uttering a word, his nose visibly running, Lazy Zan fished a yam out of his ox-dung fire and proceeded to eat it. The emperor's envoy suggested that he might at least wipe his nose, but Zan replied that he didn't have time to clear his snot for an ordinary man. When this was reported to him, the emperor was vastly impressed, or so the story goes.[11]

That knowing enough became an aspirational standard in Chan institutions is evident from *Precious Advice for the Chan Forest*, the monastic leadership manual I've cited several times. One of its selections extolls the virtue of the master Yuantong Juna (or Yuan-t'ung Chu-na; J., Entsu Kyototsu), who in 1050 declined an imperial summons to assume the abbacy of a new monastery in the capital. Asked why he declined, Yuantong at first pleaded unworthiness, next noted the precedent of Śākyamuni Buddha refusing royal requests, then finally put his decision down to zhizu:

> An insightful predecessor had the saying, "A big name makes it hard to remain settled." My whole life I've practiced the principle of knowing enough and haven't gotten myself bound up in reputation and profit. Weighed down by such concerns of heartmind, when could you have enough?

Rounding out this explanation, Yuantong quoted the Chan layman and famed poet Su Dongpo (or Su Tung-p'o): "Dongpo once said, 'Know peace and you flourish; know enough and you're rich.'"[12]

The teaching of reducing desires and knowing enough was also established early in the Japanese assimilations of Chan. In 1253, Dōgen incorporated portions of Śākyamuni's supposed deathbed speech from the *Sūtra of Bequeathed Teachings* into what Dōgen probably saw as his own final composition, "The Eight Realizations of a Great Person." The first of those eight is titled Reducing Desires, the second Knowing Enough.[13] Two centuries later, the Rinzai master, poet, and contrarian par excellence Ikkyū Sōjun left a pair of verses on these virtues, titling both with those same words: "Reducing Desires, Knowing Enough."[14]

For a Japanese embodiment of contentment, however, our best candidate may be the Sōtō priest and poet Ryōkan. From the closing years of the eighteenth century into the first decades of the nineteenth, Ryōkan lived solitarily, thirteen of those years in a one-room mountain hut where he had few possessions other than his priest's robe, alms bowl, staff, and a set of cherished texts. To supplement the foods that he could gather in the forest, he carried his bowl into nearby farm communities, receiving from supportive villagers what little they could spare—rice, miso, some vegetables, and occasional luxuries like saké or fruit. "Desire nothing, and you're content with everything," he wrote, stating the ethic he lived by and often took as his theme:

How long has it been since I came to this place?
With no one to tend them, the grounds have run wild
My begging bag and bowl just sit gathering dust
A solitary lantern lights the bare walls
Evening rain patters on my lonely door
Every detail is complete
Ah! What else is there that I need?[15]

It remains to be seen if Chan and Zen communities in the West will come to understand "knowing enough" as an integral element of our tradition and to consider its realization a critical aspect of maturing in practice. In the first hundred-plus years of efforts to root the Dharma here, as far as I can tell, contentment has remained a minor theme for teachers and little appreciated in the sangha.[16] Our glossy magazines brim with ads for costly Buddhist accoutrements, Asian tours, programs featuring Dharma celebrities, investment opportunities, and the like. Some prominent figures in the U.S. Zen universe, far from encouraging contentment, have headed conspicuously in the opposite direction, exhibiting fast-lane behavior and One Percent habits.

Of early teachers here in the United States, it may have been Nyogen Senzaki who most expressly taught and exemplified the way of living contentedly within limits. He addressed that theme with particular poignancy in a poem commemorating the Buddha's *parinirvāna*, written for his fellow Japanese-American inmates— the "evacuees" of the poem—incarcerated during World War II in Wyoming's high desert:

"Those who live without unreasonable desires
Are walking on the road of Nirvana."
So Buddha said on his deathbed.
Evacuees who follow him, learning contentment,
Should attain peace of mind
Even in this frozen desert of internment.
See a break in the clouds in the East!
The winter sun rises calmly,
Illuminating the light of wisdom.[17]

We can only speculate as to how this message registered with the small sangha he led behind the barbwire at Heart Mountain. Was it unreasonable to desire justice at the hands of the government and the courts? Was it unreasonable to desire decent food and housing during their internment? Do desires of that sort put contentment out of reach?

One thing is sure: for Senzaki Sensei, maintaining modest desires was a lifelong practice, and now it's our turn. What desires shall we deem unreasonable? On what basis shall we decide such questions? How can we know enough (in the usual sense) to know how much is enough?

These challenges come at us from every direction. Let's start at home, where relatively small scope and familiarity with the issues would seem to simplify any question of enoughness. Even here, though, the questions proliferate, and the answers are rarely no-brainers. How much can we afford? How much space do we need? How much furniture and lighting? And how nice should it be? How much should we do to protect ourselves against intruders? How much should we save for that proverbial rainy day? If you have kids, the questions mount: How long to let them cry, how strictly to require naps or the consumption of broccoli, how much to tell them about sex (and at what age), how many hours of screen time is good for them or for you? Is it the same amount or different? And so on.

The studious among us often look to experts for answers or at least for information that could lead to answers, but if the experts differ, as they frequently do, the question soon becomes how much time you're willing to spend consulting experts and sorting out their various opinions. Most of us don't have time enough (check) or patience enough (check?) to pursue expertise on a wide array of domestic issues, so we make many decisions on the basis of what we notice around us. The key factor in such matters, social scientists say, is who serves as our "reference group"—who we take, consciously or unconsciously, as our standard in how to live, what's appropriate, satisfactory, or desirable. For much of the twentieth century, Americans ran hard to keep up with the Joneses, but as it turned out, finally the Joneses themselves couldn't keep up, and soon after the turn of the century, they got bumped by the younger, more photogenic Kardashians.

I doubt that you or any other reader of this book has ever undertaken to keep up with the Kardashians except, perhaps, to keep up with their doings as an indicator of how fast civilization is speeding toward a wall. Social scientists know their business, though, and have demonstrated that the more a product, service, or experience is seen as common, cool, de rigueur, happenin', or simply the norm among people in your reference group, the more likely that you'll be buying it, too. A destination wedding maybe? A Rolex? Cool bling? A $75,000 electric truck?

In days of yore, kin and neighbors typically constituted the reference group, with customs a strong binding force, but that's mostly no longer true. How life is lived in our parents' homes or next door still affects us, no doubt, but what we see by other means—in the media, in the lives of our virtual neighbors—may affect us even more. Studies by economist Juliet Schor indicated that annual spending increases $200 for every hour of TV viewing a person does weekly. Every hour! Average three hours of TV a day and by this calculus, your yearly spending would jump $4,200 beyond what you'd spend if you skipped TV. "The likely explanation," Dr. Schor concluded, "is that what we see on television inflates our sense of what is normal. With a few exceptions, TV characters are upper-middle-class, or even rich."[18]

Schor reported the impact of TV viewing on personal spending in her 1999 book *The Overspent American*, so her $200-per-hour figure probably understates the effect today, and the many new means by which streaming and digital media "capture eyeballs" would make a study of TV habits less useful now. I find it hard to imagine, though, that the productions of the Hollywood dream machine, the glossy come-ons of Madison Avenue, and the glittering, infinite clickbait of the Worldwide Web haven't pushed expectations still higher. All by itself, the practice of uploading Instagram shots of mouthwatering meals, holiday scenes, glamorous parties, and enviable acquisitions seems sure to have further inflated our sense of what's normal or at least acceptable to our peers.

The virtual Joneses, not to mention the Kardashians, do seem to have spacious homes and fancy kitchens. To whatever degree media imagery drove the increase, the fact that American homes grew from an average of 983 square feet at mid-twentieth century to 2350 square feet at the start of this century is unlikely to be mere coincidence. Since that expansion, our homes provide each U.S.

citizen, on average, 721 square feet of living space, almost twice as much as people have in homes of the wealthy western European nations.[19] How much is enough? And why does that differ so greatly from one place to another? Is it a function of available wealth, buildable land, zoning, and the like, or are some societies better at knowing enough? Dunno!

In any case, there's no question that rising expectations are a global reality or that for many years the United States has ridden high, heading that curve along with other favored nations, or that now China is leading the trend to a large extent. The phrase "rising expectations" permits us to think and speak about these developments as though the rise has a life of its own, as natural as grass growing in the spring, but it's not really so, is it? Our expectations do not *have* to rise. They rise under the influence, yes, of our reference groups and of the messages we receive via the media, but ultimately it all comes back to us and the choices we make. Those who "know enough" also become members of a reference group, after all, and thus have a potential to flatten the curve of expectations or even to start the needed downturn.

Liberating ourselves and others from the endless, hopeless course of rising expectations won't be easy, but anyone paying attention knows it has to happen. Some claim—and appear to honestly believe—that civilization can continue its sky's-the-limit course through "efficiencies" in energy, manufacturing, and other sectors of the economy and by acquiring elements needed to meet humanity's escalating needs from new sources, namely mining the ocean floor, the moon, and maybe passing asteroids. Whether or not you accept these claims (or assurances, to attach a more exact label), please don't neglect the word hiding in plain view in the preceding sentence: *needs*.[20] It's clear that none of us *needs* to go joyriding in space, as our billionaires have started to do, but look around you: How much of what you see could *you* do without? Where do needs stop and desires take over?

Framing it this way personalizes the problem of knowing enough, making it a matter of your and my needs and wishes, of who we take as our reference groups, of the way we allow experience through the media or in the flesh to shape our expectations. Nothing about this is strictly personal, though; we aren't separated from others by even so much as a cell wall. We feel others' influence and, at the same time, exert influence on others. While the media shape us, our choices shape the media. The problem of knowing enough is a shared problem.

And we've only started. As I noted earlier, questions of knowing enough arise in every quarter. Besides facing them at home, we face them on the street, in the marketplace, on the job, in clubs and on teams, in churches and temples, and especially, dizzyingly, in the vast domain of public policy and law. In this last arena, the difficulty of the questions compounds, as competing interests clash, political posturing clouds the facts, and frequently the game being played is, or is thought to be, of the zero-sum variety in which a victory for one is regarded as a loss for another. Contentment is correspondingly rare. The solutions settled upon often aren't satisfactory, either to those directly involved (a.k.a. stakeholders) or as a means of resolving problems in a lasting manner.

What's enough when it comes to compensating families who lost members in the infernos of 9/11? Congress approved a pot of money and handed over the problem of distributing it justly to a respected attorney serving as a "special master." He came up with a three-part compensation formula: $250,000 for each life (its "noneconomic value") plus $100,000 for a spouse and every additional dependent (called the "dependent value") plus an amount (the "economic value") that varied according to an individual's expected earnings, calculated on the basis of age and annual income. Final "awards" ranged from the minimum of $250,000 to $7.1 million. What do you think? Did U.S. taxpayers give heirs of the 9/11 victims enough compensation? What would be enough for relatives of a single, elderly, minimum-wage worker? What about for a family of five whose breadwinner collected a salary upward of $231,000? Should differences among the needs of recipients have been taken into consideration? If so, under what definition of needs?[21]

That may seem like a difficult and painful set of questions, but imagine the problem if a decision were reached to pay reparations to the descendants of slaves or of Black citizens robbed, lynched, denied the vote, and abused in other ways during the Jim Crow era. What would enough compensation be, and how would it rightly be apportioned? In 1988, the Japanese locked up with Senzaki Sensei at Heart Mountain and elsewhere in the United States finally received an apology and payment of $20,000 per living survivor.[22] Was that enough? What sort of actions would suffice to requite the debt that the United States has to Native Americans or to indigenous citizens of the formerly independent nation of Hawai'i?

The scope and nature of these issues makes them particularly mind-boggling examples of the difficulty of knowing enough, but school boards, city councils, legislatures, courts, and other government entities weigh less dramatic issues of that kind every week. How much funding shall we allocate for water purity, sewage treatment, library resources, firefighting, public transit, low-income housing, road repair, parks?[23] What's enough for an insurance company to pay in order to "make whole" an old woman who's suffered a broken leg in a freak accident at her church? On what basis shall we compute her pain and suffering or the long-term impact of her disability?

Rational means of answering such questions can be found or invented, as in the 9/11 case, but purely objective and perfect answers don't exist. At every scale, from personal to cosmic, we have to make judgment calls; facts help but, in themselves, can't tell us what's enough. Probably the hardest of all the what's-enough questions are those involving great intangibles like freedom, safety, wildness, community, sanctity. Philosopher and mountain guide Jack Turner writes,

> Much of the best intellectual labor of this century [the twentieth] has led to the admission of various limits in science and mathematics—of axiom systems, observation, objectivity, measurement. This should have a humbling effect on all of us, and the

limits of our knowledge should define the limits of our practice. The biological sciences should draw the line of their operations at wilderness...for the same reason atomic scientists should accept limits on messing with the atom and geneticists should accept limits on messing with the structure of DNA: *We are not that wise, nor can we be.*[24]

I'm happy to acknowledge that some scientists *are* calling for limits on genetic modification, AI, and geoengineering, and some of the influential breed known as policymakers have joined them. Others insist on the importance of open-ended "disinterested" research, and the debate soon gets abstract, the going extremely difficult. No surprise, really.

Wherever we encounter the problem of "knowing enough," its subtleties and complexities make it a problem best addressed with a settled heartmind and beyond that, as my friend Turner says, with humility and wisdom. It's for good reason that contentment became a subject of profound inquiry in traditions of long standing and that the foundational texts of Daoism and, later, those of Chan and Zen recognized zhizu as a high achievement. With the very habitability of Earth already at risk, the need to know enough is more pressing than ever. How well we rise to that challenge—and thus decide what to do and to desist from doing—will go a long way to determining the future of untold billions of beings.

—

Reserving the joys of desistance for my final chapter, I'm going to pivot here from zhizu as knowing enough to zhizu as knowing *contentment*. That, you may remember, is among the definitions of *zu* and was what Senzaki encouraged fellow "evacuees" to learn. When I swap this alternate translation into passages I cited earlier, it lends them a different quality:

• "The dharma of knowing contentment is precisely the abode of plenty, joy, peace, and seclusion. People who know contentment experience joy and peace even if they sleep on the ground; people who don't know contentment still complain if they dwell in the heavens. Those who don't know contentment feel poor even when rich; people who know contentment feel rich even when poor."

- "Reducing desires and knowing contentment, you leave behind wealth and appearances. This we call 'honor among the two-legged.'"
- "My whole life I've practiced the principle of knowing contentment and haven't gotten myself bound up in reputation and profit. Weighed down by such concerns of heartmind, when could you have contentment?"
- Dongpo once said, "Know peace and you flourish; know contentment and you're rich."

Contentment, says the *Oxford English Dictionary*, is "Having one's desires bounded by what one has (though that may be less than one could have wished)"—a crucial qualification—or not being "disturbed by desire of anything more or of anything different." Contentment, in other words, doesn't require a hair-shirt asceticism, a warring against desires; it's a pleasure available to anyone whose desires don't exceed their circumstances. It allows us to wish for, and even to desire, more and different things or conditions than exist at present, as long as those wishes and desires don't *disturb* us.

Contentment has certainly had advocates outside of Chan and Zen and outside of Asia, too, Thoreau being among the most prominent. He may have found his understanding confirmed in the Asian classics he was able to read, but the pleasure he took in unadorned phenomena, wild or domestic, seems native and basic to his character and likewise the "amusement" (his word) he derived from accomplishing simple tasks. In journal entries, he recounts the satisfaction he found in gathering driftwood for his fireplace from as much as three miles away, deducing the history of each stick, studying its grain as he split it, and so on. Acquaintances couldn't understand why he preferred to get his firewood that way instead of just buying it, and he found he couldn't convey his "profound secret" to them. It was plain to him, though: when he purchased such necessities, he said, "I cheat myself to some extent, I deprive myself of the pleasure, the inexpressible joy, which is the unfailing reward of satisfying any want of our nature simply and directly."[25]

In the interest of credibility, I should probably note that Thoreau's secret is no secret to me. I too feel a happiness hard to explain in gathering firewood and in meeting other household needs with my own two hands. Where firewood is concerned, part of the satisfaction comes from a tree falling where I was aiming it, without damaging its neighbors on its way down, or from a stroke of the maul landing on a hairline crack in a dry round, splitting it with one blow. But I don't always hit my mark, and the elation of such successes is short-lived in any case, displaced by the demands of the next cut or round.

A pleasure more peculiar and more durable arises from awareness that my competence, such as it is, really has very little to do with me and much more to do with the boon of hand-eye coordination, a product of evolutionary processes unimaginably ancient and continuing. It makes perfect sense to me that Layman Pang identified woodcutting as one of his supernatural powers, ordinary as it is.[26] Satisfying the need for winter heat, a bona fide "want of our nature," in this old, intensely physical way brings, yes, "inexpressible joy."

There's contentment to be had in the incidental pleasures of the work, too. The colors, from brilliant reds to deep plum, often revealed in cutting manzanita. The fragrances of fresh-cut oak, cedar, and pine. The surprises that hours in the forest dependably yield—a pile of bear scat, an unexpected spray of larkspur, a lovely old bottle, a scattering of quail, a bright red madrone leaf twirling on a strand of spider silk. In our part of the world, where forests are overgrown due to decades of well-intended but mistaken fire suppression, cutting firewood brings the additional satisfaction of knowing that we reduce the threat of catastrophic wildfire. All things considered, getting our winter heat by setting a thermostat and paying a bill would amount to a tremendous and sad loss.

Thoreau famously did *not* feel content with the politics of his day or the direction he saw society heading, and neither do I. But contentment with life's immediacies is another matter, and Thoreau did his best to impress it upon his readers. He pulls out the stops in the final paragraphs of *Walden*, pitching this form of contentment with a fervor that puts some people off:

> However mean your life is, meet it and live it; do not shun it and call it hard names....Love your life, poor as it is. You may perhaps have some pleasant, thrilling, glorious hours, even in a poorhouse. The setting sun is reflected from the windows of the alms-house as brightly as from the rich man's abode; the snow melts before its door as early in the spring. I do not see but that a quiet mind may live as contentedly there, and have as cheering thoughts, as in a palace.

Whether you buy this or not, please take note of the prerequisite Thoreau embedded in his appeal: "a quiet mind." The *Oxford English Dictionary* definition of contentment agrees, though it frames the issue in reverse—as a matter of not being "disturbed" by the desire for something other than what one has. Senzaki's poem and several of the other Asian precedents I've quoted make this connection, and Chan or Zen have long presented arrival at *anxin*, a peaceful heart-mind, as a crucial point on the path to maturity.[27] "Fail to exhaust the road of heartmind," warns a great thirteenth-century kōan text, "and you clutch at grasses and hang onto trees—a wraith, a ghost."[28] Conversely, the Zen phrase books contain many sayings extolling the pleasures and happy consequences of a heartmind at rest:

> Lately the dharma of anxin has come down to me:
> to lie back and hear the soughing pines of a thousand river
>   valleys.

Such equanimity curbs the impulse to compare and impugn:

> Just secure a heartmind of ease, and everywhere brings
> delight;
> you don't weigh the morning market against the cloudy
> mountain.

And it encourages contentment:

> The disgrace of disgraces: having many desires;
> the joy of joys: having nothing to seek.[29]

Whatever its cause, a disturbance of heartmind is odious in itself and crowds out all but the sharpest stimuli, leaving little room for the varied delicate sounds, sights, tastes, aromas, and sensations— the nuances of perception—that further contentment. A mind needn't be especially agitated or distracted to overlook the flash of sunlight off a window pane that Thoreau describes, to delight in a puff of wind, to enjoy the heft and balance of a well-made hand tool, or to register the wondrous dexterity of your own tongue working in your mouth, moving a bite of food about as you chew and only getting bitten itself one chew in a million. The world affords us subliminal pleasures of this kind every day in numbers beyond counting, but the vast majority we squander for want of anxin. Some will dismiss them as cheap thrills; to me, the fact that they come free, as gifts, not at the price of a fine bottle of Cabernet Sauvignon or from watching a $200 million Hollywood blockbuster, enhances their value.

The contentment realized with anxin is wonderful yet isn't alone sufficient to meet the challenge of zhizu: for that, we need to marry the two senses of zhizu. Knowing enough, a function of insight, enables us to distinguish necessities from superfluities, but it remains merely intellectual unless it's complemented with a capacity to know contentment under circumstances more restricted than we'd prefer. Similarly, since one can know contentment under a wide range of conditions, including conditions of extreme luxury, it won't have any teeth unless it's coupled with the discernment of knowing enough.

I've long relished an English proverb that unites the two aspects of zhizu: "Enough is as good as a feast."[30] Enough brings satisfaction. Beyond that lies excess, not greater satisfaction. It says a lot about us (and about contentment) that people often wake up to the feast of plain life only when they reach death's door. There, under the most "reduced circumstances" of all, many a person has discovered the sweetness of things previously too ordinary for them to notice.

Whether humanity will ever have enough zhizu for its own good or for the good of the rest of the planet we cannot know. It's a lot to ask of ourselves, and history offers precious little reason to suppose that we'll meet the challenge en masse. Still, it's a project that every one of us can undertake and, in that sense, is fully within our power. To take it a step further: it's a project each of us *must* undertake in order to preserve even the possibility that our collective answer will someday be yes.

Am I really recommending contentment to women, say, or Black Americans or citizens of totalitarian states—to people who live in circumstances unjust, exploitive, violent, possibly all of those at once? Yes, I am, but please let's not confuse contentment with complacency or passivity. Knowing enough is always a question of where to draw the line between enough and not enough, and it wouldn't be much of a question if the right answer always had to be "enough." There are, of course, situations we can't be content with. Even then, though, those who know contentment may experience it in moments and in ostensibly small, intangible things—Thoreau's spring melt, Ryōkan's satisfaction in stretching his legs, Senzaki's break in the clouds at dawn. Or in a nap, a breeze, a friendly gesture, a dignified act, a visit from a squirrel.

I'd go so far as to suggest that unjust, exploitive, and violent conditions have, more than ever, become our common lot, widely felt among people and inflicted still more widely on other species, beings with no means to resist. That makes it imperative for us to cultivate contentment within the modest limits we discern through knowing enough. And it makes contented living the true opposite of complacency, in fact a form of activism—a campaign for contentment, through contentment, by the contented.

The most hopeful evidence that such a campaign could succeed today, in this country, is that it already has, albeit on a relatively small scale. I refer you to David Kline's description, in his books *Great Possessions* and *Scratching the Woodchuck*, of the life in rural Ohio that he and his family enjoy as members of an Old Order Amish community established by their ancestors almost two centuries ago. Here's a random specimen of the pleasures Kline takes in working his farm, in this case the result of taking a roundabout route to bring his plow horses in from pasture:

> Since it was a splendid morning I took the long way, which was through the woods, for the same reason that the bear went over the mountain—to see what I could see. I soon spotted a Canada warbler as it was moving through some brambles. This beautiful warbler has a bright yellow breast with a black necklace across it and is most often seen toward the end of the migration. I followed it for quite a while as it foraged through the undergrowth. As it entered a thick tangle, I got down on my hands and knees to get a better look, when suddenly my attention was diverted from the warbler to several big yellow morel mushrooms. Blending in so well with the forest litter, I'm sure I would have missed them if I hadn't been on my knees. After picking a hatful I left the rest....[31]

Let me hasten to say that I realize some people are immune to such delights and that I certainly don't expect my fellow Americans to undergo a mass conversion to Amish ways. I simply hold it out as an example of a group that drew its line (out of faith and deep contentment) and within its bounds has managed to maintain, if Mr. Kline's reports are indicative, a culture richly satisfying to its members, no threat to the planet, and good to other residents of the place, plant or animal, human or nonhuman.

Half a century ago, the cultural anthropologist Marshall Sahlins observed that "there are two possible courses to affluence. Wants may be 'easily satisfied' either by producing much or by desiring little." The latter course he saw fit to designate "the Zen road to affluence."[32] Thanks, Professor! At that time in this country, the word *Zen* commonly meant something like "cool" or "offbeat," but even if that's all that the insightful Sahlins intended, okay, let's accept the compliment and pass it on. Speaking anthropologically, he might better have dubbed it "the Amish road to affluence" or still better, judging from the fieldwork he cites, he could have called it the road being taken (even then) by relatively small, close-knit, indigenous societies all over the world. *Zen* is snappier, though.

I don't know how the Amish reached their version of zhizu, but their success at it has placed them in my "reference group." They keep company there with others I've been fortunate to meet along the way, including the farm people I visited in 1985 at their hamlet in northeastern Thailand, introduced by my friend Wisit Wangwinyoo. In that cluster of houses too small to call a village, a TV set that faced out a window was revealing the marvels of the metropole to a dozen rapt children sitting on the ground, and one of their sisters, a preteen, performed for us with her face caked in some white substance, perhaps clay, in heart-rending homage to women she'd seen on that screen. She joined my reference group as a kind of cautionary member.

By the time she did, I'd accepted air travel, personal computers, and many other features of modernity as normal. I'd come a good ways toward knowing contentment and could regularly find it in folding a paper bag or in the taste of water, and "enough" was starting to dawn on me, but the process of aligning my life with zhizu had barely begun. It's not easy to disentangle from patterns established by personal habit, family routine, social expectations, demands of work, and structures of commerce. Those difficulties are nothing, though, next to the ones that come if your reference group widens beyond *people*, as mine finally did—strangely late, it seems to me now.

After all, if our commitment is to carry all beings to liberation, how could we leave caterpillars, sand dunes, lichen, and cottonwood groves out of the project? They maintain zhizu impeccably and elegantly themselves, never exceeding their needs, and their long-term welfare depends on our practicing it likewise. I aspire to, but I haven't reached the point where I know contentment as well as I know enough. For instance, though I know that I never truly *need* to fly again and that it would be best for the ten thousand things if I quit, I find myself content—so far—only to curtail my air travel sharply; I don't yet know the contentment of never flying again. That's what I mean: the process of aligning my behavior with zhizu has only begun.

So sure, I admit it: a movement to live contentedly within the limits of our needs is more than unlikely. It's far-fetched. Still, it might be our last best chance to calm our lives, pull the plug on our insane economy, change the course of civilization as we know it, and protect the viability of earthly life. Put it that way, and it seems churlish not to take it on. Such a movement is wholly within our capacity, too: it'll cost nothing to start, require no budget or staff, and be hard, maybe impossible, to derail or repress. Imagine it. We can begin today.

14 | Recognizing the Unrecognized

It took me decades of study to recognize the peculiar saliency of the word 識 *shi* (or *shih*; J., *shiki*) in Chan and Zen texts. Its semantic range and flexibility made it extremely useful to the teachers, translators, and writers interpreting the Dharma to Chinese audiences, and they adopted it to convey many important terms and experiences, including the Sanskrit term *vijñāna*. Usually rendered into English as "consciousness," *vijñāna* is the standard noun for what we typically call a sense, so Chinese texts such as the *Heart Sūtra* name a 識 each for vision, hearing, taste, and the rest. *Shi* also figures in the translation of *kalyānamitra*, literally "good friend" in Sanskrit, which is frequently used in sūtras and commentaries to refer to a reliable teacher, guide, or companion on the path—a 善知 識 *shanzhishi* (or *shan-chih-shih*; J., *zenchishiki*). Here, *shi* stands in for *mitra*, Sanskrit for "friend."

It may seem odd that *shi* could be taken to mean things as different as "consciousness" and "friend," but those meanings are linked logically and experientially to the word's central meaning: "familiar with, knowledgeable about, informed about; aware of; recognize; acquainted with."[1] *Shi* denotes a sort of knowing that goes beyond mere facts, a familiarity born of intimacy with a person, place, event, or subject. If you know something like the back of your hand, that's shi. It's the way you know your home, your best friend, the work of a favorite recording artist, painter, or author. It's how someone who "knows the tune" understands what the musician is feeling.

Note the verb *recognize* in the definition. Our senses enable awareness of all manner of things but recognition only of some things. What you recognize depends on contextual factors, especially on previous experience or training. You can hear the coo of a mourning dove without recognizing it as a mourning dove's call. Or maybe you do recognize it as a mourning dove's call but don't recognize the whistling sound that the dove's wings make as it takes flight. Recognition comes in a variety of forms and degrees of intimacy.

Once I tumbled to the importance and multifarious usages of *shi*, I paid more attention to the work it does in Chan and Zen writings, beginning with the legend that marks the tradition's advent in China. In the oft-told tale of the monk Bodhidharma's arrival from the Western Heavens, now commonly referred to as India, he showed up one day at the court of Emperor Wu, a ruler with a reputation for personal interest in the buddhadharma and support of its institutions. When the emperor questioned the unfamiliar monk, he received answers that seem calculated to shock:

> "What is the prime import of the Buddha's holy insights?"
> Bodhidharma said, "Vast as can be, no trace of 'holiness.'"
> "Who is confronting Us?" the emperor then asked.
> "I don't know," Bodhidharma replied.

Recognizing that Emperor Wu had no aptitude for the teaching he'd come to transmit, the text tells us, Bodhidharma gave up on him, exiting not merely his court but his whole domain as well. Later, when the emperor consulted his advisor Baozhi (or Pao Chih; J., Hōshi) about what had transpired with his strange visitor, he received a second shock, even greater than the first:

> Baozhi asked, "Does Your Eminence know who that was or not?"
> The emperor replied, "I don't know."
> "That was the mahāsattva Guanyin," said Baozhi, "transmitting the heartmind-seal of the Buddha!"

In this account, the first case in *The Blue Cliff Record, shi* occurs three times, once from the mouth of each of the three speakers, and translators have persistently rendered it as above, using the English verb *to know*. But another word, 知 *zhi* (or *chih*; J., *chi*), was available to the authors of the story and was commonly used to express knowing of various kinds, including the intellectual sort and more subtle forms such as "knowing the tune" and "knowing enough." It's safe to conclude that the authors selected *shi* for the richness of its implications. Owing to his studies, the emperor knew something about the buddhadharma, but unlike Baozhi, he was unable to recognize Bodhidharma as Guanyin—Avalokiteśvara, embodiment of compassion. Baozhi's perspicacity brought him esteem as a Chan master avant la lettre, and the tradition awarded him an epithet that recognized both the clarity of his eye and the deadliness of his grasp: 鏡容鷹爪 Mirror Countenance, Hawk Talons.

Here's the kicker: the emperor's answer to Baozhi is exactly the same as Bodhidharma's answer to the emperor—just two words, 不識, not *shi*—but it would be a mistake to assume that they meant the same thing. Commenting in *The Blue Cliff Record*, Yuanwu categorically rejects that assumption. After acknowledging the symmetry of the two men's responses, he demands, "Tell me, is this"—emperor Wu's 不識—"the same as what Bodhidharma said or different?" Answering himself, he declares, "The resemblance is exactly a resemblance; it's exactly what it's not!"[2] Within the superficial sameness of the men's words, that is, a significant difference lurks.

The Chinese text invites us to complete the men's sentences by supplying pronouns. In the emperor's case, context makes it easy to fill in the words: Baozhi has asked if he recognized Bodhidharma, and the emperor says, "[I] didn't recognize [him]." What Bodhidharma meant by 不識, however, is much less clear and becomes a point to consider. "[You] don't recognize [me]" and "[I'm] unrecognized" are possible interpretations, but if that's all he meant, the difference between his reply and the emperor's is negligible, and Yuanwu's comment makes little sense. A pronounced difference emerges only if we read the First Ancestor's 不識 the way that translators consistently have—as a first-person statement: "[I] don't know."

But not to know, not to be aware of or to recognize oneself, what does *that* mean? Unless we suppose Bodhidharma suffered temporary amnesia under the emperor's questioning, we can credit him with knowing who he was in the everyday sense. So what else might he have intended in saying, "Not 識"? What would it be not to recognize yourself? Not to recognize yourself as a discrete self? Not to recognize yourself as any self at all? Not to recognize the existence of self? Maybe something else? In any event, this is where the case gets juicy, raising issues at the heart of Mahāyāna teaching, not just of Chan and Zen. Devotees of Dōgen will recall a saying of his that touches on the question: "To study the buddha-way is to study oneself. To study oneself is to forget oneself. To forget oneself is to be verified by the ten thousand things."[3] Hmmm.

—

Before teasing out other aspects and implications of shi, I want to zero in on the social dimension of recognition manifest in this story so central to the mythos of our tradition. Baozhi's identification of Bodhidharma as Avalokiteśvara links shi as an intimate knowing with shi as an overt acknowledgment—the express recognition, in this instance, of Bodhidharma's bodhisattvic nature. Such recognitions became a staple of Chan and Zen literature, particularly in accounts of a master singling out a student, even on first encounter, as a person with the potential to become a Dharma successor and to carry on the teaching. Take, for example, the narrative of the initial encounter between Hongren, still a boy at the time, and the master whom our tradition long has numbered as its Fourth Chinese Ancestor, Daoxin (or Tao-hsin; J., Dōshin). Straining credibility to the breaking point, if not beyond, the story involves an intricate play on words that are written similarly and both pronounced *xing* (or *hsing*). This would have made a live exchange beautifully ambiguous, but in writing, the two meanings are distinct: 姓 means "surname" and 性 means "nature." The conversation ends abruptly with Daoxin recognizing Hongren as his Dharma heir:

Hongren met Daoxin on the road to Huangmei. The Ancestor questioned him, saying, "What's your hsing [surname]?"

Hongren said, "The hsing [nature] I have isn't a common hsing [surname]."

The Ancestor said, "What hsing [surname] is it?"

The master said, "Buddha-hsing [nature]."

The Ancestor said, "So you don't have a hsing [surname]?"

The master said, "Hsing [nature] is empty, so I haven't."

Silently recognizing [shi] him as a vessel of the Dharma, the Ancestor handed on the Dharma and the robe.[4]

Elsewhere, it's reported that Hongren received transmission following a period of training under Daoxin when he wasn't so young, but whether or not we put any stock in the legend, clearly the tradition incorporated into its mytho-history a sense of shi as recognition of Dharma excellence.

Besides exemplifying usage of 識 to indicate overt, transactional recognition, the story of Bodhidharma, Emperor Wu, and Baozhi involves two more senses of shi that became prominent in Chan and Zen parlance. Both of them allude to personal awakening. I've already noted the first of these and will return to it below: using the word backward, so to speak, associating a type of *non*-recognition with the wisdom of Bodhidharma. The second, "forward" use of shi equates it positively with awakening and is implicit in Baozhi's recognition of Bodhidharma; he manifests a degree of discernment that the emperor lacked.

More explicit usage of shi in the latter sense can be seen in numerous Chan texts. To wit, a line from the *Wumenguan*: "Recognizing [shi] self-nature, you immediately get free from birth-and-death."[5] In a lineage history, the master Baizhang quotes a teaching of Śākyamuni:

If you wish to recognize [shi] the import of "buddha-nature," you must respect the causes and conditions of seasons. If its season arrives, the pattern [of buddha-nature] will show itself distinctively.[6]

Likewise, from another lineage history comes this dictum of a Korean master known as Damao Heshang (or Ta-mao Ho-shang; J., Daibō Oshō):

> If you want to recognize [shi] the teacher of all buddhas, face the ignorance [wuming, darkness] within the heartmind, and recognition [shi] is accomplished. If you want to recognize [shi] our ever-present, unchanging nature, face the point where the myriad inert things move and morph, and recognition [shi] is accomplished.[7]

Conversely, absence of such recognition indicates that awakening hasn't occurred. Thus Emperor Wu's failure to "tally." An oft-repeated verse by Changsha puts it succinctly:

> People who study the tao don't recognize [shi] reality;
> they just continue the old, familiar consciousness [shi].
> Countless kalpas of birth-and-death issue from this root;
> imbeciles make it out to be the original person.[8]

Changsha calls out a more specific failure of recognition in a story that appears as a kōan in the *Ancestral Gate of Entangling Vines*:

> Officiant-at-court Haoyue (or Hao-yueh; J., Kōgetsu) asked Changsha, "A worthy of old said, 'With understanding, karmic obstructions are empty from the start; / Without understanding, karmic obstructions still must be repaid.' How could masters the likes of the Venerable Siṃha and the august master the Second Ancestor have had to repay their debts?"
> Changsha said, "Great worthy, you don't recognize [shi] original emptiness."
> Haoyue said, "What is original emptiness?"
> "It's karmic hindrances," said Changsha.
> Once more, Haoyue asked, "What are karmic hindrances?"
> Changsha said, "They're original emptiness." Haoyue had no reply.[9]

Haoyue, a priest responsible for conducting rites at the imperial court, begins by quoting lines from the now-familiar "Song of Realizing the Way." He presumes, wrongly, that the wretched deaths that befell the Indian master Siṃha (or Sim-ha; J., Shishi) and the Second Chinese Ancestor following Bodhidharma—both of whom held honored places in the traditional account of Chan's transmission from Śākyamuni—as signifying that the two men had been obliged to "repay" karmic obstructions and thus must have failed to understand the Dharma.

These two aspects of shi—as overt recognition and as private realization—poignantly and potently collide in a dialogue between Longtan (or Lung-t'an; J., Ryūtan), a widely known ninth-century master, and a woman of his community:

> A nun from the assembly asked, "Getting to become a monk—what about that?"
>
> "Since you became a nun," the master countered, "has it been a long or a short time?"
>
> The nun said, "Not long enough to return as a monk, I suppose."
>
> "Right now, exactly what are you?" asked the master.
>
> "At present, this is a nun's body!" the nun exclaimed. "How could anyone fail to recognize [shi] it?"
>
> The master said, "Who recognizes [shi] you?"[10]

Well, I do! At least I think I do. Her words are open to interpretation, including an interpretation very unfavorable to her: namely, that she raises her initial question out of naïveté or ignorance and that, throughout their exchange, she has no sense of what Longtan is driving at. I don't read the story that way; I recognize her differently. How about you? Let's take it again, from the top, slowly.

"Getting to become a monk—what about that?" The nun's question concerns doctrines handed down in early sūtras, doctrines rooted in Indian culture but consistent with longstanding Chinese norms, that privileged men over women in numerous ways. In addition to placing nuns in roles subservient to monks, these doctrines held that their gender precluded great awakening and becoming bodhisattvas. The best that a woman could hope to do, under these doctrines, was to contain her sexuality thoroughly in her present life so that she could gain rebirth as a man, become a monk, then maybe rise to the status of a bodhisattva or even, sacré bleu, a buddha. This was common knowledge in the sangha, so it seems untenable to suppose that the nun is asking Longtan for information. I believe she's checking him, asking whether he actually buys into those culture-bound concepts about women.

I think I recognize Longtan, too. His answer, "Since you became a nun, has it been a long or a short time?" reads like a non sequitur and is just as open to unflattering interpretation as her question. You could say that he's dodging her question or at least deaf to it. But that underestimates him. He's coming at the subject from a different angle, doing his job as a Chan master by redirecting her to a question of fundamental identity. Did she actually "become" a nun at some point in time? What did this becoming consist of? When did it occur?

Her response turns the conversation back around: "Not long enough to return as a monk, I suppose." In this dry, indeed acid reply, I detect a note of frustration. She wants Longtan to deal with the issue she's raised, not to carry on as usual, as if buddha-nature were the only issue and as if it has nothing to do with the one she's brought up.

But no, he pointedly returns to the matter of identity: "Right now, exactly what are you?" That's a big question, one all of us would do well to consider. What exactly am I? What exactly are you? No glib answers, please! In an era when identity has become a fraught issue, one that regularly spills into the news, social interactions, political discourse, and law, it's often reduced to a matter of categories and labels, which do a miserable job of expressing what you and I "are exactly." That gives all categories the slip. How would you respond without recourse to labels?

There's an intriguing parallel to this exchange in the *Vimalakīrti Sūtra* in which the arhat Śāriputra, reputedly the wisest of Śākyamuni's disciples, matches wits with a goddess who lives in Vimalakīrti's small house.[11] She's dwelled there invisibly but decides to make herself known on this occasion when Śāriputra has come, along with Manjuśri and tens of thousands of other bodhisattvas, arhats, and celestial entities, to ask after the ailing layman. She impresses Śāriputra with her wisdom in answering his initial question, about how long she's lived there: "As long as the Elder's been in a state of liberation." Not very long then, he responds modestly, and back she comes with a question corresponding squarely with the one that Longtan puts to the nun: "How long have you been in a state of liberation?" Śāriputra keeps quiet at first but, when pressed, explains that liberation is beyond words, so he doesn't know what to say.

The goddess sets him straight on that point and goes on to stagger him with her astute observations on other matters. Finally, Śāriputra asks why she doesn't give up female form, and she answers that, despite years of searching, she hasn't found "femaleness" and then, exercising her magical powers, transforms him into a woman and takes on his appearance herself. He's bewildered and finds himself unable to resume the body he considers his, which sets the goddess up to say,

> If the Elder could drop his female form, then women would be able to do so as well. Just as Śāriputra isn't a woman yet appears to be a woman, so it is with all women: they appear to be women but aren't. That's what the Buddha meant when he taught, "Among existent things, there are no men or women."

So, dear reader, what do you say? You're exactly *what*? Perhaps you fall silent, but our nun doesn't hesitate in fielding Longtan's question: "At present, this is a nun's body! How could anyone fail to recognize it?" Note the exactitude of her answer. At *present*, she's a nun in nun's form, a woman leading a woman's life in a strictly gendered society. And given the dual implications of the verb *shi*, her closing question—"How could anyone fail to *recognize* it?"— strikes with considerable force. Has Longtan failed to recognize her the same way the emperor failed to recognize Bodhidharma? Surely Longtan recognized her as a nun, but did he overlook her true nature?

Maybe, but I doubt it. If I recognize *him* correctly, his questions implicitly recognize her. By posing them as he does, Longtan demonstrates from the get-go that he regards her as worthy of incisive instruction. Far from dismissing her, he pushes her—and pushes her hard—to recognize three realities: the folly inherent in the idea of "becoming" something (a nun, a monk, a buddha), the completeness of what she is already, and finally, most pointedly and of paramount importance, the true identity and nature of the one who recognizes. His last question, "Who recognizes you?" tacitly recognizes her capacity to realize the Great Matter. Like Bassui's kōan "Who hears?" it drives to the very heart of experience.[12]

I applaud Longtan's readiness to engage the nun in this manner, and as a teacher, I admire his skill in turning her questions around and prodding her to recognize her own self-nature; that's his job and mine, and by this account, he did it very ably. At the same time, I mourn his failure to address the strictures, doctrinal and practical, that the woman there before him, along with others near and far, have had to live under.

The story of Bodhidharma's encounter with Emperor Wu balances recognition as profound realization with recognition as social fact, while the Longtan story sets the two in opposition and comes down on the side of shi as realization. That emphasis aligns with Chan's historic mission, so it's hardly surprising to find a master enacting it, but in scanting the nun's concerns, Longtan scants a central teaching of Mahāyāna Buddhism, too: the unconditioned is inextricable from the conditioned. Recognizing that fact through personal awakening is vital and wonderful, but then failing to recognize and enact it "on the ground," in social, economic, political, and ecological arrangements, is to be the sort of person that our ancestors dubbed a "board carrier"—a person capable of seeing only half of reality.

At least a few of our male predecessors long ago noticed the failure to recognize women in the public sense. Of this we can be sure thanks to a Chan anthology dating from the thirteenth century that preserves the tale of exactly such a board carrier:

> Once there was a monk studying with Mihu. On the road, he happened upon an old woman living in a hermitage and asked the old woman if she had a sangha or not. She said she did. "Where are the members?" asked the monk.
>
> "The mountains, rivers, and great earth, these grasses and these trees," she said, "they're all my sangha."
>
> The monk responded, "Old woman, don't pretend to be my teacher, alright?"
>
> "What do you see me as?" she asked.
>
> The monk said, "An ordinary person."
>
> "You can't be a monk!" the old woman exclaimed.
>
> The monk responded, "Old woman, don't muddy up and abuse the most excellent buddhadharma."
>
> "I'm not muddying up and abusing the buddhadharma!" she said.
>
> The monk said, "How can you think that you haven't muddied up and abused the buddhadharma?"
>
> The old woman replied, "You're a man. I'm a woman. Where's all this muddiness and abuse?"[13]

A contemporary scholar suggests that this tale and others like it were intended to motivate monks to gain enough insight to avoid ignominious defeat at the hands of a woman.[14] Even if so, the story presents incontestable evidence that long ago at least some members of the Chan leadership recognized the perfect Dharma capability of women. At the same time, it affords mute testimony to the fact that the institutions of Chan (and of Zen, too) remained trapped in the social prejudices of their culture. Individual masters did much better, but it's taken centuries—right down to the present—even to begin dismantling institutional barriers to women's rightful recognition.[15]

Since such outward recognition unquestionably affects everyone's lives, individually and collectively, a detour into matters of everyday life seems warranted. I'll start with the confession that I pursued personal recognition greedily during my precollege years and received plenty but that it meant nothing relative to two family events. One was my elder brother taking me, at age nineteen, into his confidence, recognizing me as trustworthy and, as never before, his peer. The second, about a decade later, was my aged grandmother remarking, out of the blue, "Nelson, I'm proud to be related to you." *You?* Proud of being related to *me*? Her words took me utterly by surprise and struck me as upside down. I was proud to be related to *her*. I have no idea why she said that or why my brother chose to let me in on his private life as he did, but their recognition affected me powerfully, to a degree that more conspicuous honors never have.

I mention these moments to foreground two points: that recognition can have substantial impact without any public or material element and that it's often close relationships that make it ours to give, especially to our juniors. The life of Rachel Carson offers a consequential example: at twenty-eight, forced by the Depression to discontinue graduate study and support a houseful of relatives, she took a part-time job as a writer with the U.S. Bureau of Fisheries. One day, her boss rejected the introduction she'd drafted for a brochure titled "The World of Waters," telling her, "Better try again. But send this one to the *Atlantic*."[16]

Thus began Carson's career as what used to be called a public intellectual, contributing thoughtfully to discussion of crucial issues in a manner that today's "influencer" rarely does, if ever. The *Atlantic* published that first piece in 1937. Twenty-five years (and three books) later, Carson shook the nation with *Silent Spring*. It's possible, of course, that she'd have made her outsized contribution to public understanding even if Elmer Higgins, her otherwise forgotten supervisor, had turned a blind eye to her talent or had simply neglected to add the seven simple words "But send this one to the *Atlantic*." No doubt his recognition was important to her, though; we wouldn't even know of it otherwise. I say, hats off to Mr. Higgins!

In this example, as in the episodes from my own life, one person bestows recognition on another, but recognition operates in many ways, at many social scales. This book results from an instance of recognition at the near end of the scale, as described in the first chapter—just me, no grandmother or Mr. Higgins to point out my ignorance of this tradition. At the distant end of the scale lie recognitions of national, if not civilizational and international, proportions and in realms of thought I'm ill-equipped and uneager to enter: philosophy, psychology, political theory, human development, and so on. I'll defer to a noted contemporary historian and philosopher:

> We need recognition from others as a condition for being ourselves. We need it not only in the innermost spheres of love and friendship but also in the outermost reaches of public life, where it assumes an institutional form. Recognition, we might say, is a dynamic force that quickens our institutions and prevents them from hardening into an unresponsive mass. The right to vote, for example, is not only a matter of law; it is an expression of recognition for others as agents who deserve a say in determining the course of their lives.[17]

Point this lens at history or today's news, and they immediately snap into focus as continuing sagas of groups and individuals clamoring for public recognition of their causes, travails, achievements, or needs, of their way of life, of their rights, of their sovereignty or territorial claims, of injustices done to them, sometimes simply of their humanity.

It's not only people who need recognition, however; fellow occupants of planet Earth do, too. Again we can look to the example of Rachel Carson as a person who herself recognized, and helped many thousands of others begin to recognize, the importance of the oceans and the diverse, often wondrous forms of life that dwell within and depend upon them. And of course she then brought the world to recognize the damage DDT and other toxic chemicals were doing and the disasters they would wreak if left unchecked. She lifted people toward recognition of ecosystems—their intricacy and susceptibility to disruption—even as (let's not idolize her) she failed to recognize that the means of remediation she promoted, biological controls, could also do severe damage.[18]

Unless we become skillful at recognizing "other kinds," we stand a very poor chance of appreciating their uniquenesses, their needs, their interactions, and their part in ecological balances. That, in turn, puts us at a terrible disadvantage in understanding how to interact with them in the interest of our common welfare. I was impressed recently to learn of an American entomologist who's dedicated his life to, yes, recognizing caterpillars—finding, documenting, identifying, and describing them—and frames his work as serving the caterpillars. Convening a 2023 conference to initiate a five-year, federally funded research program on insect decline, he told his fellow scientists something delightfully suprascientific: that he'd undertaken the project "because the bugs demanded that I do this."[19] Even if he spoke those words a little tongue in cheek, they mark him as a person who, beyond recognizing larval lives in their mind-boggling, distinctive forms, also recognizes the obligation this places him under (and you and me with him) to do right by these small fellow citizens of contingent systems much larger than ourselves. As a species, out of gratitude and shame, surely we're much obliged.

———

Okay, I've said enough, perhaps more than enough, about recognition as overt event and, before that, about recognition as realization. Now let's double back to the curious matter of *non*-recognition—of Bodhidharma, that paragon of *prajñā*, saying "Not shi" in reply to Emperor Wu's question of who was confronting him. What might Bodhidharma have meant by saying "[I] don't recognize [myself]"? A strong clue comes in an exchange between two men that Chan claimed in its fanciful Indian lineage, Punyayaśas and the great

Buddhist poet held to be his successor, Aśvaghosa. When Aśvaghosa inquires, "I want to recognize the buddha. What is that?" the ancestor responds, "You want to recognize the buddha. The one who doesn't recognize is it."[20] Who could *that* be?

Interactions among Chinese masters developed the theme:

> When Xuefeng took leave of Dongshan, the master said, "Where are you going?"
>
> "Back among the high passes," said Xuefeng.
>
> "Before, when you came out," the master asked, "what road did you follow?" Xuefeng said he'd followed flying gibbons as he came out over the passes.
>
> The master said, "Now, returning there, on which road will you depart?" and Xuefeng answered that he'd follow the flying gibbons as he went back over the passes.
>
> "There's someone who doesn't follow flying gibbons over the passes," the master said. "Have you looked around and recognized him?" Xuefeng said he hadn't, whereupon the master asked, "Why didn't you recognize him?"
>
> "He has no face!" said Xuefeng.
>
> The master said, "You just said you don't you recognize him, so how do you know he has no face?" Xuefeng had no comeback.[21]

Point well taken! And here's an instance of *non*-recognition releasing a monk from great despair:

> When the future master Yungai Zhian (or Yun-k'ai Chih-an; J., Ungai Shian) was residing in the assembly of Shishuang (or Shih-shuang; J., Sekisō), a monk asked Shishuang, "When the myriad doors are all locked, what about that?"
>
> Shishuang said, "Inside the hall, what's going on?"
>
> The monk went half a year before he was able to reply, "Nobody touches him."
>
> Shishuang said, "You speak grandly but have only said eighty or ninety percent."

When Zhian heard this, he respectfully implored Shishuang to say something more, but Shishuang didn't speak. The master then locked Shishuang in his arms, took him behind the abbot's quarters, set him down, and declared, "Honored priest, if you don't say something, I'll have to hit you."

"So be it," said Shishuang. At this, the master made prostrations without cease. As he was doing so, Shishuang commented, "Nobody recognizes him!" and the master, hearing those words, tumbled into great awakening.[22]

Whatever else you take from these stories, they demonstrate that *shi* and not *shi*, recognizing and not recognizing, may allude to the same experience, framed in reverse fashion. This isn't a mere toying with words. Xuefeng and Zhian recognized themselves as fundamentally unrecognizable; they unrecognized themselves. The first of Dongshan's famous verses on the "Five Positions" gestures to this experience, too, placing it late at night, in total darkness:

When the third watch begins, before moonrise,
   don't think it strange to meet and not recognize [shi] the other
   yet still somehow recall the elegance of ancient days.[23]

—

The ambiguities of 識 made it a resource, a treasure, a bit of a plaything maybe, for Chan and Zen ancestors endeavoring to communicate the Dharma, and of course this essay nominates it for continued enjoyment and use. The problem we face in that regard, if you'll forgive me for putting it this way, is that most of us can't recognize recognition when it appears in the texts we study; we're dependent on translations, and they almost always obscure it. Recognizing *that* is a good first step for those of us who receive the tradition in translation. Beyond that, we can hope that the scholars and publishers whose translations we rely on will offer more help in recognizing what lies beneath the surface of a word like *shi*.

Our larger problems of recognition will persist, no doubt. A passage from the brush of Qisong (or Chi-sung), a highly respected eleventh-century monk and literary figure, reminds us that such problems are perennial:

> Last year, in the second month of spring, [Judge Li Huishu] was about to pardon a criminal. He came to my office to discuss the matter and for an entire day was unable to leave. He said, "Long ago [Sengzhao] was called the He Yan [i.e., paragon] of monks, but now as I behold you there is no comparison." At that, I was disappointed in myself for becoming his acquaintance so late, and I sent him an epistle to let him know that he had unduly praised me. He replied, "These days, those who recognize [shi] the world's worthy people are few."[24]

How blind we can be to others! The challenges of recognition abound, continuously, day to day, with fellow humans certainly but also in realms greater than human. We have our work cut out for us. Fortunately, corresponding joys are available at each step of the way, particularly if we can bring a measure of *un*-recognizing—seeing beyond self, seeing beyond others—to each unprecedented encounter.

15 | Hundun the Beneficent, or Chaos Reconsidered

The Inner Chapters of the *Zhuangzi*, the seven chapters judged most likely to convey the teachings of Zhuangzi himself rather than additions by his followers, close with a brief story that Chan and Zen writers have frequently alluded to. Using it to sound themes central to both teaching and practice in our tradition, they've placed this story, the story of Hundun, among its treasures, and its value has, if anything, increased since it was first set down more than two thousand years ago.

> The sovereign of the southern ocean was called Shu, the sovereign of the northern ocean was called Hu, and the sovereign of the center was called Hundun. Shu and Hu sometimes met in the territory of Hundun, who always looked after them very well. Shu and Hu discussed how to repay Hundun's virtue. "All people have seven openings, for purposes of seeing, hearing, eating, and breathing," they said. "This one alone hasn't any. Let's try boring him some!" So each day they bored a hole, and on the seventh day Hundun died.[1]

Zhuangzi drops this story on the reader without a word of exposition, but its substance and placement, along with commentaries by subsequent writers, leave no doubt that Hundun's death represents human folly writ large. The sovereigns of the north and south intervened inappropriately and ruinously, and the fact that they meant well, intending to reciprocate the kindness they'd received from Hundun, makes the outcome not less horrible, I think, but more horrible and more surely telling.

Unfortunately, translators have distorted the story by persistently rendering Hundun's name as Chaos, a choice justifiable in linguistic terms but carrying a powerfully negative connotation that has no basis in the story.[2] This misleading nomenclature seems to have originated with James Legge (1815-1897), a Scottish missionary and pioneering translator of Chinese texts. Legge's comments on the story leave no doubt that he viewed Hundun as a malign presence and his death as good riddance:

> The little allegory is ingenious and amusing. "It indicates," says Lin, "how action (the opposite of non-action) injures the first condition of things."...One critic says that an "alas!" might well follow the concluding "died." But surely it was better that Chaos gave way to another state. [Shu] and [Hu] did not do a bad work.[3]

Of course an "alas!" *is* warranted when Hundun's death is seen from a Daoist perspective—the perspective of its author, first and foremost, who dedicated himself to promoting what Legge calls "non-action," wuwei. More about that in the next chapter.

A look at the Chinese characters for Hundun gives reason to reconsider Legge's translation. The graphs that comprise the name are based on the water radical and, taken at face value, seem to denote turbidity, earth suspended in water—a mixture opaque but not inherently dangerous, indeed likely to prove fertile.[4] Our finest dictionary of ancient Chinese follows the conventional English translation by identifying *hundun* as "inchoate chaos" but then defines it in terms more precise and consistent with the story: "absolutely amorphous, the primordial closed and utterly dark entity containing all potential forms...which ceases to exist when 'opened'"—in other words, when bored into by Shu and Hu in their botched attempt at reciprocation.[5]

Zhuangzi's statement that Hundun always "looked after"—literally, "attended to"—the visiting sovereigns "very well" makes Chaos at least an unsuitable translation, if not flat out incorrect. In characterizing Hundun as a good host, Zhuangzi plainly meant to present it as a beneficent force, and Legge's reluctance or inability to understand Hundun in positive terms tells us that, however good his knowledge of the Chinese language, he couldn't help reading the simple sentences of the story with the eyes of the Victorian churchman that he was. Given his background, Chaos was a nearly inevitable designation for Hundun, since it was standard biblical nomenclature for the primordial state of the world. Originating in classical Greek, it denotes a "vast gulf or chasm, the nether abyss, empty space, the first state of the universe," according to the *Oxford English Dictionary*, and apart from its generous attentions to Shu and Hu, Hundun neatly fit the account of chaos in Genesis: "earth was without form and void, and darkness was upon the face of the deep."[6]

Reverend Legge's interpretation of the Hundun story in keeping with this Abrahamic account of creation explains not only the name he assigned Hundun but also his offhand absolution of Shu and Hu for their fatal deeds. The Yahweh of Genesis instigates a series of separations—light from dark, earth from water, and more—that give the world structure and establish the basis for life. Though Legge didn't go so far as to identify Shu and Hu's acts with those of the biblical Creator, neither did he hesitate to approve the result: "But surely it was better that Chaos gave way to another state." Far from being "a bad work," to him it represented a necessary step toward the glories of creation.

Before looking at the ways Chan and Zen have deployed Hundun imagery over the centuries and considering the story's implications for present affairs, let's take note of a couple more details. Just as Hundun's name holds significance, so do the names of Shu and Hu.[7] Legge interpreted them to mean Heedless and Sudden, while subsequent translators have dubbed them Brief and Sudden, Lickety and Split, Swoosh and Oblivion. I'm partial to Flash and Rash myself, but no matter which you prefer, the point seems clear: the royal outsiders hail from realms where time is short, speed a native condition. As sovereigns of the oceans north and south, they also represent the domains of direction and difference.

These attributes, foreign to the amorphous land where Hundun presides, make Shu and Hu the hapless agents of its destruction and should remind us of ourselves. Like Shu and Hu, we're prone to project our experience upon others—in this case, the desirability of the seven human apertures and expectations of host-guest etiquette—and thus are apt to misperceive others' needs and to inflict unintended harm. Like Shu and Hu, we frequently act on the basis of deductions that, though they may satisfy the demands of logic, prove unfounded and harmful. The names Shu and Hu mock our tendency to jump to conclusions and rush into action, neglecting factors whose importance we realize too late.

—

For masters of Chan and Zen, boring holes in Hundun became a go-to metaphor for mistaken and fruitless efforts, especially for efforts to grasp the Dharma by intellectual means. In the *Record of Ease*, the master Wansong refers explicitly to the story, teaching, "If you insist on generating distinctions and forcing your efforts, that's nothing but painting eyebrows on Hundun."[8] (And for a being without eyes, what could be more superfluous than eyebrows?) Other masters alluded to the precedent more broadly, as Yuanwu did in *The Blue Cliff Record*, cautioning, "Each move, each stance, each word, each phrase—it's just in order to have a point of entry. It's like gouging a wound in healthy flesh."[9]

Treating the story in this manner, these and other writers have placed Hundun's fate in the hands of each practitioner instead of relegating it to a remote past and pinning the blame on those convenient fall guys Shu and Hu. Hanshan Deqing (or Han-shan Te-ch'ing), considered one of four great Chan monks of the Ming Dynasty, made this interpretation explicit:

> …all these obstructions to far-reaching and unfettered wandering are the fault of clever understanding and calculating skill.

They are all holes drilled in Hundun, destroying him, so that the Heavenly genuineness is lost. In fact, from ancient times down to the present, in all times and places,...there is not one person who is not the driller of holes in Hundun, constantly destroying him.[10]

Hakuin Zenji likewise put the onus for Hundun's survival squarely on us, teaching that to let analytical thinking obscure the immediate vitality of our own nature is to murder Hundun with even our most mundane actions:

Who is the one that works your hands and feet?
Eats and drinks when you're thirsty and hungry?
If a hair of discrimination enters into these acts,
You've killed Mr. Hundun boring holes for his eyes.[11]

Elsewhere Hakuin semi-seriously identified Śākyamuni Buddha as Hundun's son: "This lad was born at the same instant as the great Void, / His father is Mr. Hundun, and he is nicknamed *Nameless*."[12]

Such statements go a long way toward equating Hundun with buddha-nature or original nature. From this perspective, Hundun's "turbidity," the mingling of earth and water, expresses the fundamental unity of things, and it becomes practitioners' aspiration to realize that unity personally, as the heartmind never beset by the drill bits of Flash and Rash. It should come as no big surprise to learn that Hakuin's illustrious successor Tōrei "established a strict equivalence between primeval chaos (*konton*) [i.e., Hundun] and the realization of one's intrinsic nature (*kenshō*)."[13]

Some texts emphasize Hundun's inviolate aspect by appending the phrase *weifen*, "not yet differentiated,"[14] to the name, thus making clear reference to Hundun before Shu and Hu went to work, before even the most basic polarities had emerged:

Frozen rivers exploding into flames, iron trees bursting into bloom—that doesn't come out of a process of fabrication. How could it lie within the scope of yin and yang? Regarding the epoch of Hundun not yet being differentiated, try to settle down and get a close look.[15]

The vastly creative fifteenth-century Zen master Ikkyū evoked the sufficiency and beauty of the world perceived in this fashion, without division into subject and object, in lines of a lovely verse that seems to incorporate weifen right into Hundun's name:

> Hundun weifen darkens the deepening dusk;
> the clouds and moon know who the scenery is for.[16]

Many centuries earlier, Hanshan (the early Chan recluse and poet, not to be confused with the aforementioned, much later master Hanshan Deqing) imagined the freedom of Hundun's life prior to differentiation, contrasting it to the hassles we ordinary mortals endure as a result of our "borings." Adding openings for excretion to the seven of the original story, he envisioned Hundun surviving to become the type or perhaps the progenitor of the entire human species:

> Hundun's body—how carefree!
> Not taking food, not even pissing!
> But he met with boring and cutting,
> so now we have the nine holes,
> day after day hustle for clothes and food,
> year after year worry about paying our taxes.
> People by the thousands battle for a buck,
> throngs clamoring with all their might.[17]

With such inventive, varied, and numerous evocations of Hundun, Chan and Zen have sustained a lasting allegiance to the Daoist critique of human overreach and have joined in advocating wuwei. In themselves, however, these perspectives don't require rejection of order or orderly processes. Hundun's world functioned beautifully through an order of its own, imperceptible to Shu and

Hu; their blindness to it led them to impose an *alien* order. Like anyone else, note the comparative philosophers David Hall and Roger Ames, a sage can only survive "chaos" by discriminating the prevailing order—short from long, edible from inedible, and so on—and deferring to apparent excellence. "The difference that makes all the difference," they observe, "is that the sage recognizes the arbitrariness, transitoriness, and merely conventional status of such discriminations."[18]

The sage Drs. Hall and Ames had in mind was a Daoist sage, but their observation applies equally well to a Chan or Zen sage. In treading this path, wrote master Yuanwu,

> ...it is necessary to charge past the myriad categories and types and to fly above them, to cut off the flow and brush against the heavens. How could the awakened willingly be petty creatures, confined within distinctions of high and low and victory and defeat, futilely trying to make comparative judgments of momentary experience, and being utterly turned around by gain and loss?[19]

Even in this statement, particularly in contrasting awakened people to "petty creatures," Yuanwu availed himself of categories and types, but that doesn't obviate the point he and masters before and after him have made: conceptual orders have no reliable foundation and, utilized without that awareness, promote warped understandings and ill-conceived initiatives to "bore holes" in the world. Omitting too much complexity to give us a good sense of the whole, conceptual orders don't provide a secure basis for decisions.

—

The abhorrence of chaos established in Western cultures from an early date has led, understandably, to a reciprocal, seemingly boundless desire for order—for discovery of order in all spheres of life and for imposing it where it's found to be insufficient. Such orders have frequently proven productive in the short run, destructive in the long. Perhaps the first Westerner to notice the fallacy of warring against chaos in this fashion, surely one of the first to identify it clearly, was the historian Henry Adams. In his remarkable autobiography, Adams observed, "Every fabulist has told how the human mind has always struggled like a frightened bird to escape the chaos which caged it." But escape seemed impossible to him in light of developments that he witnessed at the Great Exposition of 1900 in Paris. Wilhelm Röntgen's discovery of x-rays and Marie Curie's of radiation, along with advances in power generation and other fields, convinced him that "In plain words, Chaos was the law of nature; Order was the dream of man."[20]

Seeing this dream shattered beyond repair, Adams felt compelled to reconceive himself as "a conscious ball of vibrating motions, traversed in every direction by infinite lines of rotation or vibration,...a center of supersensual chaos"—that is, as a self formed by, and subject to, an array of natural forces undetectable to his senses and previously not even suspected. This new perspective "did not distress him" because, as a man in his late sixties, he could live with "a few illusions more or less," but it struck him as intellectually unflattering and emotionally unsatisfying that the new scientific findings had so roughly ejected humanity from the Eden of order, unity, and beauty and had left the modern mind just two options: "merge in its supersensual multiverse, or succumb to it."[21]

There may have been something in the air. In the same years, Adams's friend and fellow Boston intellectual William James, too, felt a need to consider the tension between chaos and order. Coming at the question from a very different direction, in *The Varieties of Religious Experience* he dissolved the tension in a manner amazingly consonant with the Hundun tale. He did so in a page-long footnote (in minute type!), beginning with a paragraph on the theological problem of how Christians reconcile worldly disorder with the image of God as the supreme giver of order. James then widens his lens:

When one views the world with no definite theological bias one way or the other, one sees that order and disorder, as we now recognize them, are purely human inventions. We are interested in certain types of arrangement, useful, aesthetic, or moral—so interested that whenever we find them realized, the fact emphatically rivets our attention. The result is that we work over the contents of the world selectively. It is overflowing with disorderly arrangements from our point of view, but order is the only thing we care for and look at, and by choosing, one can always find some sort of orderly arrangement in the midst of any chaos.[22]

He goes on to illustrate this observation through the example of finding order—geometric shapes—in a random scattering of a thousand beans, concluding,

> Our dealings with Nature are just like this. She is a vast plenum in which our attention draws capricious lines in innumerable directions. We count and name whatever lies upon the special lines we trace, whilst the other things and the untraced lines are neither named nor counted. There are in reality…infinitely more things with irregular relations than with regular relations between them. But we look for the regular kind of thing exclusively, and ingeniously discover and preserve it in our memory. It accumulates with other regular kinds, until the collection of them fills our encyclopaedias [sic]. Yet all the while between and around them lies an infinite anonymous chaos of objects that no one ever thought of together, of relations that never yet attracted our attention.

I regret one word in this observation: capricious. I suppose that James meant it to apply, first of all, to the lines people had drawn in the subject he was discussing, religion, or in the wider field he helped define, psychology. In both, many lines have indeed been traced capriciously in one sense of the word—changeably, inconsistently—but most have been drawn, criticized, defended, and redrawn in ways not a bit capricious in the word's other sense, of playful or fanciful. An especially pertinent and poignant example, in light of James's work, is the long, sometimes bitter struggle that has surrounded formulation of the *Diagnostic and Statistical Manual of Mental Disorders*. This supposedly authoritative text has gone through five editions since 1952, quadrupling the number of "disorders" that it describes and incorporating substantial changes of terminology, definition, and criteria for diagnosis. No doubt these lines will continue to be revised.

Though religion and psychology may have been the fields paramount in James's mind, by framing his observation as broadly as he did—in terms of the "vast plenum" of "Nature"—he implicitly included the "hard" sciences as well. Like Adams, he was keenly aware of the discoveries of the preceding decades and impressed by how profoundly they contradicted prevailing notions of how the world works. (In his case, evidence of unseen physical forces fed a long-held interest in such "psychic phenomena" as communication with the dead.[23]) If "by choosing, one can always find some sort of orderly arrangement in the midst of any chaos," then no order, however widely accepted, is immune to doubt or reconsideration. This doesn't mean that every perceived arrangement—natural selection, for instance—is necessarily mistaken. It only demands that we regard the lines we draw as tentative and incomplete, as simplifications likely to need revision to take into account "relations that never yet attracted our attention."

Whichever domains James had in mind, his footnote put him in agreement with the Daoist sage described by Hall and Ames: he obviously recognized "the arbitrariness, transitoriness, and merely conventional status" of regularities that most of us perceive in the complex, ever-changing bean pile of reality. Whether or not Professor James deserves to be elevated to sagehood, it seems probable that if he, instead of Flash and Rash, had been the recipient of Hundun's hospitality, he'd have accepted his beneficent treatment with respect and refrained from boring holes.

A similar receptivity to chaos has been rare in European and American cultures since the Renaissance, but theoreticians in a number of fields started to embrace it in the decades after Adams and James, and today mathematicians and scientists apply the word in a value-neutral way, without the dread-full connotations it carried previously. This new Western conception of chaos, commonly applied in attempts to model and understand the behavior of nonlinear, dynamical systems—the weather, ecological interactions, social influence, financial markets, and the like—bears a much closer resemblance to Hundun than earlier conceptions did.[24]

Not only have the developers of chaos theory attributed no negativity to chaos, in their work they've also accepted, so far at least, a large measure of turbidity, if I may call it that. Although they're able to discern patterns in chaotic systems, they can't predict the position of a given element in the flux—where a stick tossed into a stream will wash up, for example. Also, despite truly impressive thinking devoted to this new research, so far even a consensus on a scientific definition of chaos remains out of reach. That might be cause for frustration from the math and science perspectives, but in the nebulous domain of Hundun, keeping the lines sketchy is a recipe for success, not failure, and gives reason to hope for subfatal results.

Chaos also has received application of a positive, less arcane sort in the field of urban design. Jane Jacobs, an eloquent advocate of neighborhood in metropolitan settings like Manhattan, begged city planners to respect "strips of chaos that have a weird wisdom of their own."[25] Such respect would require planners to examine without prejudice, indeed with appreciation, the jumbled factors at play in an existing cityscape and to initiate only modest interventions in support of its organic configurations instead of imposing large, high-concept solutions. Dramatically extending Jacobs's argument for minimally intrusive approaches, a contemporary Dutch planner has demonstrated that streets with little or no signage are functionally safer than those marked in the typical fashion, apparently because drivers, cyclists, and pedestrians sharing such "naked streets" pay closer attention to one another. His conclusion: "Chaos equals cooperation."[26]

I was surprised to see chaos also receiving respectful, well-informed notice in, of all places, a recent opera review: "Order, whether cosmic or artistic, doesn't come from rational planning or a god's imperious command. Rather, it's an emergent property that chaos mysteriously distills out of itself."[27] That's exactly the way that Hundun has been serving the cosmos forever, distilling out of itself suns, planets, oceans, volcanos, ferns, bees, corals, people, operas, opera reviews, and this chapter, too, of course. Might chaos be making a comeback like this, distilling out of itself an enhanced human understanding of our place in the schemeless scheme of things? I hope so.

But this much is certain: with the era of big data now hard upon us, we face continuing tests of our capacity to avoid killing off Hundun. In theory, analysis of gigantic data sets should enable researchers to identify relationships otherwise too obscure to find, but it may instead make it easier than ever to draw the "special lines" that, as William James observed, so interest and obsess us. The impossibility of extracting a reliable chronicle of events from a database containing hundreds of thousands of email messages moved the journalist Nathan Heller to reflect on our "tendency to weave stories" that result in erroneous ideas and foolhardy behavior. "Broadening the data pool," he wrote,

> has no chance of dissolving these delusions, because people generally deal with huge volumes of information the same way they deal with small ones: by sifting and discarding, then connecting dots to make a picture out of what remains. They latch onto results that bear out narrative and hopeful theory. They seek a private order in the chaos of the world.[28]

The notion of life as a struggle to stave off chaos by carving out an order has a powerful grip on us legatees of Western thought, and breaking its hold anytime soon is a long shot at best. Yet in some quarters, clearly, chaos has outlived its representation as a universal bogeyman, and it behooves us to remember that we have reason to be suspicious of order. The word is martial at its root, referring to the order of troops. Yes, it may make the trains run on time as it goes goose-stepping through history but at a price we don't always want to pay. I like to think that those who "know the tune" and other clear-sighted people might show us how to cool our ardor for ordering the world and instead lead us in a conspiracy to recuperate Hundun. Better late than never.

Our tardy emergency response probably needs to start, as Confucius advised, with "the rectification of names"—in this case, rectification of a skewed translation. Although *turbidity* seems etymologically appropriate, Zhuangzi's sketch of Hundun points in the direction of wild nature as a whole, a dynamic, self-organizing system or, better, a *process*. The more we learn about it, the more we see how this process has produced the world we love and depend on and the more we see, too, if we're honest, that our undertakings have tended to disrupt and diminish it. No example is more salient today than our penchant for "climate control," which has contributed, and continues to contribute, to throwing earth's inherent climate control disastrously out of whack.

As a wild process, Hundun has not only met the needs of humankind in the sense of providing us means for sustenance and shelter; it's also "attended to us" in terms of bodily makeup, suffusing our being in every detail. Recent findings in biology have revealed the wildness within us as never before, especially in bringing to light the fantastically diverse microbiome that occupies and operates our innards and the hugely complicated neuronal networks of our brains that enable our perceptions, reflexes, dreams, memories, thoughts, and actions. Every year, research gives us more reasons to regard ourselves, each of us, as a walking, talking ecosystem embedded and participating in larger ecosystems, never apart from their influences, subtle or not so subtle.

Of course, the beneficence of wild nature includes many things that people wish it didn't. Blizzards and floods, scorpions and sidewinders, mosquitos, flies, lice, headaches, hunger, the agonies of childbirth, cancer—the hardships posed by such things have driven many of our efforts to reconfigure Hundun to our liking. No wonder, and no blame either. A desire to improve upon given conditions seems universal among life-forms, part of our wild endowment. The pines and oaks around our house reach out for the sun. Dragonflies congregate where their prey is rich.

The question now, even more than in Zhuangzi's time, is whether we'll rein in the impulse to rearrange the ten thousand things in service to human designs. From where I sit, the need to do so is apparent; Flash and Rash have drilled dangerously many holes. Accumulating evidence of complexity at every level of wild process—from subatomic to supragalactic, intestinal to intellectual—in itself seems sufficient to warrant humility before chaos and a reluctance to intervene further. Humanity has amassed such a long and terrible record of unintended consequences that, smart as we are, sophisticated as our sciences are, we can't rightly claim to know what we're doing.

It seems imperative to apply the Hundun paradigm in our personal and collective responses to ecological issues of our day, including the overarching emergency of climate change. British author and "recovering environmentalist" Paul Kingsnorth is among those who have surrendered hope that humanity is farsighted enough or has means enough to repair the damage already done. Although the ancient abyssal, fearful conception of chaos clings to Kingsnorth's sentences, he shows no inclination to resist chaos through an imposition of order. To the contrary, he rejects pretensions of control and condemns the notion that our problems can be solved like problems in mathematics:

> The future offers chaos, uncertainty, loss. To deny this is to deny reality. To pretend we have more control than we have, and to cling to glib "solutions" as if the world were a maths puzzle we could solve with the right equations, is a similar form of denial. There is an abyss opening up before us. It challenges everything we thought we knew about our culture and about nature. We need to look into it and concentrate on what we can see.[29]

Both in these words and in his choices about how he and his family now live, it's evident that Kingsnorth has undertaken to align himself with the world as given rather than to look toward some new iteration of our long-running Masters of the Universe fantasy. He isn't interested at all in the "glib 'solutions'" ballyhooed these days by technocrats—artificial intelligence, nanotechnology, bioengineering, geoengineering, emigration to Mars, and such.

What remains to be seen is how many of us will face up to our circumstances in Kingsnorth's forthright fashion, especially if it requires taking up a scythe and following him into the fields. It's undeniably more convenient to persist in our well-worn ways and to count on the same ingenuity that's gotten us into our predicament to get our children or grandchildren out of it. Reorienting human relations to the ten thousand things in the way the Hundun story suggests—removing ourselves from the planetary driver's seat—would require a trust in the world's capacity for self-organization much firmer than the populace at large apparently feels, perhaps firmer and greater than many of us can even conceive.

Persuading billions of us habitual "decision-makers" to kick the Shu-and-Hu habit of knowing what's needed, persuading us to sit back, relax, and enjoy the ride....Fat chance, huh? That very phrase of mine above—"would require a trust..."—manifests the problem, I'll admit; it's a specimen of my own "knowing what's needed." Retirement from running the show is bound to be tricky business. Having asserted human willpower pretty freely for a few millennia, we're deeply implicated in its operations mentally and physically.

Still, it seems to me that one good look around—the sort of look Paul Kingsnorth begs us to take, the sort that William James postulated, "with no definite theological bias one way or the other"—reveals beyond doubt the world's robust self-organizing capacity, brilliantly successful at every scale. Even those of us committed to belief in a Supreme Being find it hard to imagine their Creator designing every one of the tens of thousands of species of beetle and instead often posit a Prime Mover, who set the world in motion and then...what? Left most of the details to the beetles themselves, to the weather, and so forth. Divine trust in the self-organizing capacity of the world seems to recommend equal human faith.

Granted, however, even we who recognize and embrace the self-organizing capacity of the ten thousand things may find it hard to accept a place in the universe for ourselves and other people that's much more modest than the one we claim today. Harder still, probably, will be finding a way to assume, or actually to *resume*, that place. Here, I dare say, Zen training has something to offer. Our tradition's affinities for Hundun spring from more than a love of literary allusion. Actually, at every stage Zen training requires engagement with Hundun, and its fruits typically include unusual equanimity even when things appear "out of control."

During a question-and-answer session Aitken Rōshi had with American Buddhist teachers from various schools, someone took the opportunity to ask my elderly teacher what his mind was like after more than four decades of Zen practice. "Oh," he declared, "it's a mess!" The audience fell silent, then roared with laughter when, widening his eyes and casting up his hands, he exclaimed, "But you should've seen it *before!*"[30]

That sort of lightness arises, first, from experiencing mental perturbations as a neutral fact of life and, second, from learning to negotiate them with a measure of grace. Note that I didn't say "learning to *manage* them." Attempting to manage the blameless energies of your neuronal circuits puts you in a command relationship to them; you've fallen into a project of imposing order, of trying to force things in a direction you deem correct or productive. Cautioning his disciples against this error, Dōgen told them, "A Buddha ancestor said that it is better to have the mind of a wily fox than to follow a narrow way of self-regulation."[31] Practice in the latter way amounts to joining up with Shu and Hu. It may not kill off Hundun, but it'll leave you tired and sorry for your exertions.

The negativity still so common in considering chaos might make Zhuangzi's story even more important for Western audiences today than it was to Asian disciples and readers in days of yore. In four decades of close work with Zen practitioners, I've repeatedly witnessed eruptions of overwhelming fear when they get their first whiff of what Chan and Zen texts frequently call "emptiness" but might just as well be called Hundun weifen, not yet differentiated. Sometimes they describe the experience in words uncannily echoing the etymology of *chaos*: coming to the edge of a cliff, teetering on the brink, about to fall into an abyss, absolute darkness. Our culture, I suppose, has set us up for terror.

I'd like the vision of Hundun as a beneficent amorphous force to relieve people of that debilitating fear. We who take the path of Zen will need at least to relax our trepidation if we want to follow that path all the way home. And whether or not we're interested in Zen, as our societies drift into chaos of various kinds, the too many billions of us will need, and need badly, a capacity to inhabit Hundun's world with some measure of equanimity. Lacking that, the allure of further rash and flashy interventions will very likely prove irresistible.

We might take courage from the fact that Henry Adams, despite his deep personal qualms about chaos, saw in it a life-giving power even when it took its most destructive form. Reflecting on the Civil War, which he'd witnessed as a young man, Adams wrote, "Chaos often breeds life, when order breeds habit. The Civil War had bred life."[32] Nobody should wish upon their country a rerun of that epic bloodbath, but perhaps Adams's experience can encourage us to see chaos as a realm of possibility and to look for the renewal that, at least sometimes, lies beyond disaster.

16|Wuwei and the Power to Desist

The wise have nothing to do;
foolish people tie themselves in knots.

—*Xinxin ming*

These lines, from a versified teaching I've quoted in a couple of previous chapters, are ascribed to an obscure personage known as Sengcan (or Seng-ts'an; J., Sōzan), which translates literally as Glittering Monk. Although he's considered the Third Ancestor of Chan, the school's own texts contain virtually no information about him. A leading scholar of the formative period in Chinese Buddhism dismisses wholesale all assertions about his life, calling them "completely unusable as historical data," and warns that "Only the most foolhardy or avowedly myopic student of early Chan would suggest that Sengcan had any knowable impact on the school's historical development or any actual connection whatsoever with the text usually attributed to him...."[1]

In fact, the historical process seems to have worked in reverse: somebody else composed the poem, then Chan writers, wittingly or unwittingly, assigned it to this nebulous personage, at once backdating it and giving it prestige in family lore. Such dubious origins didn't prevent the *Xinxin ming*, the "Trusting Heartmind Inscription," from becoming a revered statement of the Dharma-according-to-Chan. It has inspired numerous commentaries through the centuries and is recited all around the world in monasteries, temples, and training centers.

The two words in the title romanized as *xin* are different, the first referring to trust itself, the second meaning the heartmind we're encouraged to place trust in.[2] Both words point beyond conventional understandings of what they signify. The heartmind the poem urges us to trust—to have confidence in and rely upon—is yours and mine but isn't merely personal, isn't even just a human phenomenon, and the trust in question is unconditional and existential in kind.

The couplet that I've quoted names a profound difference between people who feel the sort of trust the *Xinxin ming* recommends and those who don't. Their trust enables the wise to live at ease, to "have nothing to do," while the lack of trust that foolish people feel prompts them to "tie themselves in knots" in attempting to make themselves secure.[3] Although the poem frames this difference in absolute, dichotomous terms, it's better understood as a continuum, with people ranging from utterly wise, trusting, and at ease to terribly foolish, anxious, and struggling.

The phrase I've translated as "have nothing to do" is the now-familiar wuwei. Although primarily associated with Laozi and others in the Daoist tradition, it also has a very long history of usage in Chan and Zen, as reflected in preceding chapters. The famous Chan layman Pang Yun identified wuwei as the focus of training and accomplishment under his teacher, Mazu:

> Joining the assembly from all directions,
> one person after another masters wuwei.
> This is where buddhas are identified:
> heartmind empty, they pass the test and go home.[4]

Chan so deeply integrated wuwei into its teaching and its characterization of mature, awakened functioning that a seventeenth-century Western writer, Pierre Bayle, designated Chan "the Wuwei Sect,"[5] and this connection warrants further inspection than it usually gets.

The *wu* of *wuwei* means "has not" or "doesn't have," possibly "lacks" or "without," and is the famous one-word response that the master Zhaozhou gave when a monk asked whether a dog has buddha-nature. *Wei* means "to do, make, or contrive," so the familiar translation of *wuwei* as "nondoing" or "inaction" is perfectly legitimate. It risks the impression, however, that the term indicates doing nothing at all, an interpretation that neither Daoist nor Buddhist teachings support. The *Daodejing* says,

> Those doing study each day accumulate;
> those learning dao each day relinquish.
> They relinquish and relinquish again
> until they reach the point of wuwei—
> without doing yet with nothing undone.[6]

The ten thousand things exemplify "without doing yet with nothing undone." This is the ziran or "self-so" working of the world—the way a stone sits in the dirt, moss grows on a tree, a cup holds water, a mirror reflects, a shark strikes, a baby cries and takes a nipple, clouds form, rain falls, the moon orbits the earth, hearts beat. Without plans or program objectives, things proceed very nicely on their own. Science has discovered many physical and biological "laws" that seem to govern all this activity, but it never has located a doer, a "lawgiver" initiating or directing it.

Our tradition shares with the author of the *Daodejing*—Laozi or whoever wrote the book that bears his name—an appreciation of the fact that doing tends to "tie us in knots." Thus the advocacy of wuwei and wushi documented in the preceding essays. But what's simple on its face isn't necessarily easy. If one needn't and indeed *shouldn't* make an effort for the sake of realizing buddhadharma, then why did Linji preach? Didn't that involve an effort on his part, and in telling monks just to behave ordinarily, wasn't he encouraging *some* sort of effort on their parts, too? What about you and me? How could my writing and your reading take place without "doing," consistent with the teachings of wuwei and wushi? Just pondering this, a person could get tied in knots.

Another wrinkle before we delve into this further: among the distinctions that Buddhist texts brought to China was one between *samskrita* and *asamskrita*, between the conditioned and the unconditioned—in other words, between phenomena that arise, persist awhile, decay, and die and what's free from that birth-to-death-to-rebirth cycle, namely nirvāna, space, dao, things of that sort. As translators went to convert the Sanskrit terms into Chinese, they made the fascinating decision to borrow *wuwei* for *asamskrita* and to use its opposite, *youwei* (literally, "with doing" or "to have doing") for *samskrita*. Consequently, when *wuwei* crops up in a Chinese Buddhist text it can be read in its original Daoist sense, in the Buddhist sense of *asamskrita*, or as a word blurring and merging the two. In that third case, it might be glossed as "unconditioned existence entailing no 'doing' or not 'doing' in a conditioned way."

This verges on gibberish, unfortunately, and Chan and Zen texts portray masters of the tradition avoiding such convoluted and conceptual talk—talking *about* the Dharma—and instead presenting it with gestures or a few nonexplanatory words. According to their records, they usually elucidated the dao of doing-yet-not-doing through dialogues such as the following, said to have taken place in the eighth century and centering on a monk who later emerged as the noted Chan master Yaoshan (or Yao-shan, also Yueh-shan; J., Yakusan). When his teacher, Shitou, found him sitting silent and still, "doing zazen" as we are wont to say, Shitou asked,

> "You there, what internal activity are you undertaking?"
> "Wholly not doing," Yaoshan answered.
> "Reflecting?" pressed Shitou. "That's merely sitting idle."
> "If I were sitting idle," Yaoshan replied, "that would actually be doing something."
> Shitou asked, "You speak of not doing, but not doing what?"
> "Even a thousand sages couldn't tell," said Yaoshan.[7]

Too bad sages can't say at least a little bit more! How *can* anyone just sit like that, not idle yet doing nothing at all? Yaoshan's retort that sitting idle "would actually be doing something" is a strong clue: not-doing requires surrendering any thought of not-doing, any thought of just sitting idle, along with everything else. It makes sense of "without doing yet with nothing undone."

A contemporary story may clarify this old one. When my friend Blanche Hartman, late abbot of the San Francisco Zen Center, was beginning her training, she told her teacher, Zen Center founder Shunryū Suzuki Rōshi, that she felt she was finally getting a sense of how to do zazen. "*You* can't do zazen!" Suzuki Rōshi corrected her. "Zazen does zazen!"[8] Clear as that counsel is, it still leaves the imponderable problem of how to remove ourselves so that zazen can do zazen on its own, ziran—a problem that only experience will at last dissolve.

As if wuwei isn't enough of a challenge when you're sitting still, how about when you take action, purposefully doing something? Actually, though active doing heightens the logical contradiction of "doing not-doing," many people find it somewhat easier to approximate Suzuki Rōshi's pointer in action than while meditating: *you* don't scrub the dishes; scrubbing the dishes scrubs the dishes. An athlete who speaks of "playing out of my head" or being "in the zone" plainly is referring to similar total absorption in activity, and many others experience it, too—dancers, emergency first responders, lovers.

Wuwei of this intimate sort, as a matter of forgetting oneself thoroughly enough to slip the categories of "doing" and "not-doing," may be wonderful, but early Chinese thinkers went on to identify human avidity for doing as the cause of needless, ruinous interference with the rest of the ten thousand things. This critique of our tendencies to overdo wasn't confined to the Daoists. One of the stories most vividly advancing it comes from Mengzi, a great master from the house of Confucius rather than of Laozi. He alludes to the story in an exchange about 義 *yi* (or *i*; J., *gi*), the virtue of appropriateness,[9] criticizing a colleague's understanding of that virtue because he considered it in merely external terms:

"You must devote yourself to it, never forgetting it," he tells his inquirer, "yet at the same time, you mustn't try to force its growth. If you do that, you're like the man of Song. One day, the man of Song, worried that his rice seedlings weren't growing fast enough, went around his fields tugging at the plants one after another. At day's end, he got home worn out, telling his family, 'I'm exhausted. I've been helping the rice grow.' His son dashed out to look and found the rice shoots all drooping and dying."[10]

Mengzi concludes, "Under the heavens, few can resist 'helping the rice grow,'" but he goes on to reject a strict construction of wuwei, too: "Others suppose that nothing they do can be of use and neglect their plants, not even bothering to weed." Appropriateness lies somewhere between these extremes, in actions that actually serve the rice rather than beleaguer it with human hopes, needs, and expectations.

While this parable makes sense on its own restricted terms and provides an evaluative framework I find useful, it obscures the complexities we encounter in real-world circumstances. For instance, the man-of-Song story presupposes rice monoculture, which many would see as a form of overdoing in itself. Even if we accept rice monoculture as a given, every farmer knows that there comes a point where a beneficial activity like weeding (or watering or fertilizing) can go too far, crossing from the range of appropriate doing into overdoing. The key to the Mencian principle is an ability to discern where the line falls between doing enough and doing too much, which relates it both to ganying—responding to the rice by giving just what it "calls for"—and, of course, to the perennial challenge of knowing enough.

One of my favorite scholars of classical Chinese thinking proposes a nonquantitative approach to wuwei that also meshes neatly with the tale from Mengzi: he interprets wuwei as "action that, by taking the other on its own terms, defers to what it actually is"—in other words, as doing that which respects and conforms to the nature and needs of other beings. He continues, "Wuwei involves recognizing the continuity between oneself and the other, and responding in such a way that one's own actions promote the well-being of both oneself and the other."[11] Again there's a connection to the subtle communication among beings that ganying describes.

Of course many things may impede such delicate communication: if we can't tell what's called for, we have little hope of aligning our words and behavior to squarely meet the needs and potentials of a situation. Among the factors that complicate clear perception of circumstances and appropriateness in responding, two stand out in my mind. A Chan dialogue addresses the first, with direct bearing on wuwei:

> The Twenty-Fourth Dharma Ancestor, Āryasimha, questioned the Twenty-Third Ancestor, saying, "I want to seek the dao. How should I put the heartmind to use?"
>
> The Twenty-Third Ancestor answered, "If you seek the dao, refrain from putting the heartmind to use."
>
> The master asked, "If one refrains from putting the heartmind to use, who will do the buddhas' deeds?"
>
> The Ancestor said, "If you have 'putting to use,' it lacks liberative benefit. If you have no 'doing,' that's the buddhas' deeds. A sūtra says, 'The liberative benefit of my doing has no self in it.'"[12]

An intrusive *I* obstructs perception and warps activity, depriving "my" undertakings of the power to serve or liberate either oneself or others. A seasoned ability to forget oneself and one's "doing" improves our chances of realizing both what a particular configuration of circumstances calls for and what sort of response would be suitable. In his verse for this kōan, Zen master Keizan wryly comments, "If you want to reveal the sky, you mustn't cover it over."

The second major impediment to discerning circumstances clearly and responding in an appropriate way is a sort of inherent, universal bias favoring youwei over wuwei. In considering this, I find it helpful to utilize the age-old Chinese concepts of yin and yang. Though this pair is understood as complementary, balancing one another and mutually entailed, by definition yang phenomena tend to dominate yin, and that tendency, left unchecked, causes problems.

For example, silence (yin) enables us to hear sounds plainly, while sound (yang) makes silence impossible. Sound overwhelms silence; silence can't compete with sound, can do nothing but yield to it. No doubt we've all experienced the practical effect of this dynamic: someone who talks so much or so loudly that nobody else can "get a word in edgewise," a job site so noisy that you can't bear it for long or at least find it difficult to concentrate. I remember my father raising his voice angrily one afternoon when my siblings and I were making a racket, shouting, "It's so noisy in here, I can't hear myself think!" He *had* to yell—to resort to yang—because yin has no means of asserting itself. Yang phenomena often generate vicious cycles like that, the most flagrant being the arms races, great and small, that have escalated since time immemorial.

Chinese convention equates yang with male and yin with female, but whatever that may say about the gender relations that prevailed in ancient Chinese society, I don't think it helps us to understand yin and yang. It seems much more useful to visualize their relationship in terms of foreground and background, where yin phenomena constitute the background, and yang is what occurs in the foreground. In this dynamic, yin affords the context necessary for yang to appear, and yang, by its appearance, tends to obscure yin. Another example: under the yin condition of darkness, we can see far-distant stars, a tiny glowworm on a stone wall, any light at all, but only when light is blocked or entirely absent will darkness be found. It's dark under a stone, we can intuit; lift the stone to look, though, and of course we let in the light.

In Zen practice, we encounter a vexing version of this dynamic: when thinking occupies the foreground, as it often does, exerting its yang dominance, nonthinking is out of the question. Attempt to suppress thoughts, and you pitch yourself into a vicious cycle. Suppression belongs to that yang realm of doing, to youwei rather than wuwei, so we have to realize and learn to rely on the strength of yin, which resides in its receptive and perduring nature. The background just remains the background, outlasting whatever happens in the foreground: noise eventually subsides, sooner or later lights go out, engines seize up or run out of gas, thoughts lose their sizzle. It isn't wordplay to say that Zen practice requires discovering how to not-do it. We have to learn to accommodate our eagerness to "do" it or to "do" it better, to gain, to break through, to "get enlightened."

Without succumbing to this directing, controlling impulse, though, in the most practical sense we also have to do something—to engage in Zen training, to commit ourselves to years of sometimes frustrating practice. Unless we apply ourselves in this way, Zen will amount to little more than a word game, a thought experiment, a hollow rationale for idleness, an occasion for spiritual pretensions. Yang has its place, in other words; any attempt to quit it altogether would be mistaken and sure to fail. We need to find the sweet spot, to strike a very subtle balance.

But as Mengzi said, "few can resist 'helping the rice grow.'" When the late Thich Nhat Hanh, beloved master of the Vietnamese variant of Chan, began making teaching trips to the United States in the early 1980s, he found American Buddhists so eager for activism that he felt a need to turn one of our familiar phrases around on us, saying in his firm, gentle manner, "Don't just *do* something. Sit there!" I wasn't the only one who saw, in the way he spoke and behaved, that he might embody a sort of not-doing in action.

A propensity for doing and overdoing seems ingrained in our species, though, enough to be considered our besetting vice. I don't doubt the sincerity of oft-stated aspirations to "make the world a better place," but honesty compels us to acknowledge that, on the whole, we've done the opposite. Is the world better now that the rain is laden with tiny particles of plastic? Now that its finest farmlands have been largely destroyed? Now that the Amazonian rainforest, "the lungs of the planet," is being ruthlessly cut? Now that the human population has exceeded eight billion? Now that populations of other species are declining, if not disappearing altogether, at the most rapid pace in tens of millions of years? Now that the world is heating up, seas are rising, and storms and wildfires are growing in severity?

What I want to suggest and will explore at some length in the remainder of this chapter—fair warning!—is that wuwei offers a path out of this debacle. Intimate practice of not-doing not only can teach us to quit bossing around our own thoughts and feelings but also can inspire us in the greater project of not bossing around the rest of the world, even in the name of improving or "saving" it. Call this the path of desistance rather than resistance. Resist when it makes sense to do so, but desist we must.

Desistance has become crucial because, to undo the damage that civilization has already inflicted upon the world and its ziran processes, numerous new doings have been proposed or begun, including varieties of doing never before attempted. Obviously, people will continue our doing at some level and in various forms, but to place our faith mainly in doing would amount to doubling down on a failed theory—boring more holes in Hundun in the belief that we can restore its wholeness. Our existential challenge, it seems to me, will be to shift in the direction of wuwei—to downshift from *over*doing, from tugging at the seedlings, in favor of the sort of doing that occurs of itself.

Instead of following the lead of Mengzi's overdoing farmer, I hope that we'll cultivate the way of desistance modeled by a farmer in *Zhuangzi*. The story begins with a well-meaning disciple of Confucius who, observing an old man laboriously hauling jars of water to irrigate his crops, tells him about the well sweep, a new device he could use to achieve the same result with much less effort. The farmer rejects this technology on grounds that seem freshly pertinent today, when it's become commonplace to feel flummoxed by our devices, frustrated and disempowered when they fail us:

> "I've heard from my master, 'Have mechanical equipment, and you'll surely have mechanical concerns. Have mechanical concerns, and you'll surely have a mechanical heartmind.' With a mechanical heartmind lodged in your breast, purity and simplic-

ity become unavailable. With purity and simplicity unavailable, your vital spirits are unsettled. Those with unsettled vital spirits the dao won't bear. I'm not ignorant of such equipment! I'm humble and don't use it!"[13]

We needn't give up our garden hoses to appreciate this sharp prod to approach decisions about tools with careful regard for the ways their use may shape us. Whether to opt for a dishwasher or wash dishes by hand, whether to clear the yard with a rake or a leaf blower—such decisions often get made on the basis of speed, convenience, and social norms, without consideration or perhaps even awareness of the unquantifiable effects crucial to Zhuangzi's farmer.

The farmer's refusal provides a beautiful illustration of the logic of wuwei, of how and particularly why one might choose to refrain from adopting a device purported to "save" energy. His argument unspools in if-then fashion, tracing a series of causes and effects that soon jumps the line we're wont to draw between external and internal. Its basis lies in correlations (and noncorrelations): mechanical equipment "goes together" with mechanical concerns, which in turn go together with a mechanical heartminds, which *don't* go together with purity and simplicity—and thus run counter to the dao. An entirely practical argument against the new technology could also be made: "Use the well sweep, and you'll deliver water swiftly and easily. Deliver water swiftly and easily, and you'll use water more freely than when you have to carry it by hand. Use water more freely, and you're likely to waste water." A good argument, too, but significantly different.

The farmer's rejection of the well sweep is invoked as a model of something larger—of wisely chosen priorities, of what's at stake in technology decisions. If we take the story seriously, we have to apply his standard when evaluating devices, old as well as new: not how much work, time, money, or even "raw material" they might "save," not how cool and cutting-edge they are, not how much they might impress others, but rather the inconspicuous, detrimental impact they stand to exert on our heartminds. To the extent that we buy into complex contrivances, the tale strongly warns, we burden and deform ourselves, separating ourselves from everything that works self-so, subjecting ourselves to thinking, feeling, and behaving mechanically in a universe that inherently isn't mechanical. The fact that hand tools remain the tools of choice in Zen temples and in many institutions of a similar nature is due not to antiquarian impulses but to the recognition that how we do things matters to us profoundly and intimately.

Of course, decisions about technology affect vastly more than our own heartminds, and the calculus for reaching them becomes overwhelmingly complicated as the equation expands to include factors of energy consumption, sourcing of raw materials, water use, pollution, shipping, labor conditions, noise, and so on. No easy answers. I certainly don't presume there's a "correct" solution to questions of technology that will fit all places, climates, needs, households, cultures, and characters, nor do I presume that I or anyone else can "know enough" on behalf of others. I have no doubt, however, that our circumstances will require hard decisions about tools and that desistance from technologies, existing as well as new, will deserve consideration.

—

We can look to old societies besides those of East Asia for precedents in technological restraint since, as soon as hominids learned to make fire, it became imperative to address the danger of "playing with fire" and to inculcate practices to discourage it. We can imagine these regimes of instruction, formal and informal, growing in diverse cultures as the centuries passed, with the original means—a growl of disapproval, swat, or sharp word—getting complemented and eventually displaced by increasingly sophisticated domestic rituals and practices, taboos, customs, proverbs, folktales, etiquettes, religious doctrines, and ethical and philosophical principles.

Sure enough, sedimented into European and European-descended cultures we find Greek myths that teach the wisdom of desisting—the tales of Midas, Icarus, Pandora, Prometheus, and Phaethon, among others; hubris appears again and again as humanity's root problem. The three Abrahamic traditions campaigned against overweening pride as well, all teaching its sinfulness in their distinctive fashions. With the explosion of learning and technology in the Renaissance, these themes gained fresh pertinence and energetic expression, with the French philosopher Montaigne in the sixteenth century vividly calling out the human tendency to reach beyond our innate capacity: "To make a fistful bigger than our fist, an armful bigger than our arm, to hope to step further than the length of our legs—these actions are impossible and monstrous."[14]

Well, monstrous maybe but hardly impossible, as the Industrial Revolution soon proved. With its clatter and roar, the chorus of concern too grew larger and louder. Among others raising their voices was William Blake, who married Montaigne's insight to the myth of Icarus in one of his jewel-like aphorisms: "No bird soars too high, if he soars with his own wings."[15] The Romantic writers who came after Blake—Wordsworth, Coleridge, De Quincey, Byron, Keats, and others—condemned the drift of things in stronger terms, but it fell to the younger Mary Shelley to present a critique of technology in suitably horrifying and potent form with her 1818 novel *Frankenstein*. Her warning couldn't be more explicit: "You are my creator," Dr. Frankenstein's android admits, "but I *am your master*; Obey!"[16] Across the Atlantic, the transcendentalists worried, too, in a less feverish way. "Things are in the saddle," Emerson lamented, "And ride mankind."[17] Thoreau put it more bluntly: "But lo! men have become the tools of their tools."[18]

As his country sprinted to modernize in the early twentieth century, that concern haunted the great Japanese potter Yanagi Sōetsu. Whether his views followed consciously from Daoist or Buddhist teachings or emerged entirely from personal observations, he brought the critique of technology full circle, writing in his book *The Unknown Craftsman*, "The more complex machinery becomes, the more fully men become slaves to it."[19]

Rather than heeding such pleas for restraint, societies everywhere have plunged ahead, adopting technologies helter-skelter, as if there were no tomorrow, and recognizing their mistakes only when tomorrow dawns. In retrospect, it wouldn't seem terribly difficult to anticipate some of our oversights. When plastics came under development, for example, even if no one foresaw the danger of introducing a little-known suite of petrochemicals into our homes and workplaces, into our landfills, and (as we now know) into the seas, the air, and the cells of plants and animals, including ourselves—even if no one foresaw all that, the qualities that made plastics attractive to captains of industry made it possible to anticipate that they'd cause colossal problems sooner or later: synthetic, cheap, malleable, useful in many forms and for many purposes, durable but also ostensibly disposable, they were bound to proliferate and become, in one way or another, a blight upon the planet.

Likewise, it seems apparent in retrospect that the automobile, guzzling gas and belching fumes, would impose heavy long-term ecological costs, but its ruinous impact outran scientific detection, quantification, and consensus as well as effective government action. Dams are a third instance, engineering triumphs constructed at extraordinary expense—and not only immediately destructive of the landscape but also harmful long term in ways that, looking back, seem obvious and that now are powering a movement to remove them. And what about digital communication? Ballyhooed as a technology that would unite the world in a "global village," instead it's yielding social fragmentation. Heralded as an instantaneous source of good information, it now presents a grave, intractable problem of bad information. Once imagined as a democratizing force, it shows itself to endanger democracy. Initially promoted as a field of free expression, today its nefarious uses have governments scrambling to implement effective means of policing it (when they aren't utilizing it themselves for surveillance of citizens or to interfere in the affairs of other countries).

Positive things can be said about these troublesome technologies; I don't mean to deny the benefits they've brought, such as they are. But that we collectively missed, downplayed, or at least neglected the problems they'd create ought to humble us—that is, to temper our hubris. It certainly ought to shake whatever confidence we feel in our ability to spot and reject innovations before their long-term hazards become apparent. Two and a half centuries ago, after accidentally plowing up the nest of an unoffending field mouse, Robert Burns concisely summed up the situation:

> The best-laid schemes o' *Mice* an' *Men*,
>   Gang aft a-gley,
> An' lea'e us nought but grief an' pain,
>   For promis'd joy.[20]

Of course, it's not just the best-laid plans that go awry, and the grief and pain left in the wake of our plows has spread far beyond local fields and forests.

So far, humankind has managed to curtail use of its most heinous weapons and a few of the toxic chemicals we've created (think DDT and Freon), but the usual approach, here in the United States if not elsewhere, has been to adopt technologies now and pay their costs to human health and to the rest of life later. We've just reached another such reckoning with "forever chemicals." Particularly at present, as both world population and the power of our devices increase, we—we in the broadest sense, we who share the ecosphere—can't afford to continue on this course, so blithe and headlong. We no longer have the leeway we once had, or thought we had, to take the unknown risks that stem from willy-nilly adoption of attractive, untried technologies.

I'm happy to acknowledge that people are starting to call for technological restraint and, more important, that these calls are starting to receive public notice, especially when they come from recognized leaders in high tech and when they pertain to cutting-edge developments in AI, synthetic biology, and geoengineering. In that group, one of the first people to raise the cry was cyber innovator Bill Joy, whose 2000 article "Why the Future Doesn't Need Us" caused a brief stir. Troubled by the growing power of emerging technologies in genetics, nanotechnology, and robotics, Joy made a case for "relinquishment: to limit development of the technologies that are too dangerous, by limiting our pursuit of certain kinds of knowledge." He appealed to "common sense...that there is a limit to our material needs—and that certain knowledge is too dangerous and best foregone."[21]

Relinquishment is a hard sell under any circumstances and especially so when, as in this instance, the dangers in question haven't become manifest "on the ground" or at least haven't yet featured prominently in newscasts or created a big buzz on social media. Nonetheless, the option to desist, the wuwei option, remains available to us. Like Zhuangzi's farmer, you and I have a full and immediate capacity to decline technologies that are marketed to us as the latest load lighteners but are likely to compromise our heartminds, deplete our skills, impoverish the lives of generations not yet born, and threaten the current health and continuation of wombats, puffballs, and other fellow tenants of this marvelous earth.

But the not-doing that present circumstances demand of us will almost certainly have to go beyond restraint in adopting *new* technologies, extending to relinquishment of technologies considered normal or even inevitable today. We won't know how far such relinquishment needs to go, but if we accept a definition of *wuwei* that "involves recognizing the continuity between" ourselves and others of all kinds (including earth, water, and air) and "responding in such a way that one's own actions promote the well-being of both," then we're past due in giving up many things. Coal-fired power plants, for sure, but what about the air-conditioning those plants provide electricity to run? How about the immense, power-sucking server "farms" that make the internet possible? How about traveling halfway around the world for fun in the sun or to visit the Sphinx?

In considering where to draw the line, I've long relied on rubrics offered by Ivan Illich, one of the twentieth century's most farsighted and conscientious thinkers on technological issues.[22] Bringing specificity to the concern that Montaigne expressed about human overreach, in *Tools for Conviviality* Illich delineates "two ranges in the growth of tools": those in the first range serving "to extend human capability," while those in the second "contract, eliminate, or replace human functions."[23] Among means of transportation, for example, Illich reckoned that the first range ends with technologies like bicycles and small sailboats. Beyond that, the tools—cars, trains, ships, planes—become too complex for nonspecialists to build, operate, or repair and make their users, in effect, hostage to systems beyond their control—oil and gas extraction and refinement, electric power generation, computerized engines, road construction, airline routing and scheduling, and satellite-based guidance systems, among others. Illich's terms are by no means perfect, but I find them "good to think with." When my computer won't do what I want it to, I hear Illich whispering, "See what I mean?"

If you find it hard to imagine forgoing all second-range technologies, okay, Illich did too. His vision permitted some trains, phones, even TV, and I confess, in the spirit of full disclosure, that I too cross the line, using a select group of second-range technologies in addition to the computer I've just mentioned. Other than that electronic gadget, my most advanced tool—the one that I understand least and definitely couldn't repair—is a solar system (a subsidiary of the original solar system) that lights the house, pumps the well, and keeps the computer purring. I ceased using a gas-fueled hydraulic wood splitter some years ago, stepping "down" to quieter, far more pleasant work with the old tools of axe, maul, and wedges. My wife and I enjoy using other technologies that meet Illich's standard for first-range tools, too: an utterly simple solar rig that heats our hot water, an equally simple solar oven that cooks much of our food in the summertime (thus helping to keep the house cool), woodstoves that warm us in the winter and often heat food as well. Such things bring us joy, and that was a theme in Illich's work.

I've put forward his definition of technological ranges as a means of gauging which tools to choose, refuse, or discontinue in order to avoid mechanical heartminds and to diminish the harm we do, but his chief purpose in drawing the distinction, he wrote, was to name and prevent the loss a society incurs through a heavy reliance on second-range technologies—the conviviality of the book's title. Illich, a former Catholic priest and scholarly man, termed it *"eutrapelia* (or graceful playfulness) in personal relations,"[24] but there's nothing esoteric about what he meant: the diverse pleasures of collaborating with friends, not only in work but also in many other facets of life, by entertaining ourselves, for instance, instead of consuming products of the entertainment industry.

I'm well enough acquainted with the pleasures of local collaboration to endorse Illich's point enthusiastically, but I would go a big step farther to include the pleasures of wielding first-range tools all by oneself. Performing tasks, even modest tasks, by means within my own power and competence brings me a delight that often seems quite out of proportion to the job I've done. Stirring up pancakes from scratch, replacing a leaky valve on the sink, writing a letter by hand, patching a hole in the fingertip of a good work glove—there's nothing even remotely impressive about accomplishments on this order, yet they dependably provide me great satisfaction, and the strength of today's do-it-yourself movement suggests that many others feel similarly.[25]

I emphasize this because technological self-restraint may sound like self-punishment to many ears, and I experience it, and advocate it, the other way around. I understand it as a prudent and necessary response to ever-louder alarms that the world is issuing but also as an opportunity, a motivation, to reorient toward ways of living that will prove richer, lovelier, and more fulfilling than any possible technofuture.

Illich, writing in long-ago 1973, couched the argument for desisting from the adoption of second-range tools in very stark terms:

> Survival depends on establishing procedures which permit ordinary people to recognize these two ranges and to opt for survival in freedom, to evaluate the structure built into tools and institutions so they can exclude those which by their structure are destructive, and control those which are useful.[26]

That seemed like hyperbole to me when I read it decades ago, but as second-range technology has metastasized to mediate, imitate, or all but eliminate an increasing number of once-normal human functions and as surveillance and repression have become increasingly prevalent, it's become hard to deny that survival, particularly "survival in freedom," *will* hang to a large degree on choices we make about "advanced" technologies.

Unfortunately, although society notices cautionary voices like Bill Joy's and those of the Romantic and transcendentalist writers before him, rarely do they inspire the restraint proposed; until well-documented disasters occur—a Love Canal or a Chernobyl—new technologies emerge and come into use without large-scale public opposition. And when disasters do occur, the usual response is to call for, and eventually to require, restraint by means of another sort of technology: the apparatus of government bureaucracy, backed by the threat of punishment. Thus ceaselessly expanding systems of not only laws, courts, police forces, and penal systems but also of patents, deeds, codes, labeling standards, permits, inspections, vaccination requirements, licenses, and all the rest—systems that, in modern nations, structure and regulate almost the entire spectrum of human endeavor.

To my eyes, this looks more and more like a losing game, with our bureaucracies, no matter how large, no matter how competent, always at least a step behind in a multilevel, high-stakes game of cat and mouse. People intent on defeating these systems have consistently been able to find or carve loopholes in them, loopholes so big that sometimes they've been able to fly airplanes through them. No sooner is a loophole plugged than another appears. Miniaturization, digital media, drones, robotics, 3-D printing, data mining, bioweapons, cryptocurrencies…Innovation is proceeding at too fast a clip across too numerous and too broad an array of fronts for governments—even totalitarian governments—to stay abreast of it, much less to get ahead. Try as we might, in this way, too, we're tying ourselves in knots.

The difficulty doesn't lie entirely with the rapidity of innovation and the comparatively plodding pace and burdensome costs of bureaucratic regimes. It also stems from inertial forces in society: deeply entrenched beliefs in the world as a zone of limitless possibility, past successes in overcoming obstacles to growth, our still-expanding powers to manipulate materials, pride in the ingenuity of our species, the firm hold that vested interests have on the levers of government, and an all but sacrosanct belief in economic growth as the sine qua non of national well-being. These are enormous forces. Though surely susceptible to change, they seem, even more surely, unlikely to change at the rate and to the degree that our profligacy has made necessary.

Thus far, most pleas for restraint frame their argument in terms of threats to human well-being, giving relatively short shrift to the disastrous effects that the increasingly expensive tastes of our ever-swelling populations have inflicted on other species and critical natural systems.[27] That's true of Illich's book, of E. F. Schumacher's *Small Is Beautiful: Economics as if People Mattered*,[28] and of Joy's more recent essay as well. Joy nods to "the risk that we might destroy the biosphere on which all life depends," but his overwhelming concern is that rapidly advancing technologies will endanger *us* as a species.[29]

Over the centuries, of course, the cultural West has always included individuals—poets, philosophers, saints and sages, pastoralists—who spoke for the importance and prerogatives of other beings,[30] but not until the rise of a specifically "environmental" movement have the interests of other beings been consistently set on a par with those of people. Aldo Leopold's essay "The Land Ethic," published in 1949, sounded this theme early, exhorting us to see ourselves and to behave as "plain members and citizens" of the "biotic community" rather than its "conqueror."[31] Even now, though, with the harmful effects of our high-handed conduct wreaking havoc, it's evident that only a tiny fraction of the populace has come to accept the modest status Leopold urged upon us and that even fewer have changed their ways to live as lightly as "plain membership" would require.

This brings us back to the question of relinquishment, a question current circumstances raise in multiple contexts: Will we step down from the highly privileged position we've claimed for ourselves as a species, the dominion we've assumed over other species and the liberty we've taken to reroute rivers and blast away mountains? Are we willing at least to temper, if not to give up, our propensity to do, to do more, and to do it bigger and better and faster? Can we forgo some, perhaps many, of the powerful technologies available now or on the horizon? And—bottom line, I suppose—will we be able to find contentment as we wean ourselves off comforts, conveniences, pleasures, and spectacles that the ravishing powers of modernity provide?

However you formulate the question, our collective answer so far is a foot-stomping NO! Don't wanna! We may view relinquishment as saintly behavior in others poised atop pedestals far away, but we seem indisposed to it ourselves or for our families and communities. It's not in our DNA, some would say. Raise the subject and, if it's not laughed off, talk soon turns to hair shirts, asceticism, self-hatred. U.S. president Jimmy Carter met with derision when, as a response to the so-called oil crisis of 1979, he went on national TV to say that the country "simply [had] no way to avoid sacrifice" and urged citizens to take a few baby steps in that direction:

> And I'm asking you for your good and for your Nation's security to take no unnecessary trips, to use carpools or public transportation whenever you can, to park your car one extra day per week, to obey the speed limit, and to set your thermostats to save fuel. Every act of energy conservation like this is more than just common sense—I tell you it is an act of patriotism.[32]

As far as I can tell, such proposals fall on deaf ears pretty much everywhere, but inhabitants of wealthy nations like ours may resist them most staunchly, attached as we are to the spoils of our war on the planet. Moves toward relinquishment are almost sure to be inconvenient, sometimes uncomfortable or perhaps painful. Even stout good intentions won't make it easy or pleasant for us, much less for our children, to give up technologies, goods, and services that, at the moment, constitute much of Life as We Know It.

For that reason, if for no other, humankind is likely to give up its ruinous ways on a large scale only when circumstances leave no choice. Whether the force that compels change arrives in the form of economic pressure, in the form of someone wearing a badge and gun, in the form of terrorism or warfare (a cyberattack that disables the power grid, for instance), or in the form of one or more natural forces—a hurricane, flood, wildfire, heat wave, pandemic, you name it—it seems only a matter of time until one or more forces we can't effectively resist impose drastic changes on a society-wide basis. Such forces have begun to make themselves felt, and some people have begun pulling back from today's improvident ways, but the overall direction of research, policy, legislation, and funding so far has been to develop means of sustaining "business as usual"—that is, of consuming all we please, with scant regard for anything except our own pocketbooks or the public treasury.

That accentuates rather than diminishes the rightness of starting today to exercise the option of desistance in our habits and purchases, in what we do for recreation and entertainment, in educating ourselves and others, in coping with illness, aging, and debility, in how and what we communicate, and so forth ad infinitum. We need no organization behind us. We don't even need a plan or definite target. The power to desist is ours as soon as we think to claim it. We can freely start not-doing, promptly and noncoercively sponsoring and effecting change through voluntary withdrawal from the status quo. "Nelson," my mother used to tell me as a child, "you *must* learn to leave well-enough *alone!*" Indeed. Across the board.

This ultimately low-tech method of containing human impulses has attractions, I think, beyond its immediacy. For starters, it seems a more honorable means of reducing our demands upon the ten thousand things than stalling until I (and others like me) wreak maximum damage and there's a gun, literally or figuratively, at my head. Also, it should allow a modicum of flexibility and creativity in how we effect the transition to life within limits—allow us to ease into new patterns, experiment, find solutions suitable to our locales, and learn now what we may need to know later instead of getting caught ill-prepared, when the need to do things differently is abruptly upon us. It will, perhaps most importantly, equip us to serve as useful members of our communities, with competent help to offer others making that transition with less preparation.

In expressing such views, I've often received the response that we can't affect the change needed, on the scale needed, with the necessary rapidity, by changing the behavior of individuals, households, and small groups. The rapidity objection is plainly and completely mistaken. Change on one's own initiative is the *only* kind that can take place swiftly, actually overnight, whereas improvement at the corporate, governmental, and international levels will come, when it comes at all, only after a great deal of wrangling, drawn out over months and years as "interested parties," apparent or in hiding, fight to defend and advance their special interests against the assertions of other "stakeholders" who themselves often differ over preferred remedies.

The objection about scale has greater merit, no doubt, considering the systemic nature of our problems. It's hard to imagine that decisions personal, familial, or otherwise local and small could wield significant influence in sectors involving huge infrastructures and sunk investments—mining, manufacturing, transportation, communications, and the like—and there are those, committed to solutions on a grand scale, who actively pooh-pooh the possibility. While writing this chapter, I had a chance to discuss my concerns about our snowballing ecological catastrophe with a friend who shares those concerns but works in Washington, D.C., deep into efforts to foment change from the top. After he returned to the capital, he sent a book by a colleague titled *But Will the Planet Notice?* that rejects the way of personal restraint as hopeless, powerless to affect change at large scale, especially in the time remaining before the climate is projected to go completely haywire.[33]

That may be so, I admit. But it may also be so that the author's top-down mega solution (given away by his subtitle: *How Smart*

Economics Can Save the World) wouldn't emerge intact and in time from the political meat grinder to achieve what he hopes. My friend's friend clearly has a much more robust faith in governmental solutions than I do, but I don't know why he felt a need to denigrate the value of small, practical steps to reduce abuse of the planet. (He tells us he practices some of them himself.) In any event, yes, Mr. Economist, the planet *will* "notice" every action we take or desist from taking. It has no choice in the matter. It registers the smallest, least visible changes all day, every day; that's elementary physical causality.

It's also elementary Buddhism. Without pretending that our Dharma ancestors foresaw modern scientific understanding, it's nevertheless true that they envisioned the cosmos as a vast, complex, indivisible system, sometimes referring to it as 森羅萬象 *sen-luo wanxiang* (or *sen-lo wan-hsiang*; J., *shinra banshō*)—the dense mesh, weave, or fabric of the ten thousand things.[34] That term turns up frequently in Chan and Zen texts, including the kōan capping phrase

> Mountains, rivers, the great earth, the ten-thousand things of
>   the dense weave—
> fungi, insects, plants large and small, people, livestock—
> one after another emits the great light,
> each one sheer, firm, an eighty-thousand-foot cliff.[35]

It also appears in lines from the "Song of Realizing the Way" that I've quoted in other contexts:

> The mirror of heartmind shines brilliantly, without
>   obstruction,
> its light limitlessly pervading worlds countless as sands of the
>   Ganges.
> The dense weave of the ten-thousand phenomena is reflected
>   therein,
> each one of them fully illumined, no inside, no outside.[36]

Nothing goes missing in this system. In our bodies, our families, our communities, our polities, in the markets, in ecosystems at every scale, nothing occurs without consequences. That makes each concrete action, no matter how modest, a sure bet. We can depend on them to bear fruit in the fullness of time, perhaps in an indirect way that no one predicted or that goes undetected for a long time. To live in such confidence is radical—and liberating. We don't need to Get Results, much less to claim credit; results are guaranteed.

To answer the good economist's question in terms of his own discipline, according to no less an authority than the U.S. Bureau of Economic Analysis, consumer spending accounts for nearly 70 percent of the economy in this country. Whatever else you make of that figure, it must mean that we who do the consuming possess enormous power to affect the economy and thus to reduce human impact in myriad ways. Desisting from business as usual can't help but reshape business as usual.

I've framed this pitch for desistance as a matter of individual initiative because readers, obviously, are individuals but also because many people feel powerless and because decisions to desist will necessarily involve individual determination. I don't intend to understate the need for collaboration, however, much less to downplay its value; it's likely that change sufficient to foreclose environmental and social collapse will come *only* if we organize, mobilizing in ever-larger groups to sway corporate and political elites thus far clinging to the status quo. I'd simply beg that such efforts be coupled with, not instead of, personal desistance.

The unanswerable question is if and when such voluntary desistance could reach a scale sufficient to propel, indeed compel, changes that, at this point, have already become urgent. As I've acknowledged, a large percentage of the population is likely to cling to life as usual until compounding crises take that option off the table. So it's certainly not optimism that moves me to recognize the possibility—just barely a possibility—that a multitude of other people, before it's too late, will harken to ever-mounting evidence, fervent urging, and good example and start desisting from habits and institutions that otherwise pave the way to hell on earth. The potency of such desistance, let's recall, was demonstrated during the Covid shutdown. Brief though it was, that widespread withdrawal from routine behaviors sufficed to clear murky waters, put a substantial dent in energy use, relieve the air pollution in major cities, give animals new room to roam, and so on. The results were irregular, but we got a basic "proof of concept" in the form of a health emergency.

Of course, I'm not holding my breath for—well, for anything, really, but certainly not for a mass conversion to Zen practice or a sudden outburst of public enthusiasm for wuwei. I dare to hope only that those of us who've chosen the way of Zen will take seriously the ancient wisdom of avoiding overdoing, consider the implications of that wisdom for our daily lives, and embrace every good opportunity to give up foolish, destructive ways that the toxic combination of human genius and greed have made the civilizational norm. In my own crude attempt at humanity, such desistance feels necessary, both to fulfill a boundless obligation to others' welfare and as a happy step away from doing. It isn't easy, of course, for me or any member of a doing-addicted species to realize wuwei, but the vow to carry over all beings makes it a challenge I want to live up to. It ought to go without saying, I suppose, but the wise not only have nothing to do; they also have nothing *better* to do.

Notes

Preface

1. In romanizing Mandarin Chinese, I've chosen to use pinyin renderings, supplying romanizations in the Wade-Giles system parenthetically or in notes, as well as Japanese pronunciations. Neither Wade-Giles nor pinyin makes it easy for English speakers to approximate the sounds of Chinese, unfortunately, but comparing the two may be somewhat helpful.

2. In discussing *bao, zang*, and *baozang*, I've relied heavily on Robert Sharf's *Coming to Terms with Chinese Buddhism: A Reading of the Treasure Store Treatise* (Honolulu: University of Hawai'i Press, 2002), 143-45. The excerpts I cite are on p. 144.

3. Inexhaustible storehouse: one of Chan's rivals among the schools of Chinese Buddhism literalized the wujinzang concept, amassing wealth and power through a sort of banking system premised on the accumulation of merit. Cf. Wendi L. Adamek, *The Mystique of Transmission: On an Early Chan History and Its Contexts* (New York: Columbia University Press, 2007), 125-27.

4. Cf. Ruth Fuller Sasaki, trans. and Thomas Yūhō Kirchner, ed., *The Record of Linji* (Honolulu: University of Hawai'i Press, 2009), 117.

5. "On Ruth Fuller Sasaki," *Wind Bell* 8, nos. 1-2 (fall 1969): 22.

6. "On Rinzai Masters and Western Students in Japan," *Wind Bell* 8, nos. 1-2 (fall 1969): 24. Lightly emended.

7. Tōrei's plea: quoted by Michel Mohr in "Imagining Indian Zen: Tōrei's Commentary on the *Ta-mo-to-lo Chan ching* and the Rediscovery of Early Meditation Techniques during the Tokugawa Era," in *Zen Classics: Formative Texts in the History of Zen Buddhism*, ed. Steven Heine and Dale Wright (Oxford: Oxford University Press, 2006), 236. Lightly emended.

8. For the text, sources, and a different translation of this saying, see Victor Sōgen Hori, *Zen Sand: The Book of Capping Phrases for Kōan Practice* (Honolulu: University of Hawai'i Press, 2003), item 7.498.

1. Getting to the Spring—and Beyond

1. This is my translation, as are all others herein, unless otherwise credited. "Mt. Nan" is short for Zhongnan-shan, which in this case refers to the Zhongnan (Chung-nan) Mountains in central China. Many good translations of the poem are available, including C. H. Kwock and Vincent McHugh, *Old Friend from Far Away* (San Francisco: North Point Press, 1980), 106; Tony Barnstone et al., *Laughing Lost in the Mountains: Poems of Wang Wei* (Hanover, NH: University of New England Press, 1991), 3; and Jonathan Chaves in Thomas J. Rimer et al., *Shisendo: Hall of the Poetry Immortals* (New York: Weatherhill, 1991), 62. Victor Sōgen Hori translates the famous couplet in *Zen Sand: The Book of Capping Phrases for Kōan Practice* (Honolulu: University of Hawai'i Press, 2003), item 10.515.

2. Wu's comment appeared, with accompanying translation, in *The Golden Age of Zen* in 1967, but I didn't see it until Doubleday reissued the book in 1996 (p. 203).

3. "Tracing Dao to Its Source" is part one of the second-century B.C.E. Daoist classic *Huainan zi*. For the Chinese of the passage I've quoted and a different translation, see D. C. Lau and Roger T. Ames, *Yuan Dao: Tracing Dao to Its Source* (New York: Random House, 1998), 103. Dōgen Zenji incorporated the second of the couplets in "Sansuikyō," his "Mountains and Waters Sūtra."

4. "Song of Realizing the Way": *Zhengdao ge* (or *Cheng-tao ke*; J., *Shōdōka*), lines 228-29, translated in collaboration with Benjamin Brose.

2. The Taste of Water

1. This quatrain has been translated many times with minor variations. A convenient one, with Chinese graphs, is Victor Sōgen Hori, *Zen Sand: The Book of Capping Phrases for Kōan Practice* (Honolulu: University of Hawai'i Press, 2003), 643.

2. The story of Huineng's encounter with Ming turns up in late editions of the *Platform Sūtra* and numerous other texts. My informal retelling is based on case 23 of the *Wumenguan* (or *Wu-men kuan*; J., *Mumonkan*), of which several English translations exist, including Robert Aitken, *The Gateless Barrier* (San Francisco: North Point Press, 1990) and Zenkei Shibayama, *Zen Comments on the Mumonkan* (New York: Harper & Row, 1974).

3. Paul W. Kroll, *A Student's Dictionary of Classical and Medieval Chinese*, rev. ed. (Leiden: Brill, 2017), 76. Dr. Kroll gives a secondary set of definitions: "pale, pallid, light (color); faded, etiolated."

4. For an eye-opening account of dan as a Chinese aesthetic, I'm indebted to François Jullien's *In Praise of Blandness: Proceeding from Chinese Thought and Aesthetics* (New York: Zone Books, 2004).

5. *Daodejing* 35.

6. I've drawn the excerpt of the *Zhuangzi* from one of its "outer" chapters, "The Mountain Tree." Cf. Burton Watson, *The Complete Works of Chuang Tzu* (New York: Columbia University Press, 1968), 215.

7. The *Zhongyong* verse appears in section 33.1. For comparison, see Roger T. Ames and David L. Hall, *Focusing the Familiar: A Translation and Philosophical Interpretation of the* Zhongyong (Honolulu: University of Hawai'i Press, 2001), 114.

8. I've simplified the aesthetics of *dan* here. In Chinese literary circles, it was often paired with a second word to form the terms *pingdan* (or *p'ing-tan*), even and plain, and *danbo* (or *tan-p'o*), plain and tranquil. Concerning *dan* as a literary quality, see Robert E. Buswell, Jr., and Robert M. Gimello, eds., *Paths to Liberation: The Mārga and Its Transformations in Buddhist Thought* (Honolulu: University of Hawai'i Press, 1992), 402-03, and Kang-i Sun Chang and Stephen Owen, eds., *The Cambridge History of Chinese Literature*, vol. 1 (Cambridge: Cambridge University Press, 2010), 389-90, 429-30.

9. For the Chinese text of the poem and Burton Watson's translation, see Red Pine and Mike O'Connor, eds., *The Clouds Should Know Me by Now: Buddhist Poet Monks of China* (Boston: Wisdom Publications, 1998), 60.

10. Dongshan's caution comes from an unpublished translation by Peter Wong Yih Jiun, for which I'm very grateful. It appears in an edition of Dongshan's record dated 1761, almost nine hundred years after his death, so how much Dongshan, in fact, had to do with writing it is open to question.

11. I've adapted Yuanwu's comment from Thomas and J. C. Cleary, trans., *The Blue Cliff Record* (Boulder, CO: Shambhala Publications, 1977), 1:81.

12. Hongzhi's line begins his verse for *Congrong lu* case 23. For another translation, see Thomas Cleary, trans., *Book of Serenity: One Hundred Zen Dialogues* (Hudson, NY: Lindisfarne Press, 1990), 102.

13. Verse for *Wumenguan*, case 23. For alternative translations, see Aitken, *Gateless Barrier*, 149, or Shibayama, *Zen Comments*, 167, among others.

3. To Mingle with Friends

1. The *Congrong lu* (1224), a compilation of kōans with companion poems and commentaries, is commonly titled in English the *Book of Equanimity*. Cf. Thomas Cleary, trans., *Book of Serenity: One Hundred Zen Dialogues* (Hudson, NY: Lindisfarne Press, 1990), 38-39. I've cited just part of the verse; Cleary gives a full translation.

2. A. C. Graham, trans., *The Book of Lieh-tzu* (New York: Columbia University Press, 1990), 109-10, emended to give names their pinyin romanization and to revise Graham's "lute" to "zither." Daoist classics more widely known in the West would be, of course, the *Daodejing* and the *Zhuangzi*.

3. "Zhiyin" is a chapter in the *Wenxin diaolong* (or *Wen-hsin tiao-lung*) by Liu Xie. The passage I've translated is quoted in Stephen Owen, *Traditional Chinese Poetry and Poetics: Omen of the World* (Madison, WI: University of Wisconsin Press, 1985), 59.

4. For another translation of his poem, see David Hinton, *Selected Poems of Li Po* (New York: New Directions, 1996), 28. Li Bai refers to Lu Zishun, the qin player, as a 幽人, literally a "dark, hidden, or secluded person"—a term sometimes applied to people who lived in isolation. I've opted for a sense of physical darkness, of a man playing by moonlight, shrouded in shadows.

5. The *Wumenguan* presents the story of the so-called Flower Sermon as its sixth case. Numerous translations are available, including Aitken, *The Gateless Barrier*, 46, and Shibayama, *Zen Comments on the Mumonkan*, 58.

6. Kuo'an's oft-cited verses on the "Ten Oxherding Pictures" receive extended treatment in Yamada Mumon, *Lectures on the Ten Oxherding Pictures*, trans. Victor Sōgen Hori (Honolulu: University of Hawai'i Press, 2004).

7. Thomas and J. C. Cleary, trans., *The Blue Cliff Record* (Boulder, CO: Shambhala Publications, 1977), 2:409.

8. *Analects* 7.8.

9. Yuanwu's opening words: Cleary and Cleary, *Blue Cliff Record*, 1:1. For additional instances of his use of the Confucian formula, see 1:14, 88, 139, 176, and 198. Such references continue in vols. 2 and 3 of the Cleary brothers' translation.

10. Furong's dialogue is translated from Keizan Zenji's commentary on case 45 of the *Denkōroku*. Cf. Francis H. Cook, trans., *The Record of Transmitting the Light* (Los Angeles: Center Publications, 1991), 207–08. For another version, see Andrew Ferguson, trans., *Zen's Chinese Heritage* (Boston: Wisdom Publications, 2000), 385–86.

11. *Guanyin*: 觀音. *Guanshiyin*: 觀世音. It may not be coincidental that the same verb, *guan*, appears in Liu Xie's description of reading quoted above: "In contemplating (guan) a text, one enters the [writer's] emotions...."

12. Dōgen Zenji devotes a chapter of the *Shōbōgenzō* to the subject of saindhava. "Ōsaku sendaba," translated by Steven Heine in *Dōgen and the Koan Tradition: A Tale of Two Shōbōgenzō Texts* (Albany: State University of New York Press, 1994), 249–53.

13. *Jingde chuandeng lu*, fasc. 9. Cf. Sohaku Ogata, trans., *The Transmission of the Lamp: Early Masters* (Wolfeboro, NH: Longwood Academic, 1990), 305–06, and Chang Chung-Yuan, *Original Teachings of Ch'an Buddhism* (New York: Pantheon, 1969), 207.

14. 符 (also romanized as *fu* in Japanese). Bernard Faure treats the topic of fu in *Visions of Power: Imagining Medieval Japanese Buddhism* (Princeton,

NJ: Princeton University Press, 1996), 225-28, as does Jeff Broughton in "Tsung-mi's *Zen Prolegomenon*: Introduction to an Exemplary Zen Canon," in Steven Heine and Dale Wright, eds., *The Zen Canon: Understanding the Classic Texts* (Oxford: Oxford University Press, 2004), 16-18.

15. Usage of "tallying" appears, for example, in the *Daodejing* 79, in the title (and arguably is the subject) of the fifth chapter of the *Zhuangzi*, and in the *Mengzi* 4B1.

16. This early Buddhist use occurs in a preface to *The Dhyāna [Meditation] Sūtra of Dharmatrāta*. For a translation of the passage, see Wendi L. Adamek, *The Mystique of Transmission: On an Early Chan History and Its Contents* (New York: Columbia University Press, 2007), 35.

17. Keizan Jōkin, *Denkōroku*, case 15.

18. Cf. *Blue Cliff Record*, case 1, and *Congrong lu* case 2. I treat this case in more detail in chapter 14.

19. Many English translations of the *Cantong qi* are available, including Thomas Cleary, trans., *Timeless Spring: A Soto Zen Anthology* (Tokyo: Weatherhill, 1980), 36-39; Sheng-Yen, trans., *The Poetry of Enlightenment: Poems by Ancient Chan Masters* (Elmhurst, NY: Dharma Drum Publications, 1987), 67-70; and Stephen Addiss et al., eds., *Zen Sourcebook: Traditional Documents from China, Korea, and Japan* (Indianapolis: Hackett Publishing, 2008), 31-33.

20. For the biography and work of Baisaō, see Norman Waddell, *The Old Tea Seller: Life and Zen Poetry in 18th Century Kyoto* (Berkeley: Counterpoint Press, 2008). The poem itself is on p. 149. I owe the translator both thanks for confirming that *zhiyin* appears in its last line and apologies for presuming to add punctuation where he omitted it.

4. Cutting and Polishing: A Matter of Character

1. Aitken Rōshi's quotation of Yamada Rōshi's dictum and his comment to Brother David both are from Robert Aitken and David Steindl-Rast, *The Ground We Share: Everyday Practice, Christian and Buddhist* (Liguori, MO: Triumph Books, 1994), 83.

2. I owe awareness of the phrase *sessa takuma*, of its origin in the *Analects* 1:15, and of its importance in Zen training to Victor Sōgen Hori, "Teaching and Learning in the Rinzai Zen Monastery," *Journal of Japanese Studies* 20, no. 1 (1994): 17-18. The examples Hori gives, though undoubtedly faithful to his monastic experience, are blunt and harsh, almost fierce in tenor, as if the only tool useful for cutting and polishing were a sledgehammer.

3. *Shijing*, verse 55. Cf. Arthur Waley, trans., Joseph R. Allen trans. and ed., *The Book of Songs* rev. 2nd ed. (New York: Grove Press, 1996), 46. Ezra Pound's

translation in *The Confucian Odes* (New York: New Directions, 1954), 26-27, is far off the mark.

4. Cf. Yifa, *The Origins of Buddhist Monastic Codes in China: An Annotated Translation and Study of the* Chanyuan Qinggui (Honolulu: University of Hawai'i Press, 2002), 139.

5. Aitken and Steindl-Rast, *Ground We Share*, 82. Aitken Rōshi also acknowledges Shintō as a source of moral guidance for the Japanese sangha.

6. Sheng Yen, *Footprints in the Snow: The Autobiography of a Chinese Buddhist Monk* (New York: Doubleday, 2008), 32-33.

7. D. T. Suzuki, *Essays in Zen Buddhism: First Series* (New York: Grove Press, 1961), 74.

8. Suzuki, *Essays in Zen*, 76.

9. Suzuki, *Essays in Zen*, 77. To his credit, Suzuki goes on to acknowledge that "This was most slippery ground for the Mahāyānists" because it made objective assessment of a person's actions impossible, "and consequently who could ever distinguish libertinism from spiritualism?"

10. D. T. Suzuki, "Self the Unattainable," collected in Frederick Franck, ed., *The Buddha Eye: An Anthology of the Kyoto School* (New York: Crossroad Publishing Co., 1991), 21.

11. "Samsāra is exactly nirvāna": 生死即菩提. A variant is "Kleśa are exactly nirvāna": 煩惱即菩提.

12. Fayan, 宗門十規論 *Treatise on Ten Admonitions for the Ancestral Gate*, part 6. Cf. Benjamin Brose, "Disorienting Medicine: Fayan Wenyi's *Ten Admonitions for the Lineage*," *Journal of Chinese Buddhist Studies* 28 (2015), 153-88, and Thomas Cleary, trans., *The Five Houses of Zen* (Boston: Shambhala Publications, 1997), 133-44.

13. Cf. Ruth Fuller Sasaki, trans. and Thomas Yūhō Kirchner, ed., *The Record of Linji* (Honolulu: University of Hawai'i Press, 2009), 235, and Burton Watson, trans., *The Zen Teachings of Master Lin-chi* (Boston: Shambhala Publications, 1993), 52.

14. Thomas Cleary, trans., *Zen Lessons: The Art of Leadership* (Boston: Shambhala Publications, 1989), xvi.

15. 禪林寶訓 *Chanlin baoxun* (or *Chan-lin pao-hsun*). The *bao* of the title is the same as in *baozang*, and the title could just as well be *Treasured Models* (or *Examples*) *for the Chan Forest*. Cleary, *Zen Lessons,* is a partial translation, and this passage is lightly emended from pp. 41-42.

16. My version of *Shōbōgenzō Zuimonki* 4:5. Cf. Reihō Masunaga, trans., *A Primer of Sōtō Zen* (Honolulu: University of Hawai'i Press, 1971), 64, and Thomas Cleary, trans., *Record of Things Heard: From the Treasury of the Eye of the True Teaching* (Boulder, CO: Prajna Press, 1980), 73. Also partially translated in Hee-jin Kim, *Dōgen Kigen: Mystical Realist*, rev. ed. (Tucson:

University of Arizona Press, 1987), 223. In the *Eihei Kōroku*, Dōgen again carefully advances the need to "polish," this time in counterpoint to the categorical statement "For a luminous jewel without flaw, if you carve a pattern its virtue is lost," made by Hongzhi, a predecessor he highly esteemed. Cf. Taigen Dan Leighton and Shohaku Okamura, trans., *Dōgen's Extensive Record: A Translation of the Eihei Kōroku* (Boston: Wisdom Publications, 2010), 163.

17. *Denkōroku*, case 42. Cf. Cook, *Record of Transmitting*, 193, and T. Griffith Foulk, ed., *Record of the Transmission of Illumination* (Honolulu: University of Hawai'i Press, 2021), 1:434.

18. Cf. Chang Chung-Yuan, trans., *Original Teachings of Ch'an Buddhism* (New York: Pantheon, 1969), 58; William F. Powell, trans., *The Record of Tungshan* (Honolulu: University of Hawai'i Press, 1985), 23; Sohaku Ogata, trans., *The Transmission of the Lamp: Early Masters* (Wolfeboro, NH: Longwood Academic, 1990), 266.

19. Recounted by Gary Snyder, *The Practice of the Wild* (San Francisco: North Point Press, 1990), 149.

20. *Daodejing* 41.

21. Fayan, *Treatise on Ten Admonitions*, part 10.

22. 三教合一 *sanjiao heyi* (or *san-chiao ho-i*; J., *sankyō gōitsu*) and 三教一致 *sanjiao yizhi* (or *san-chiao i-chih*; J., *sankyō ichi*).

23. Robert N. Bellah, "The Meaning of Dōgen Today," in William R. LaFleur, *Dōgen Studies* (Honolulu: University of Hawai'i Press, 1985), 153-54.

24. Aitken and Steindl-Rast, *Ground We Share*, 54.

5. A Good, Hard Look in the Mirror

1. Paul Demiéville made a rich, early exploration of mirror imagery both East and West, republished as "The Mirror of Mind," Neal Donner, trans., in Peter Gregory, ed., *Sudden and Gradual: Approaches to Enlightenment in Chinese Thought* (Honolulu: University of Hawai'i Press, 1987).

2. Emperor Qin's mirror is described in T. Griffith Foulk, ed., *Record of the Transmission of Illumination* (Honolulu: University of Hawai'i Press, 2021), 2:606. Regarding the Yellow Emperor's mirror, see Victor Sōgen Hori, *Zen Sand: The Book of Capping Phrases for Kōan Practice* (Honolulu: University of Hawai'i Press, 2003), item 10.142 and p. 727.

3. The usual terms are ancient mirror 古鏡 *gujing* (or *ku-ching*; J., *kokyō*); round mirror 圓鏡 *yuanjing* (or *yuan-ching*; J., *enkyō*) or, using a synonym for mirror, 圓鑑 *yuanjian* (or *yuan-chien*; J., *enkan*); bright mirror 明鏡 *mingjing* (or *ming-ching*; J., *meikyō*); and broken mirror 破鏡 *pojing* (or *p'o-ching*; J., *hakyō*).

4. "The Jewel Mirror Samādhi," attributed to Dongshan Liangjie (or Tung-shan Liang-chieh; J., Tōzan Ryōkai).

5. Donald S. Lopez Jr. provides a critical history of this notion in *Buddhism and Science: A Guide for the Perplexed* (Chicago: University of Chicago Press, 2008).

6. Great Perfect Mirror Wisdom 大圓鏡智 *dayuanjing zhi* (or *ta-yuan ching chih*; J., *daienkyōchi*) derives from the Sanskrit *ādjarśajñana*.

7. From the *True Summary Treatise on Opening Heartmind and Manifesting [Buddha-] Nature in the Sudden Awakening of the Mahāyāna*, the *Dasheng kaixin xianxing dunwu zhenzong lun* (or *Ta-sheng k'ai-hsin hsien-hsing tun-wu chen-tsung lun*; J., *Daijō kaishin kenshō tongo shinshū ron*). Translated in J. C. Cleary, trans., *Zen Dawn: Early Zen Texts from Tun Huang* (Boston: Shambhala Publications, 1986), 121.

8. From a brief Chinese compilation of sūtras discussed and translated in Heng-ching Shih, "The Sutra of Forty-two Sections [四十二章經]," *Apocryphal Scriptures* (Berkeley: Numata Center for Buddhist Translation and Research, 2005); the passage quoted is on p. 37. See also Robert H. Sharf, "The Scripture in Forty-Two Sections," in Donald S. Lopez Jr., ed., *Religions of China in Practice* (Princeton: Princeton University Press, 1996).

9. 客塵煩惱 *kechen fannao* (or *k'e-ch'en fan-nao*; J., *kyakujin bonnō*) from the Skt., *āgantukakleśa*.

10. Yongjia, "Song of Realizing the Way," lines 20–21 of an unpublished translation by Benjamin Brose and myself. The title of the poem appears in a document dated 838, and the poem itself is quoted in an 857 text, so it came relatively early in Chan's development but probably wasn't written by Yongjia, who died in 713.

11. Yongjia, "Song of Realizing," lines 116–19 (with emendations).

12. Yongjia, lines 180–83.

13. This verse and Huineng's responses all appear in the earliest iteration of the *Platform Sutra*. Cf. Philip B. Yampolsky, *The Platform Sutra of the Sixth Patriarch* (New York: Columbia University Press, 1967), 130 and 132. He gives the Chinese texts in an appendix. Slightly different translations have been proposed by other translators.

14. Cited in Demiéville, "Mirror of Mind," 17.

15. *Jingde zhuandeng lu* 5, record of Nanyue. Cf. Sohaku Ogata, trans., *The Transmission of the Lamp: Early Masters* (Wolfeboro, NH: Longwood Academic, 1990), 162–63, and Randolph S. Whitfield, trans., *Records of the Transmission of the Lamp*, vol. 2 (Books On Demand, 2015), 113. The text identifies Daoyi as a 沙門 *shamen*, the standard Chinese transliteration of the Sanskrit *śramaṇa*, probably indicating that he maintained the monastic practice with unusual rigor; I've paraphrased it here as "diligent monk."

16. 磨 *mo* (J., *ma*), translated as "polish" in, e.g., Ogata, *Transmission of the Lamp,* and Thomas Yūhō Kirchner, trans., *Entangling Vines: A Classic Collection of Zen Koans,* 2nd ed. (Boston: Wisdom Publications, 2013), 122.

17. *Jingde chuandeng lu* 21, record of Guotai Yuantao. Cf. Whitfield, *Records of the Transmission of the Lamp,* vol. 5, 225.

18. Hori, *Zen Sand,* item 14.453.

19. *Jingde chuandeng lu* 16. Cf. Chang Chung-Yuan, trans., *Original Teachings of Ch'an Buddhism* (New York: Pantheon, 1969), 281–82, and Whitfield, *Records of the Transmission of the Lamp,* vol. 4, 148. For a variant, see Thomas and J. C. Cleary, trans., *The Blue Cliff Record* (Boulder, CO: Shambhala Publications, 1977), 2:430.

20. Dōgen, "Kokyō," Sōtō Zen Text Project, trans., *Treasury of the True Dharma Eye: Dōgen's* Shōbōgenzō (Tokyo: Sotoshu Shumucho, 2023), 2:153. I owe Carl Bielefeldt a deep bow for all of his assistance with this text.

21. Hori, *Zen Sand,* item 8.304.

22. Both Hakuin passages are from Norman Waddell, trans., *The Essential Teachings of Zen Master Hakuin* (Boston: Shambhala Publications, 1994), 49, 80.

23. *Eihei Kōroku* 4. Cf. Taigen Dan Leighton and Shohaku Okamura, trans., *Dōgen's Extensive Record: A Translation of the Eihei Kōroku* (Boston: Wisdom Publications, 2010), 305. In a note attached to the passage, the praiseworthy translators of this enormous text deem Dōgen's fruitful misquotation an "abbreviation." Even Homer nods!

24. Dōgen, "Kokyō," *Treasury of the True Dharma Eye* 2:139.

25. Cf. Thomas Yūhō Kirchner, trans., *Entangling Vines: A Classic Collection of Zen Koans,* 2nd ed. (Boston: Wisdom Publications, 2013), 41. This story also appears in Lingyun's entry in the *Zongmen wudeng huiyuan.*

26. Arthur Braverman, trans., *A Quiet Room: The Poetry of Zen Master Jakushitsu* (Boston: Tuttle Publishing, 2000), 94.

6. Putting Integrity Back into *Integrity*

1. Cf. Chang Chung-Yuan, trans., *Original Teachings of Ch'an Buddhism* (New York: Pantheon, 1969), 202; Sohaku Ogata, trans., *Transmission of the Lamp: Early Masters* (Wolfeboro, NH: Longwood Academic, 1990), 299; Andrew Ferguson, trans., *Zen's Chinese Heritage* (Boston: Wisdom Publications, 2000), 129; and Thomas and J. C. Cleary, trans., *The Blue Cliff Record* (Boulder, CO: Shambhala Publications, 1977), 1:232.

2. Danner made this observation during Trump's reelection campaign: "Moving Backward: Hypocrisy and Human Rights," *New York Review Daily* (June 1, 2020). In *Character: The History of a Cultural Obsession* (New York:

Farrar, Straus and Giroux, 2020), 42–43, Marjorie Garber quotes a journalist's related observation during the 2016 election: "The character Mr. Trump plays may be more honest than that of any of his rivals: He's the ambitious businessman who cares only about winning."

3. Quoted in Michael Gerson, "The Last Temptation," *Atlantic* (April, 2018): 51. It has since emerged that Falwell's paean to Trump may be explained, at least in part, by his own failures of integrity—a sex scandal that prompted his removal from leadership of Liberty University.

4. Brooks Atkinson, ed., *The Selected Writings of Ralph Waldo Emerson* (New York: The Modern Library, 1950), 148, 152.

5. Quoted in Nicholas Lemann, "The After-Party," *New Yorker* (October 26, 2020): 63.

6. The Trump campaign's senior communications adviser, Jason Miller, seized the opportunity to criticize Clinton on exactly these grounds, charging her with wearing a false face: "Just when Hillary Clinton said she was going to start running a positive campaign, she ripped off her mask and revealed her true contempt for everyday Americans."

7. *Cheng* becomes *sei* or *makoto* in Japanese, usually conveying a stronger sense of sincerity than of integrity.

8. *Daxue* (or *Ta Hsueh*) 6.2.

9. *Zhongyong* (or *Chung-yung*) 25. Cf. Roger T. Ames and David L. Hall, *Focusing the Familiar: A Translation and Philosophical Interpretation of the Zhongyong* (Honolulu: University of Hawai'i Press, 2001), 106. The Ames and Hall title greatly improves upon James Legge's *Doctrine of the Mean*. I like *Balancing Amidst the Everyday* as another possibility.

10. *Mengzi* 4A.12. Cf. D. C. Lau, trans., *Mencius* (London: Penguin Books, 1970), 123.

11. *Zhuangzi* 31. For alternative translations, see Burton Watson, *The Complete Works of Chuang Tzu* (New York: Columbia University Press, 1968), 349; Victor H. Mair, *Wandering on the Way: Early Taoist Tales and Parables of Chuang Tzu* (Honolulu: University of Hawai'i Press, 1994), 321; and David L. Hall and Roger T. Ames, *Thinking from the Han: Self, Truth, and Transcendence in Chinese and Western Culture* (Albany: State University of New York Press, 1998), 164.

12. From the *Shangshu* (or *Shang-shu*), also called the *Shujing* (or *Shu-ching*), a title often translated as the *Classic of History*.

13. John Rohsenow, *ABC Dictionary of Chinese Proverbs* (Honolulu: University of Hawai'i Press, 2002), 193.

14. Ames and Hall make a case for translating *cheng* as "creativity" in *Focusing the Familiar*, 61–63.

15. Ari Borrell, "*Ko-wu* or *Kung-an*? Practice, Realization, and Teaching in the

Thought of Chang Chiu-ch'eng," in Peter N. Gregory and Daniel A. Getz, Jr., eds., *Buddhism in the Sung* (Honolulu: University of Hawai'i Press, 1999), 92. I've changed Borrell's romanizations to pinyin. See pp. 63-64 for his account of Zhang's relationship with Dahui and p. 106 (n. 114) for a twelfth-century Neo-Confucian leader's comment that in his exchange with the emperor Zhang "was using Chan masters' method of sudden repartee," *jifeng* (literally, "dynamic spearpoint"). See chapter 12 for a discussion of *ji*.

16. From the *Xiuxing yao lun* (or *Hsiu-hsin yao lun*). Cf. John R. McRae, *The Northern School and the Formation of Early Ch'an Buddhism* (Honolulu: University of Hawai'i Press, 1986). McRae dates the text to "around the year 700" (p. 120), translates the passage (p. 128), and provides the Chinese text in the backmatter (p. 十, i.e., p. 10; the pagination there is given in Chinese).

17. For the eighteen distinguishing traits of a buddha, see Robert E. Buswell Jr. and Donald S. Lopez Jr., *The Princeton Dictionary of Buddhism* (Princeton, NJ: Princeton University Press, 2014), 85 and 1092.

18. "Good friends" approximates the meaning of Sanskrit *kalyānamitra*, which Chinese translators converted to 善知識 *shanzhishi* (or *shan-chih-shih*; J., *zenchishiki*).

19. Adapted from Ruth Fuller Sasaki, trans., and Thomas Yuhō Kirchner, ed., *The Record of Linji* (Honolulu: University of Hawai'i Press, 2009), 174. Since not killing is the first Buddhist precept and Right Views the first step on the Eightfold Noble Path, it seems reasonable to interpret this reference to them as alluding to the precepts and the Eightfold Path in their entirety.

20. Yuanwu's statement appears in the *Chanlin baoxun* (or *Chan-lin p'ao-hsun*), a twelfth-century handbook on proper leadership of Chan assemblies. Thomas Cleary's partial translation, *Zen Lessons: The Art of Leadership* (Boston: Shambhala Publications, 1989), includes this passage on p. 51. I owe thanks to Benjamin Brose for the Chinese text and advice on translating it.

21. Yuanwu, *Chanlin baoxun*. The "ancient" Yuanwu cites here must be Confucius, but he's either misremembered or intentionally toned down the even more radical statement recorded in *Analects* 12.7, where Confucius teaches that governance requires "Enough food, enough troops, and enough trust" but that, if necessary, he'd give up the first two in order to preserve the third.

22. Concerning the Shintō teaching of *makoto* (as *cheng* is read in Japanese) and for a fascinating example of its personal impact in a Zen context, see Sallie B. King, trans., *Passionate Journey: The Spiritual Autobiography of Satomi Myōdō* (Boston: Shambhala Publications, 1987), 7-10 and 152-55.

23. Cf. Victor Sōgen Hori, *Zen Sand: The Book of Capping Phrases for Kōan Practice* (Honolulu: University of Hawai'i Press, 2003), item 14.593.

24. Dōgen is quoting the *Xiaojing* (or *Hsiao ching*), a classic text attributed to

Confucius, espousing the dao of familial relations. Cf. Henry Rosemont, Jr., and Roger T. Ames, *The Chinese Classic of Family Reverence: A Philosophical Translation of the Xiaojing* (Honolulu: University of Hawai'i Press, 2009), 106-07. For Dōgen's statement, cf. Reihō Masunaga, trans., *A Primer of Sōtō Zen: A Translation of Dōgen's Shōbōgenzō Zuimonki* (Honolulu: University of Hawai'i Press, 1971), 108, or Thomas Cleary, trans., *Record of Things Heard: From the Treasury of the Eye of the True Teaching* (Boulder, CO: Prajna Press, 1980), 123-24.

25. I've adapted Shaku Sōen's admonition from two sources: Paul Reps, ed., *Zen Flesh, Zen Bones: A Collection of Zen and Pre-Zen Writings* (Rutland, VT: Charles Tuttle Company, 1957), 43, and Eido Shimano, ed., *Like a Dream, Like a Fantasy: The Zen Writings and Translations of Nyogen Senzaki* (Tokyo: Japan Publications, 1978), 116. His admonition parallels a passage from the ancient Chinese *Book of Songs*, no. 256.

26. Reported in Robert Aitken and David Steindl-Rast, *The Ground We Share: Everyday Practice, Christian and Buddhist* (Liguori, MO: Triumph Books, 1994), 182.

27. King, *Passionate Journey*, 109.

28. Senzaki in Reps, *Zen Flesh, Zen Bones*, 47-48. A different version of the blind seer's words, perhaps from another source or more precisely translated, appears in Norman Waddell, trans., *The Unborn: The Life and Teaching of Zen Master Bankei* (San Francisco: North Point Press, 1984), 137.

7. The Resource of Shame

1. The anthropologist Ruth Benedict played a leading role in establishing the concept of shame and guilt cultures. See her *The Chrysanthemum and the Sword: Patterns of Japanese Culture* (Cleveland: World Publishing Co., 1946 [reprint 1967]), especially 222-27. Marilyn Ivy offers a brief but trenchant appraisal of Benedict's thinking in "Benedict's Shame," *Cabinet*, no. 31 (fall, 2008): 64-68. For assessments of shame and guilt and their impact on culture very different from Benedict's, see Herbert Fingarette, *Confucius: The Secular as Sacred* (Prospect Heights, IL: Waveland Press, 1972, 1989), 25-34 and T. R. Reid, *Confucius Lives Next Door: What Living in the East Teaches Us about Living in the West* (New York: Vintage Books, 1999), 87-89.

2. Several Chinese words are commonly translated into English as "shame." The graphs that typically appear in Chan and Zen sayings are 慚 can (or ts'an; J., zan), also written 慙; 慚愧 cankui (or ts'an-k'uei; J., zanki), considered one of the seven personal assets; 恥 or 耻 chi (or ch'ih; J., chi or haji); and 恥辱 chiru (or ch'ih-ju; J., chijoku). The two-graph terms indicate remorse or disgrace in addition to shame.

3. Ryōkan's statement is in Ryūichi Abé and Peter Haskel, trans., *Great Fool: Zen Master Ryōkan; Poems, Letters, and Other Writings* (Honolulu: University of Hawai'i Press, 1996), 246.

4. The *Analects* quotations are from 14.27, 5.25, 8.13, 14.1, 13.20, and 2.3.

5. *Mengzi* 7A.6 and 7A.7. The two statements are consecutive in the original.

6. Victor Sōgen Hori, *Zen Sand: The Book of Capping Phrases for Kōan Practice* (Honolulu: University of Hawai'i Press, 2003), item 8.156.

7. *Zhongyong* 20.10. Cf. Roger T. Ames and David L. Hall, trans. *Focusing the Familiar: A Translation and Philosophical Interpretation of the* Zhongyong (New York: Ballantine Books, 2003), 102.

8. *Zhongyong* 33.3. Cf. Ames and Hall, *Focusing the Familiar*, 114. The *Zhongyong* is quoting the *Book of Songs*, no. 256.

9. I've degendered this stanza. Otherwise, it's as translated in Burton Watson, *The Vimalakirti Sutra* (New York: Columbia University Press, 1996), 98.

10. Liberally adapted from Burton Watson, trans., *The Lotus Sutra* (New York: Columbia University Press, 1993), 46.

11. Abé and Haskel, *Great Fool,* 245, identify Ryōkan's source as the *Sūtra of Bequeathed Teachings, Yijian jing* (or *I-chiao ching*; J., *Yuikyōgyō*). I've emended their translation slightly.

12. Benjamin Brose, "Disorienting Medicine: Fayan Wenyi's Ten Admonishments for the Lineage," *Journal of Chinese Buddhist Studies* 28 (2015): 183 (with minor emendations).

13. Thomas Cleary, trans., *Zen Lessons: The Art of Leadership* (Boston: Shambhala Publications, 1989), 71. I've substituted *dao* for Cleary's "the Way."

14. First letter to Li Bing, one of many letters to lay students that appear in Dahui's voluminous record. My translation is informed by Thomas Yūhō Kirchner's interpretation of the letter, made for a complete edition of Dahui's letters that he's preparing. The letter also appears in Christopher Cleary, trans., *Swampland Flowers: The Letters and Lectures of Zen Master Ta Hui* (New York: Grove Press, 1977), this portion on p.105. Cleary's is based on a different Chinese text, which may differ somewhat from the original.

15. Quoted in Sheng Yen, *Attaining the Way: A Guide to the Practice of Chan Buddhism* (Boston: Shambhala Publications, 2006), 94.

16. *Record of Zhaozhou*, case 194. Cf. James Green, trans., *The Recorded Sayings of Zen Master Joshu* (Boston: Shambhala Publications, 1998), 72, and Yoel Hoffman, trans., *Radical Zen: The Sayings of Jōshū* (Brookline, MA: Autumn Press, 1978), 72-73.

17. Comment on case 34 of the *Wumenguan* (*Gateless Barrier*).

18. Dōgen, *Record of Things Heard: From the Treasury of the Eye of the True Teaching,* trans. Thomas Cleary (Boulder, CO: Prajna Press, 1980), 76. Reihō Masunaga translates the passage very differently in *A Primer of Sōtō Zen:*

A Translation of Dōgen's "Shōbōgenzō Zuimonki" (Honolulu: University of Hawai'i Press, 1971), 67.

19. Keizan inserts this reflection into praise for Furong Daokai in the *Denkōroku*. The text and a more precise, scholarly translation are in T. Griffith Foulk, ed., *Record of the Transmission of Illumination* (Honolulu: University of Hawai'i Press, 2021), 1:471. Prior translations are in Thomas Cleary, trans., *Transmission of Light: Zen in the Art of Enlightenment* (San Francisco: North Point Press, 1990), 199, and Francis H. Cook, trans., *The Record of Transmitting the Light* (Los Angeles: Center Publications, 1991), 208.

20. For the full story of the river porter, see Norman Waddell, trans., *Complete Poison Blossoms from a Thicket of Thorn: The Zen Records of Hakuin Ekaku* (Berkeley: Counterpoint Press, 2017), 294-97.

21. "Now Is the Time to Know Shame," unpublished ms. I'm grateful to Thomas Yūhō Kirchner for sharing his translation of Kōno Rōshi's address. I haven't traced the source of Wuzu's dictum.

22. Quoted in Daniel Mendelsohn, "His Design for Living," *New York Review of Books* (January 17, 2008): 52.

23. Aldo Leopold, *A Sand County Almanac: With Essays on Conservation from Round River* (New York: Ballantine Books, 1970), 168.

24. Malcolm X, with assistance from Alex Haley (New York: Grove Press, 1966), 68. Haley's epilogue on p. 414 quotes Malcolm X reiterating his shame and remorse.

25. Republished in Merwin, *The Second Four Books of Poems* (Port Townsend, WA: Copper Canyon Press, 1993), 124.

26. Merwin, "On Being Awarded the Pulitzer Prize," *New York Review of Books* (June 3, 1971), accessed September 10, 2023, at nybooks.com/articles/1971/06/03/on-being-awarded-the-pulitzer-prize.

27. Quoted in Lincoln Kaplan, "Our Towns," *Harvard Magazine* (May-June, 2018), 48, from Fallows's essay "What Did You Do in the Class War, Daddy?" in the *Washington Monthly* (October, 1975).

28. Quoted in Fintan O'Toole, "A Moral Witness," *New York Review of Books* (October 8, 2020), from *The Selected Letters of Martha Gellhorn*, ed. Caroline Moorehead (Henry Holt, 2006).

29. Frederick Douglass, *Narrative of the Life of Frederick Douglass, an American Slave* (1845) (New York: Barnes and Noble Classics, 2005), 42.

30. Quoted in Ian Buruma, "Ghosts," *New York Review of Books* (June 26, 2008), 6. Buruma goes on to discuss later, detailed investigations of the Abu Ghraib incidents with "implications... actually more disturbing than Sontag's cultural critique."

31. Alex Ross, "The People That Walked in Darkness," *New Yorker* (January 1, 2018): 64.

32. George Packer, "Betrayed," *New Yorker* (March 26, 2007), accessed January 26, 2023, at newyorker.com/magazine/2007/03/26/betrayed.

33. David Shulman, "Israel's Irrational Rationality," *New York Review of Books* (June 22, 2017): 44.

34. Jane Kramer, "Round One," *New Yorker* (April 23, 2007): 35.

35. Bob Dylan, with Jacques Levy, "Hurricane," from Dylan's 1976 album *Desire*.

36. Quoted from *The Silent Woman* in Michael Greenberg's remembrance, "Janet Malcolm (1934-2021)," *New York Review of Books* (July 22, 2021): 15.

37. Peter Hessler, "All Due Respect," *New Yorker* (January 9, 2012): 54.

38. Atul Gawande, *Being Mortal: Medicine and What Matters in the End* (New York: Henry Holt and Company, 2014), 234.

39. Charles Taylor, *A Secular Age* (Cambridge: Harvard University Press, 2007), 142. I owe Jack Turner thanks for, among many other things, calling this sentence to my attention.

40. Robert Bringhurst, "The Mind of the Wild," in Robert Bringhurst and Jan Zwicky, *Learning to Die: Wisdom in the Age of Climate Crisis* (Saskatchewan: University of Regina Press, 2018), 38.

41. Quoted in Simon Leys (Pierre Ryckmans), *The Hall of Uselessness: Collected Essays* (New York: New York Review Books, 2013), 408.

42. The maxim came to me through the kindness of Anne Dutton, East Rock Sangha.

43. "Living in the Village, Suffering from Cold," in Burton Watson, trans., *Po Chü-i: Selected Poems* (New York: Columbia University Press, 2000), 48.

44. Rachel Sherman, "Rich People's Secrets," *New York Times* (September 10, 2017).

8. Studying with the Water Buffalo

1. Mark L. Blum analyzes the sources of contemporary Buddhist environmental thought in "The Transcendentalist Ghost in EcoBuddhism," in Nalini Bhushan, Jay L. Garfield, and Abraham Zablocki, eds., *TransBuddhism: Transmission, Translation, and Transformation* (Amherst: University of Massachusetts Press, 2009).

2. Cf. Thomas Yūhō Kirchner, trans., *Entangling Vines: A Classic Collection of Zen Koans,* 2nd ed. (Boston: Wisdom Publications, 2013), 74-75, where the kōan is translated quite differently and also interpreted to refer to beings from nonhuman births of various kinds, not just to animals. The note on the case gives examples of animals only, however.

3. Cf. Thomas Cleary, trans., *Book of Serenity: One Hundred Zen Dialogues* (Hudson, NY: Lindisfarne Press, 1990), 291. Nanquan's deathbed dialogue appears in the *Transmission of the Lamp* as well; cf. Chang Chung-Yuan,

trans., *Original Teachings of Ch'an Buddhism* (New York: Pantheon, 1969), 163 and Sohaku Ogata, trans., *The Transmission of the Lamp: Early Masters* (Wolfeboro, NH: Longwood Academic, 1990), 268.

4. Cf. James Green, trans., *The Recorded Sayings of Zen Master Joshu* (Boston: Shambhala Publications, 1998), 13, and Yoel Hoffman, trans., *Radical Zen: The Sayings of Jōshū* (Brookline, MA: Autumn Press, 1978), 16.

5. This story circulated at least as early as 952, when it was recorded in the *Zutangji*, or *Ancestral Halls Collection*, a text not yet available in English translation. The *Congrong lu* version is in Cleary, *Book of* Serenity, 291-92. Other renditions appear in Chang, *Original Teachings,* 137, and Ruth Fuller Sasaki, trans. and Thomas Yūhō Kirchner, ed., *The Record of Linji* (Honolulu: University of Hawai'i Press, 2009), 313-14.

6. Daowu is better known as Daowu Yuanzhi (or Tao-wu Yuan-chih; J., Dōgo Enchi).

7. *Congrong lu*, case 69. Cf. Cleary, *Book of Serenity*, 290, and William F. Powell, trans., *The Record of Tung-shan* (Honolulu: University of Hawai'i Press, 1985), 73 (n. 33). Other texts quote the kōan, then delve into it, including Kirchner, *Entangling Vines*, 83. Translators are reduced to guessing which mammal the Chinese term *li-nu* 狸奴 is meant to indicate. Sundry evidence led me to settle on the so-called raccoon-dog, a small canid native to eastern China, but the word *li* figures in names of a number of other animals, including civets, foxes, otters, and beavers.

8. *Jingde chuandeng lu* 9. Cf. Ogata, *Transmission of the Lamp*, 315.

9. *Jingde chuandeng lu* 9. Other translations appear in Ogata, *Transmission of the Lamp,* 315-16, and Isshū Miura and Ruth Fuller Sasaki, *Zen Dust: The History of the Koan and Koan Study in Rinzai (Lin-chi) Zen* (New York: Harcourt, Brace & World, 1966), 319.

10. *Jingde chuandeng lu* 16. Cf. Chang, *Original Teachings*, 278.

11. *Zhaozhou lu*, item 481. Cf. Hoffman, *Radical Zen*, 147, and Green, *Recorded Sayings*, 155.

12. *Zhaozhou lu*, item 13. Cf. Hoffman, *Radical Zen*, 19-20, and Green, *Recorded Sayings*, 16. Unfortunately, both of these translators badly misconstrue the key phrase "practicing among other kinds."

13. Dōgen took the story of Nanquan's interaction with Daowu and Yunyan as case 57 of his *Mana Shōbōgenzō*, frequently used the key phrase in chapters of the *Shōbōgenzō*, and took the story as the subject of a verse in his record. For the last, see Taigen Dan Leighton and Shohaku Okamura, trans., *Dōgen's Extensive Record: A Translation of the Eihei Kōroku* (Boston: Wisdom Publications, 2010), 577-78.

14. The Chinese text appears, along with her translation, in Sonja Arntzen, trans., *Ikkyū and the Crazy Cloud Anthology: A Zen Poet of Medieval Japan*, rev. 2nd ed. (Melbourne: Quirin Press, 2022), 17.

15. The oxherding sequence is available in many places. The most thorough treatment in English that I know of is Yamada Mumon, *Lectures on the Ten Oxherding Pictures*, trans. Victor Sōgen Hori (Honolulu: University of Hawai'i Press, 2004).

16. A white ox features importantly in the *Lotus Sūtra*'s well-known "burning house" parable. See Burton Watson, trans., *The Lotus Sutra* (New York: Columbia University Press, 1993), 56-62.

17. Powell, *The Record of Tung-shan*, 55; see his accompanying notes. Asked what the bird path was, Dongshan answered, "One doesn't encounter a single person." Subsequent Zen phrases enlarged the image: "Like the bird path, traceless" and "The empty sky has no front or back; / the bird path shatters east and west." For the former, see Hisao Inagaki, *A Glossary of Zen Terms* (Kyoto: Nagata Bunshodo, 1995), 30. For the latter, see Victor Sōgen Hori, *Zen Sand: The Book of Capping Phrases for Kōan Practice* (Honolulu: University of Hawai'i Press, 2003), item 10.163.

18. *Jingde chuanteng lu* 10. Cf. Ogata, *Transmission of the Lamp*, 332.

19. Hori, *Zen Sand*, item 10.130, translated differently.

20. Henry David Thoreau, "Higher Laws," in *Walden*. In fairness to him, let me note that Thoreau thought he found confirmation of such views in Asian sources. See Jeffrey S. Cramer's remarkable *Walden: A Fully Annotated Edition* (New Haven: Yale University Press, 2004), 210-11.

9. Apples and Oranges, Fruits of the Incomparable

1. John S. Rohsenow gives the text and his translation in *ABC Dictionary of Chinese Proverbs* (Honolulu: University of Hawai'i Press, 2002), 114.

2. For the Chinese text and alternative translations, see Red Pine, trans., *The Collected Songs of Cold Mountain* (Port Townsend, WA: Copper Canyon Press, 2000), 38-39, and Victor Sōgen Hori, *Zen Sand: The Book of Capping Phrases for Kōan Practice* (Honolulu: University of Hawai'i Press, 2003), items 10.559-560. Two more translations are in Burton Watson, trans., *Cold Mountain: One Hundred Poems by the T'ang Poet* (London: Jonathan Cape, 1972), 69, and Robert G. Hendricks, trans., *The Poetry of Han-shan* (Albany, NY: State University of New York Press, 1990), 95.

3. The final line of his verse for *Wumenguan* (*Gateless Barrier*), case 47.

4. R. H. Blyth, *Zen in English Literature and Oriental Classics* (Tokyo: Hoku-seido Press, 1942), 314n3. As genuinely as he appreciated "the comparison-less life" he saw in Zen, Blyth himself traded heavily in comparisons, most obviously when expressing his opinions on aesthetic points but also in addressing matters of other sorts, including his personal life. For an example of the former, see *Zen in English Literature*, 63-64. A particularly "odious" instance of the latter appears in Norman Waddell, ed., *Poetry and Zen:*

Letters and Uncollected Writings of R. H. Blyth (Boulder, CO: Shambhala Publications, 2022), 178.

5. Translations include D. T. Suzuki, *Manual of Zen Buddhism* (Kyoto: Eastern Buddhist Society,1935, and subsequent editions); Sheng-Yen, *The Poetry of Enlightenment* (Elmhurst, NY: Dharma Drum Publications, 1987); and Thomas Cleary, *Instant Zen: Waking Up in the Present* (Berkeley: North Atlantic Books, 1994).

6. Thomas Cleary, trans., *Sayings and Doings of Pai-chang* (Los Angeles: Center Publications, 1978), 35. In this passage and throughout the book, Dr. Cleary chose to use *reality* in place of the Sanskrit word *Dharma*, presumably because he felt the latter was, in 1978, unfamiliar to his readership. I've emended the text by restoring *Dharma*.

7. Christopher Cleary, trans., *Swampland Flowers: The Letters and Lectures of Zen Master Ta Hui* (New York: Grove Press, 1977), 137.

8. Peter Matthiessen, *Nine-Headed Dragon River: Zen Journals 1969-1982* (Boston: Shambhala Publications, 1986), 63

9. Hori, *Zen Sand*, items 6.266, 6.263, 6.267, 8.320, and 8.332.

10. *Zhaozhou lu*, item 231. Cf. Yoel Hoffman, trans., *Radical Zen: The Sayings of Jōshū* (Brookline, MA: Autumn Press, 1978), 83, and James Green, trans., *The Recorded Sayings of Zen Master Joshu* (Boston: Shambhala Publications, 1998), 84.

11. *Analects* 2.14. The first clause appears independently in Hori, *Zen Sand*, item 6.69.

12. *Zhuangzi* 8. One of many instances of Chan and Zen's appropriation of this passage occurs in case 27 of the *Congrong lu*. The verse for the case alludes to it, and Wansong then quotes it verbatim in his comments. Cf. Thomas Cleary, trans., *Book of Serenity: One Hundred Zen Dialogues* (Hudson, NY: Lindisfarne Press, 1990), 117, 118.

13. Adapted from Andrew Ferguson, trans., *Zen's Chinese Heritage* (Boston: Wisdom Publications, 2000), 427.

14. Thomas and J. C. Cleary, trans., *The Blue Cliff Record* (Boulder, CO: Shambhala Publications, 1977), 1:43.

15. Second half of the verse for case 31. Cf. Cleary, *Book of Serenity*, 138.

16. Ta-Nehisi Coates, *Between the World and Me* (New York: Spiegel and Grau, 2015), 43.

17. Coates, *Between the World*, 56. Coates uses the term "racecraft" on the same page, at least in part, I suspect, to acknowledge the work of Karen E. Fields and Barbara J. Fields, notably their book of that title.

18. W. S. Merwin, "The Artisan World," *The Moon before Morning* (Port Townsend, WA: Copper Canyon Press, 2014), 87.

19. Shakespeare, of course, "Sonnet 18."

20. Cf. Rohsenow, *ABC Dictionary*, 92.

21. Clifford Geertz, *Local Knowledge: Further Essays in Interpretive Anthropology* (New York: Basic Books, 1983), 233-34.

22. Geertz, *Local Knowledge*, 233.

10. Crossing Over: From Saving to Liberation

1. The form of the first vow so familiar to me was a translation by Robert Aitken, used by the Honolulu Diamond Sangha and many of its sister groups. Cf. Aitken, *Encouraging Words: Zen Buddhist Teachings for Western Students* (New York: Pantheon Books, 1993), 72.

2. Suzanne Simard, *Finding the Mother Tree: Discovering the Wisdom of the Forest* (New York: Alfred A. Knopf, 2021), 6.

3. The two forms of *du*—渡 or 度—are often but not always synonymous. Whereas 渡 usually refers to physically crossing a body of water, 度 often refers to a crossing that is more metaphorical, as in the Four Infinite Vows or as in a rite of passage (e.g., graduation or ordination).

4. 大度師. Cf. William Edward Soothill and Lewis Hodous, compilers, *A Dictionary of Chinese Buddhist Terms* (Delhi: Motilal Banarsidass Publishers, 1937), 88.

5. E.g., Wendi L. Adamek, *The Mystique of Transmission: On an Early Chan History and Its Contexts* (New York: Columbia University Press, 2007), 358 and n429. In this case, bridge is 橋樑.

6. The image of crossing to the other shore is at least as early as the "Sūtra of the Snake Metaphor," which is among the "Middle-length Discourses" of the Buddha. Cf. *Alagaddūpamasutta* in Robert E. Buswell Jr. and Donald S. Lopez Jr., *The Princeton Dictionary of Buddhism* (Princeton, NJ: Princeton University Press, 2014), 29.

7. The formulation of this point precedes Chan, occurring in Nāgārjuna's *Mūlamadhyamakakārika*. Chan and Zen texts often state it in terms of the kleśa rather than of samsāra per se: 煩惱是菩提.

8. So translated in Isshū Miura and Ruth Fuller Sasaki, *Zen Dust: The History of the Koan and Koan Study in Rinzai (Lin-chi) Zen* (New York: Harcourt, Brace & World, 1966), 39. The text they quote is *Jingde chuandeng lu 3*. Cf. Sohaku Ogata, trans., *The Transmission of the Lamp: Early Masters* (Wolfeboro, NH: Longwood Academic, 1990), 69.

9. Burton Watson, trans., *Cold Mountain: 100 Poems by the T'ang Poet* (London: Jonathan Cape, 1972), 67.

10. John R. McRae, trans., *The Platform Sutra of the Sixth Patriarch* (Berkeley: Numata Center for Buddhist Translation and Research, 1998), 35-36, lightly emended. This tale, from what McRae calls the "mature version" of the

Platform Sutra, dates from the late thirteenth century. See Philip B. Yampolsky, *The Platform Sutra of the Sixth Patriarch* (New York: Columbia University Press, 1967) for the evolution of the Huineng legend and a translation of the earliest edition of the text found thus far, set down five centuries before the "mature version."

11. Excerpted and adapted from J. C. Cleary and Thomas Cleary, trans., *Zen Letters: Teachings of Yuanwu* (Boston: Shambhala Publications, 1994), 28.

12. Soyen Shaku, *Zen for Americans* (New York: Dorset Press, 1987), 201, an unabridged reprint of his 1913 book *Sermons of a Buddhist Abbot.* Its ardent wording is likely to reflect the judgment of the translator, his student D. T. Suzuki, more than Shaku Sōen's own rhetoric. I've substituted the word *compassion* for *love,* since Suzuki noted parenthetically two pages earlier that he used *love* for the Sanskrit *karunā,* which scholars almost invariably translate as "compassion."

13. 悟性論 "The Awakening to Nature Treatise." Cf. Red Pine, trans., *The Zen Teaching of Bodhidharma* (Port Townsend, WA: Empty Bowl, 1987), 25 (Chinese text on facing page). My thanks to Peter Wong Yih Jiun for providing me the corrected text from CBETA 2022.Q1, T48, no. 2009, pp. 370c29-371a15: 迷時有此岸。悟時無此岸。何以故。為凡夫一向住此。若覺最上乘者。心不住此。亦不住彼。故能離於此彼岸也。若見彼岸異於此岸。此人之心已無禪定。.

14. *Zhaozhou lu,* item 332, and case 52 of the *Piyan lu.* Cf. Thomas and J. C. Cleary, trans., *The Blue Cliff Record* (Boulder, CO: Shambhala Publications, 1977), 2:353.

15. James Green gives the inverse translation in *The Recorded Sayings of Zen Master Joshu* (Boston: Shambhala Publications, 1998) 107-08. Cleary and Cleary make the bridge the proper subject but add the idea that the bridge "lets" the animals cross: *Blue Cliff Record,* 2:353.

16. *Zhaozhou lu,* item 506. Cf. Green, *Recorded Sayings,* 164-65, and Yoel Hoffman, trans., *Radical Zen: The Sayings of Jōshū* (Brookline, MA: Autumn Press, 1978), 155. It appears as a kōan in Thomas Yūhō Kirchner, trans., *Entangling Vines: A Classic Collection of Zen Koans,* 2nd ed. (Boston: Wisdom Publications, 2013), 202.

17. W. S. Merwin and Sōiku Shigematsu, trans., *Sun at Midnight: Poems and Sermons by Musō Soseki* (San Francisco: North Point Press, 1989), 114.

18. Specimens of both Hakuin's bridge motifs may be found in John Stevens and Alice Rae Yelen, *Zenga: Brushstrokes of Enlightenment* (New Orleans: New Orleans Museum of Art, 1990), 132-33 and 142-43. The painting I describe is illustrated in Miura and Sasaki, *Zen Dust,* 129. Many thanks to Hakuin specialist Norman Waddell for translating the inscription from p. 128 of that text. In *Penetrating Laughter: Hakuin's Zen and Art* (Woodstock, NY: Overlook Press, 1984), 103, Kazuaki Tanahashi notes that the latter works

involve a pun on the location of the bridge—a place called Mama—and the Japanese word *mama*, "just as it is."

19. Verse for *Blue Cliff Record* case 58, alluding to a legend that Bodhidharma made the river crossing on a single reed.

20. Verse for case 80 of the *Congrong lu*. Cf. Thomas Cleary, trans., *Book of Serenity: One Hundred Zen Dialogues* (Hudson, NY: Lindisfarne Press, 1990), 342.

21. *Blue Cliff Record* case 18.

22. Pointer to *Congrong lu* case 63. Cf. Cleary, *Book of Serenity,* 264.

23. In Dōgen's "Genjōkōan," of which we have several translations. I've quoted it from Francis H. Cook, *Sounds of Valley Streams* (Albany: State University of New York Press, 1989), 66.

24. This poem is well known in the West thanks to Gary Snyder's 1958 translation; cf. *Riprap and Cold Mountain Poems* (San Francisco: North Point Press, 1990), 57. See also Robert G. Henricks, trans., *The Poetry of Han-shan: A Complete, Annotated Translation of* Cold Mountain (Albany: State University of New York Press, 1990), 181, and Red Pine, trans., *The Collected Songs of Cold Mountain* (Port Townsend, WA: Copper Canyon Press, 2000), 159.

25. Excerpted from Norman Waddell, *The Old Tea Seller: Life and Zen Poetry in 18th Century Kyoto* (Berkeley: Counterpoint Press, 2008), 117.

26. Burton Watson, trans., *Po Chü-i: Selected Poems* (New York: Columbia University Press, 2000), 52.

27. Cleary, *Book of Serenity,* 251. Slightly adapted.

28. Waddell, *Old Tea Seller,* 161-62, with *yaojin* (or *yao-chin*; J., *yōshin)* there translated as "Essential Crossing." (The expression zhiyin, discussed in chapter 3, occurs in the poem's last line, given as "knowing friends.") 要津 *yaojin* crops up at least three times in the *Blue Cliff Record*: in the pointers to cases 22 and 60 and in Yuanwu's comment on the verse for case 99. The expression often appears in reverse order but with the same meaning: 津要 *jinyao.*

29. This text, the 觀心輪 or 破相論, is attributed to Bodhidharma but of later vintage. Cf. Red Pine, trans., *The Zen Teaching of Bodhidharma* (Port Townsend, WA: Empty Bowl, 1987), 55 (Chinese text on the facing page), and J.C. Cleary, trans., *Zen Dawn: Early Zen Texts from Tun Huang* (Boston: Shambhala Publications, 1986), 101. "Critical ford" *guanjin* (or *kuan-chin*; J., *kanshin)* is 關津.

30. Cf. Ruth Fuller Sasaki, trans. and Thomas Yūhō Kirchner, ed., *The Record of Linji* (Honolulu: University of Hawai'i Press, 2009), 345-46, and Burton Watson, trans., *The Zen Teachings of Master Lin-chi* (Boston: Shambhala Publications, 1993), 3. Watson presents the text as prose.

31. The story of Qingshou (or Ch'ing-shou) awakening at the ford is told in *Goads for Advancing through the Chan Barriers*, the *Changuan cejin* (or *Ch'an-kuan*

ts'e-chin; J., *Zenkan sakushin*), published in 1600. Cf. Jeffrey F. Broughton and Elise Yoko Watanabe, trans., *The Chan Whip Anthology: A Companion to Zen Practice* (Oxford: Oxford University Press, 2015), 141-42 (English) and 190 (Chinese), and J. C. Cleary, trans., *Meditating with Koans* (Berkeley: Asian Humanities Press, 1992), 90. The words I've translated as *compassion* and *joy*, 悲 and 喜, are Chinese stand-ins for *karunā* and *muditā*. If the story seems too good to be merely factual, maybe it is; his errand was taking him to a town with the suspicious name of 睢陽 Huiyang, Lifting One's Eyes to the Sunlight, and the crossing he bypassed was 趙渡 Zhaodu, Hastened-to Crossing.

32. This image dates back at least to the twelfth century, when Yuanwu utilized it in one of his letters; see Cleary and Cleary, *Zen Letters*, 38. A boat laden with moonlight also figures in the verse to case 50 of the *Congrong lu*; cf. Cleary, *Book of Serenity*, 212. The image earned a place in the Zen phrase books, too; cf. Victor Sōgen Hori, *Zen Sand: The Book of Capping Phrases for Kōan Practice* (Honolulu: University of Hawai'i Press, 2003), item 7.448.

33. The sayings "White sea grasses..." and "The old ferry landing..." appear in Hori, *Zen Sand*, items 14.549 and 16.24, respectively. The former translation is his, the latter mine.

34. Although mainstream Chan and Zen teachers, even in medieval times, have demonstrated little taste for stories of celestial intervention, they've also felt free to tell them to score a point. For example, Hakuin made outlandish tales a staple of talks and writings geared for unsophisticated audiences, utilizing the tales to persuade such audiences that misconduct reaps disaster and that Zen practice brings wondrous rewards. For example, see Norman Waddell, ed. and trans., *Hakuin's Precious Mirror Cave: A Zen Miscellany* (Berkeley: Counterpoint, 2009), 47ff.

35. A use of *jiu* in the physical sense occurs in the notorious story of Nanquan killing a cat (*Blue Cliff Record*, cases 63-64, and *Wumenguan* case 14). Had Zhaozhou been present, Nanquan concludes, the cat would have been *rescued*.

36. *Zhaozhou lu*, item 5. Cf. Green, *Recorded Sayings*, 13, and Kirchner, *Entangling Vines*, 98.

37. *Platform Sutra,* sec. 53. Cf. Yampolsky, *Platform Sutra*, 181, and Red Pine, trans., *The Platform Sutra: The Zen Teaching of Hui-neng* (Emeryville, CA: Shoemaker and Hoard, 2006), 266. Later editions of the text give it in a slightly different form.

38. Dōgen, "Bendōwa." Cf. Norman Waddell and Masao Abe, trans., *The Heart of Dōgen's Shōbōgenzō* (Albany: State University of New York Press, 2002), 9, and Kazuaki Tanahashi, trans., *Moon in a Dewdrop: Writings of Zen Master Dōgen* (San Francisco: North Point Press, 1985), 144.

39. *Wei* 為 (J., *i*).

40. The salvationist translations are from Cleary and Cleary, *Blue Cliff Record*, 3:559, and Sasaki and Kirchner, *Record of Linji*, 51. Others who adopt this reading include Hisao Inagaki in *A Glossary of Zen Terms* (Kyoto: Nagata Bunshodo, 1995), 131, and Hori, *Zen Sand*, item 7.448.

41. *Zhaozhou lu*, items 385 and 386. Cf. Green, *Recorded Sayings*, 122, and Hoffman, *Radical Zen*, 119.

42. I owe my first acquaintance with the Oxherding Pictures to Philip Kapleau's *The Three Pillars of Zen* (Boston: Beacon Press, 1965), 301-13.

43. I've chosen to use Hotei, the Japanese rendering of his name, since it's familiar to English speakers. In a Chinese pronunciation, it's 布袋 Budai or Pu-tai.

44. Suzuki's translation appears in his *Manual of Zen Buddhism* (1935) (New York: Causeway Books, 1974), 134.

45. The phrase "dangling hands," 垂手 *chuishou* (or *ch'ui-shou*; J., *suishu*), shouldn't be confused with 叉手 *chashou* (or *ch'a-shou*; J., *shashu*), a formal posture of cupping one hand over the other, held to the chest, or with 撒手 *sashou* (or *sa-shou*; J., *sasshu*), which means loosening or opening one's hands, letting go. For an interpretation of *chuishou*, see Hori, *Zen Sand*, 710.

46. He was addressing case 43 of the *Blue Cliff Record*, where the expression appears in the initial line of the verse; see *Kyō Shō*, no. 283 (July-August, 2000): 34.

47. The image of a withered or sometimes "iron" tree blossoming, besides occurring repeatedly in Chan and Zen literature, has currency in wider Chinese culture as a proverb of good luck. See John Rohsenow, *ABC Dictionary of Chinese Proverbs* (Honolulu: University of Hawai'i Press, 2002), 189. For examples in Chan and Zen texts, see *Blue Cliff Record*, case 40, pointer; Hori, *Zen Sand*, item 7.326; Ross Bolleter, *Dongshan's Five Ranks: Keys to Enlightenment* (Boston: Wisdom Publications, 2014), 5; and Morten Schlütter, *How Zen Became Zen* (Honolulu: University of Hawai'i Press, 2008), 163.

48. For such explications of the final Oxherding Picture, see Kapleau, *Three Pillars*, 312-13, especially n17, and Yamada Mumon, *Lectures on the Ten Oxherding Pictures* (Honolulu: University of Hawai'i Press, 2004), 95-102, especially p. 101.

49. *A Journey to the West*: cf. Anthony C. Yu, trans. and ed., *The Monkey and the Monk: An Abridgment of "The Journey to the West"* (Chicago: University of Chicago Press, 2006). The episode I cite comes near the book's end, pp. 452-54. For the life and work of the actual seventh-century monk, see Benjamin Brose, *Xuanzang: China's Legendary Pilgrim and Translator* (Boulder, CO: Shambhala Publications, 2021).

50. I've attributed this statement from Miura and Sasaki, *Zen Dust*, 228, to

Sasaki since she exercised full authorial control over the entire volume except for part 2.

51. As given in the *Denkōroku*, which dates from 1300. For the Chinese text and a different translation, see T. Griffith Foulk, ed., *Record of the Transmission of Illumination* (Honolulu: University of Hawai'i Press, 2021), 1:88. For the evolution of the greater bodhi tree legend as told in Chan texts, see Miura and Sasaki, *Zen Dust*, 253–55.

52. *Platform Sutra*, sec. 21. Cf. Yampolsky, *Platform Sutra of the Sixth Patriarch*, 143, and Red Pine, *Platform Sutra*, 158.

53. Instances of such expressions are numerous. See, for example, Urs App, trans., *Master Yunmen: From the Record of the Chan Teacher "Gate of the Clouds"* (New York: Kodansha International, 1994), 157; Waddell, *Hakuin's Precious Mirror Cave*, 9; and Cleary and Cleary, *Blue Cliff Record*, 1:20.

54. Scholars attribute the formula "Above, seeking bodhi; below, affecting all beings" to Zhiyi, the renowned sixth-century founder of the Tiantai school. Its incorporation into Zen is attested by, among other things, its presence in the Zen phrasebooks. See Hori, *Zen Sand*, item 8.215. The limits of its acceptance may be seen in the *Blue Cliff Record*, where Yuanwu implores students to "spit out" the above-below doctrine along with any ideas of inside and outside. See Cleary and Cleary, *Blue Cliff Record*, 1:167.

55. Eisai's gift and defense thereof are recounted in the *Shōbōgenzō Zuimonki*, a record of informal presentations by Dōgen Zenji. My version is based on three translations: Ryusaku Tsunoda et al., *Sources of Japanese Tradition* (New York: Columbia University Press, 1958), 248; Reihō Masunaga, trans., *A Primer of Sōtō Zen* (Honolulu: University of Hawai'i Press, 1971), 27–28; and Thomas Cleary, trans., *Record of Things Heard: From the Treasury of the Eye of the True Teaching* (Boulder, CO: Prajna Press, 1980), 28–29.

56. Regarding merit-making as an inferior path, see, for example, lines 92–99 of the *Zhengdao ge*, the "Song of Realizing the Way."

57. Quoted in John Kieschnick, *The Impact of Buddhism on Chinese Material Culture* (Princeton, NJ: Princeton University Press, 2003), 201.

58. Chan notables reputed to have served as ferrymen famously include Yantou (or Yen-t'ou; J., Gantō) and Chuanzi (or Ch'uan-tzu; J., Sensu).

59. Kieschnick's excellent *The Impact of Buddhism on Chinese Material Culture* also is my source for sangha involvement in bridge construction, including the statistic on the number of bridges built during the Song dynasty in Fujian (or Fu-chien) province, p. 204.

60. Bernard Faure, *The Rhetoric of Immediacy: A Cultural Critique of Chan/Zen Buddhism* (Princeton, NJ: Princeton University Press, 1991), 127–28. Quotation lightly emended.

61. Norman Waddell, trans., *Complete Poison Blossoms from a Thicket of Thorn: The Zen Records of Hakuin Ekaku* (Berkeley: Counterpoint Press, 2017),

371-72. I owe thanks again to Dr. Waddell, in this instance for furnishing the text of the key passage, enabling me to emend his own translation for purposes of this essay. Here Hakuin used 濟 *ji* (or *chi*; J., *sai* or *sei*), yet another Chinese word that denotes crossing a river or helping someone else to cross, sometimes coupled with *du* as a compound.

62. Amitābha's image has customarily been honored in monastic infirmaries but, even there, is held in a manner significantly different than in the Pure Land tradition. Cf. Marsha Weidner, ed., *Cultural Intersections in Later Chinese Buddhism* (Honolulu: University of Hawai'i Press, 2001), 28-29. For an amusing story that typifies this difference in view, see Zenkei Shibayama, *Zen Comments on the Mumonkan* (New York: Harper & Row, 1974), 81.

63. *Fengxue Chanshi yulu.* My thanks to Benjamin Brose for providing the text, from CBETA, X68, no. 1315, p. 45, a10-11 // Z 2:23, p. 121, d3-4 // R118, p. 242, b3-4: 道在乘時須濟物。遠方來慕自騰騰。他年有叟情相似。日日香烟夜夜燈.

64. Miura and Sasaki, *Zen Dust*, 271. The verb that I translate as "carry over" and that Sasaki renders "save" is *ji* 濟, the same word that Hakuin used in soliciting funds to build the Yahata bridge. Lamp is 燈 *deng* (or *teng*; J., *tō*), as in the well-worn expression "transmitting the lamp."

11. Walking in the Dark

1. Robert Macfarlane brilliantly enriches and complicates this old narrative with *Underland: A Deep Time Journey* (Hamish Hamilton, 2019).

2. Sigmund Freud, *New Introductory Lectures on Psycho-Analysis*, The Standard Edition of the Complete Psychological Works of Sigmund Freud, ed. James Strachey, vol. 22 (London: Hogarth Press, 1932-1936).

3. Alex Riley, *A Cure for Darkness: The Story of Depression and How We Treat It* (New York: Scribner, 2022).

4. Fintan O'Toole published a detailed assessment of the dark-light imagery in Biden's acceptance speech and of its implications: "Night and Day," *New York Review of Books* (September 24, 2022): 34-37. He counts seven references to dark or darkness, twelve to light or bright.

5. John 8:12.

6. Jonathan Weisman and Annie Karni, "G.O.P. Leaders Condemn Lawmakers' Appearance at White Nationalist Conference," www.nytimes.com/2022/02/28/us/politics/republicans-extremism.html. The event she addressed was the America First Political Action Conference.

7. John R. Stilgoe, *What Is Landscape?* (Cambridge, MA: MIT Press, 2015), 93-94, gives a lovely logical and etymological exposition of the positive relationship between *glade* and *glad*.

8. Dylan Thomas, "Do Not Go Gentle into That Good Night."

9. Philip B. Yampolsky, *The Platform Sutra of the Sixth Patriarch* (New York:

Columbia University Press, 1967), 173. See also p. 82: "The nature of light and darkness is not two."

10. *Cantong qi* (or *Ts'an-t'ung-ch'i*; J., *Sandōkai*), lines 27-32. The text is open to widely differing translations, examples being Sheng-Yen, *The Poetry of Enlightenment: Poems by Ancient Ch'an Masters* (Elmhurst, NY: Dharma Drum Publications, 1987), 69-70, and Stephen Addiss et al., eds., *Zen Sourcebook: Traditional Documents from China, Korea, and Japan* (Indianapolis: Hackett Publishing, 2008), 31-33. The *Cantong qi* and many other texts pair light, 明 *ming*, with the conventional term for darkness, 暗 *an*, rather than with 無明 *wuming*. *An*, too, may connote ignorance, so the metaphor remains intact. *Wuming* seems to be reserved specifically to translate *avidyā*.

11. *Wanling Record*. Cf. John Blofeld, trans., *The Zen Teaching of Huang Po: On the Transmission of Mind* (New York: Grove Weidenfeld, 1958), 76. Blofeld's translation is seriously flawed but, to the best of my knowledge, the only one in print. A scholarly translation by Jeffrey A. Leahy (with the Chinese text) is available online at ia902907.us.archive.org/24/items /wanlingrecordofchanmasterhuangboduanjithesis_78_Q/Wanling%20 Record%20of%20Chan%20Master%20Huangbo%20Duanji%20Thesis .pdf, with Leahy's translation of this passage on p. 30.

12. Cf. Thomas Cleary and J. C. Cleary, trans., *The Blue Cliff Record* (Boulder, CO: Shambhala Publications, 1977), 3:554.

13. From a poem about Zhaozhou's daily round, this verse describes the tenth of twelve periods in a medieval Chinese day, roughly corresponding to 7:00 to 9:00 p.m. Cf. James Green, trans., *The Recorded Sayings of Zen Master Joshu* (Boston: Shambhala Publications, 1998), 174.

14. *Blue Cliff Record* case 64, comment on the verse. Cf. Cleary and Cleary, *Blue Cliff Record*, 2:410.

15. Pointer for case 69 of the *Congrong lu*. Cf. Thomas Cleary, trans., *Book of Serenity* (Hudson, NY: Lindisfarne Press, 1990), 290.

16. In Kenneth Kraft, *Eloquent Zen: Daitō and Early Japanese Zen* (Honolulu: University of Hawai'i Press, 1992), 214 (Chinese text), 202 (his translation), and 197 (an example of Daitō's use). Hori's *Zen Sand: The Book of Capping Phrases for Kōan Practice* (Honolulu: University of Hawai'i Press, 2003), item 14.179, cites another phrase referring to Jiange (or Chien Ko), noting that it was a "mountain stronghold," which jibes perfectly with Daitō's phrase.

17. *Blue Cliff Record*, case 41, and *Congrong lu*, case 63. Cf. Cleary and Cleary, *Blue Cliff Record*, 2:297, and Cleary, *Book of Serenity*, 264.

12. How the World Works

1. *Jingde chuandeng lu* 3. My translation of 本 as "rootstock" is unusual but justifiable in this context and supported by Paul W. Kroll, *A Student's Dictio-*

nary of Classical and Medieval Chinese, rev. ed. (Leiden: Brill, 2017), 14. For more conventional translations, see Sohaku Ogata, trans., *The Transmission of the Lamp: Early Masters* (Wolfeboro, NH: Longwood Academic, 1990), 71, and Victor Sōgen Hori, *Zen Sand: The Book of Capping Phrases for Kōan Practice* (Honolulu: University of Hawai'i Press, 2003), items 10.566-67.

2. *Daodejing* 25. The verb used in all four lines, 法 *fa*, may be translated many ways: to model upon, to emulate, to follow, to take as a standard. As a noun, it long ago became the usual Chinese rendering of the Sanskrit *dharma*.

3. Final sentence of the latter of two texts titled *Fukanzazengi*. Writing in the form known as *kanbun*, which melds Japanese and Chinese, Dōgen rendered *ziran* as 自ずから rather than as 自然. It seems noteworthy to me that he closed the earlier iteration of the passage with an imperative instruction to open the storehouse; the revision suggests that his own appreciation of ziran may have grown in the interval between editions. Cf. Carl Bielefeldt, *Dōgen's Manuals of Meditation* (Berkeley: University of California Press, 1988), 187. Many thanks to Norman Waddell for his generous assistance in translating this passage.

4. Excerpts in my own version from the "Baika" chapter of the *Shōbōgenzō*. Cf. Kazuaki Tanahashi, trans., *Moon in a Dewdrop: Writings of Zen Master Dōgen* (San Francisco: North Point Press, 1985), 114-23. Dōgen quotes the Bodhidharma verse in full on p. 118 and alludes also to a verse by his teacher Rujing.

5. Virgil, *Georgics*, book ii, line 490.

6. Dr. Wilson made this particular statement in the 1998 Phi Beta Kappa oration at Harvard, published in *Harvard Magazine* (July-August 1998): 58. It sums up convictions he published in more detail in a book of the same year, *Consilience: The Unity of Knowledge*. His conclusions were rejected by other prominent scientists, notably Niles Eldredge and Stephen Jay Gould writing in the magazine *Civilization* (October-November 1998), and inspired a withering critique, too, from man of farm, field, and letters Wendell Berry in *Life Is a Miracle: An Essay Against Modern Superstition* (Washington, DC: Counterpoint, 2000).

7. I've drawn this brief sample of pre-1500 Chinese scientific and technological achievements from a much longer, remarkable list in Simon Winchester, *The Man Who Loved China: The Fantastic Story of the Eccentric Scientist Who Unlocked the Mysteries of the Middle Kingdom* (New York: Harper, 2008), 267-77. Why the Chinese made such great discoveries before 1500 but didn't fully exploit their potential or continue these advances is a question with a fascinating history of its own. Restraint premised on teachings of ziran jibes neatly with the concise answer Winchester gives on p. 260: "China, basically, *stopped trying* [italics his]." He recounts more explicit theories as well on pp. 260-61.

8. Needham is the subject of Winchester's *The Man Who Loved China* and originator of the multivolumed study *Science and Civilization in China*.

9. See Robert Sharf's *Coming to Terms with Chinese Buddhism: A Reading of the Treasure Store Treatise* (Honolulu: University of Hawai'i Press, 2002), 82-88, for a general exposition of 感應 *ganying* (or *kan-ying*; J., *kannō*), which he translates as "sympathetic resonance." For the *Zhuangzi* passage, cf. Burton Watson, trans., *The Complete Works of Chuang Tzu* (New York: Columbia University Press, 1968), 267-68.

10. Translated from the *Wenyen*, one of ten classical texts annotating the *Yijing*, a comment on the first hexagram thereof.

11. *Analects* 9.14.

12. From a commentary on the *Shanhai jing*, or *Classic of Mountains and Seas*, quoted in François Jullien, *In Praise of Blandness: Proceeding from Chinese Thought and Aesthetics* (New York: Zone Books, 2004), 82.

13. I'm grateful to Peter Wong Yih Jiun for notes on evolving uses and implications of *ji*. Also, for its strategic implications, see François Jullien, *A Treatise on Efficacy: Between Western and Chinese Thinking* (Honolulu: University of Hawai'i Press, 2004), 66-69.

14. *Xinxin ming*, lines 66-69 and 112-17.

15. Cf. Red Pine, trans., *The Collected Songs of Cold Mountain* (Port Townsend, WA: Copper Canyon Press, 2000), 178-79, and Robert G. Hendricks, trans., *The Poetry of Han-shan* (Albany, NY: State University of New York Press, 1990), 294. The final words 無背面 "with no back/reverse [or] face/surface" indicate an unimpeded view, vision without blind spots.

16. *Zhaozhou lu*, item 121. Cf. James Green, trans., *The Recorded Sayings of Zen Master Joshu* (Boston: Shambhala Publications, 1998), 50 and Yoel Hoffman, trans., *Radical Zen: The Sayings of Jōshū* (Brookline, MA: Autumn Press, 1978), 51.

17. *Zhengdao ge* opening: 君不見絕學無為閒道人。不除妄想不求真. The first three graphs make this a question: "Haven't you seen [or met]" such a person?

18. *Daodejing* 63 opens with these words. *Wushi* features also in chapters 48 and 57.

19. Cf. Ruth Fuller Sasaki, trans. and Thomas Yūhō Kirchner, ed., *The Record of Linji* (Honolulu: University of Hawai'i Press, 2009), 185, and Burton Watson, trans., *The Zen Teachings of Master Lin-chi* (Boston: Shambhala Publications, 1993), 31.

20. Cf. Sasaki and Kirchner, *Record of Linji*, 178 and Watson, *Zen Teachings*, 29.

21. Cf. Hori, *Zen Sand*, item 10.177.

22. Cf. Thomas Yūhō Kirchner, trans., *Entangling Vines: A Classic Collection of Zen Koans*, 2nd ed. (Boston: Wisdom Publications, 2013), 183.

23. *Jingde chuandeng lu* 2. Cf. Ogata, *Transmission of the Lamp*, 38. Hakuin Zenji affirms the unity of cause and effect in his *Zazen wasan* or "Song of

Zazen," using the phrase *inga ichinyo,* literally, cause-effect one alike: "The gate of *inga ichinyo* opens; / the way of not-two, not-three runs straight."

24. Fayan, *Zongmen shigui lun,* "Treatise on Ten Criteria for the Ancestral Gate," sec. 10.

25. J. C. Cleary and Thomas Cleary, trans., *Zen Letters: Teachings of Yuanwu* (Boston: Shambhala Publications, 1994), 26.

26. From his 中華傳心地禪門師資承襲圖 *Zhonghua chuanxindi Chanmen shizi chengxitu* (or *Chung-hua ch'uan-hsin-ti Ch'an-men shih-tzu ch'eng-hsi t'u*). I encountered this passage first in a partial translation by Robert E. Buswell, Jr., in Peter Gregory, ed., *Sudden and Gradual: Approaches to Enlightenment in Chinese Thought* (Honolulu: University of Hawai'i Press, 1987), 333. I owe thanks again to Peter Wong for obtaining the full Chinese text for me and for counsel on my translation. Its final sentence mirrors the wording of a pre-Chan text favored by masters of the school, the *Treatise on the Storehouse of Treasures* (*Baozang lun*), where it's explicitly linked to ganying. The older text reads, 應用無極 "Ying-function has no end-point," while Zongmi's statement is 應用無窮 "Ying-function has no bounds." Cf., Sharf, *Coming to Terms,* 163.

27. Yūhō Yokoi, *The Japanese-English Zen Buddhist Dictionary* (Tokyo: Sankibō Buddhist Bookstore, 1991), 342, defines *kannō dōkō* as "A spiritual communion between the Buddha and all beings or master and disciple."

28. Dōgen quotes Rujing thus in *Hōkyō-ki,* his record of his experience in China, secs. 10 and 22.

29. Dōgen, *Hotsu bodai shin,* "Bringing Forth the Mind of Bodhi," in the twelve-chapter edition of the *Shōbōgenzō,* not to be confused with a different text under the same title in the sixty-three-chapter edition. I'm grateful to Carl Bielefeldt for allowing me early access to a magisterial new translation of the *Shōbōgenzō* produced under his direction; my translation owes much to the one therein. The passage is translated also in Hee-jin Kim, *Dōgen Kigen: Mystical Realist* (Tucson: University of Arizona Press, 1987), 117.

30. Thomas Cleary, trans., *Zen Lessons: The Art of Leadership* (Boston: Shambhala Publications, 1989), 37. I've liberally emended this passage.

31. Yuanwu repeats this adage in his pointers for cases 3, 8, and 79 of *The Blue Cliff Record.* Cf. Thomas and J. C. Cleary, trans., *The Blue Cliff Record* (Boulder, CO: Shambhala Publications, 1977), 1:18, 53, and 3:514. It also passed into the Zen phrasebooks; cf. Hori, *Zen Sand,* item 8.268.

32. I've selected these from Hisao Inagaki, *A Glossary of Zen Terms* (Kyoto: Nagata Bunshodo, 1995), 41, 189, 190, 434-35, 190, 191, and 404. See chapter 6, note 15, for another such phrase, 機鋒 *jifeng,* meaning "dynamic spear-point" and referring to the incisive way a master may probe a student.

33. Hori, *Zen Sand,* 678.

34. Activating (i.e., awakening) words and corresponding verse: *jiyu* (or *chi-yu;*

J., *kigo*) and *toujiji* (or *t'ou-chi chi*; J., *tōkinoge*). An example of the latter, by Yuanwu, is in Kirchner, *Entangling Vines*, 94.

35. For a sense of ji's place in the Daoist critique of youwei, see Ellen M. Chen, trans., *The Tao Te Ching: A New Translation with Commentary* (New York: Paragon House, 1989), 228-29. She notes the word's absence from that text and points out its implied presence in a condemnation of weaponry.

36. Hori, *Zen Sand*, items 8.23 and 8.18.

37. Pointer for case 98 or, alternatively, case 100 of *The Blue Cliff Record*.

38. In Thomas Cleary, trans., *Zen Essence: The Science of Freedom* (Boston: Shambhala Publications, 1989), 65 (emended). Its line about the first step is borrowed from *Daodejing* 64.

39. Unpublished translation by Benjamin Brose and myself, lines 218-19.

40. "Business and Zen: A Dialogue between Zen Master Mumon Yamada and Supermarket Tycoon Isao Nakauchi" (Kyoto: Ittoen, 1978), 18, 19. This booklet was published to honor Yamada Mumon on the occasion of his installation as chief abbot of the Myōshin-ji branch of Rinzai Zen. Nakauchi established the Daiei chain of supermarkets.

41. The master Lingyuan, in Cleary, *Zen Lessons*, 50.

42. Fortunately we have such books available, and my sketch is indebted to them. A classic is Frederick W. Mote, *Intellectual Foundations of China* (New York: McGraw-Hill, Inc., 1971; 2nd ed., 1989). Still more deeply informed are a pair of studies by David L. Hall and Roger T. Ames, *Anticipating China: Thinking Through the Narratives of Chinese and Western Culture* (Albany: State University of New York Press, 1995) and *Thinking from the Han: Self, Truth, and Transcendence in Chinese and Western Culture* (Albany: State University of New York Press, 1998).

43. Cited by Dahui in his *Zhengfayanzang* (or *Cheng fa-yen tsang*), item 48. Thomas Cleary, trans., *Treasury of the Eye of True Teaching* (Boulder, CO: Shambhala Publications, 2022), 34. For clarity's sake, I've emended the final word of this translation, changing Cleary's "provenance" to the simpler "origin."

44. "Opens" is 開, and "opening ancestor" is 開祖. As for the five petals, two interpretations are usually made: Bodhidharma's five successors or the so-called "five houses" described in later Chan and Zen chronicles.

45. 果 *guo* (or *kuo*; J., *ka*).

13. To Know Enough, to Know Contentment

1. A shorter, much different version of this chapter appeared in the final issue of *Wild Duck Review* (winter 2000) under the title "Is There No Limit? On Cultivating Contentment." I completed its present iteration before the pub-

lication of Mary L. Trump's *Too Much and Never Enough: How My Family Created the World's Most Dangerous Man* (2020), and I haven't read it. But her title is so neatly congruent with the content of the essay as to be a bit creepy and somehow poignant.

2. Ellen M. Chen, *The Tao Te Ching: A New Translation with Commentary* (New York: Paragon House, 1989), 230.

3. *Daodejing* 46. If *zu* were translated as "enough" in each instance, the final lines would read, "So enough of knowing enough— / how perpetually enough!" Several other sections of the *Daodejing* sound the theme as well: "Those who know enough have abundance" (33) and "Knowing enough prevents dishonor" (44).

4. *Zhuangzi* 12. For other translations, see Burton Watson, trans., *The Complete Works of Chuang Tzu* (New York: Columbia University Press, 1968), 127-28, and Victor H. Mair, trans., *Wandering on the Way: Early Taoist Tales and Parables of Chuang Tzu* (Honolulu: University of Hawai'i Press, 1994), 104.

5. *Analects* 6.11. Zen phrasebooks include this passage, and modern masters have continued to quote it to their students. See, for example, Soko Morinaga, *Novice to Master: An Ongoing Lesson in the Extent of My Own Stupidity*, trans. Belinda Attaway (Boston: Wisdom Publications, 2002), 38.

6. *Analects* 7.16.

7. Cf. J. C. Cleary, trans., "The Bequeathed Teaching Sutra," in *Apocryphal Scriptures* (Berkeley: Numata Center of Buddhist Translation and Research, 2005), 11. Whoever fabricated this ersatz sūtra bolstered its credibility by attaching to it the name of the famed translator Kumārajīva and putting it into circulation during the period when Kumārajīva himself was working.

8. Cf. Burton Watson, trans., *The Vimalakirti Sutra* (New York: Columbia University Press, 1996), 127, and Luis Gómez and Paul Harrison, eds., *The Teaching of Vimalakīrti* (Berkeley: Mangalam Press, 2022), 115.

9. *Platform Sutra*, sec. 23. Cf. Philip B. Yampolsky, *The Platform Sutra of the Sixth Patriarch* (New York: Columbia University Press, 1967), 145.

10. Lanzan (or Lan-tsan; J., Ransan). *Lan* 懶 might also be translated as "slothful," "indolent," "shiftless," "reluctant," etc.

11. Thomas and J. C. Cleary, trans., *The Blue Cliff Record* (Boulder, CO: Shambhala Publications, 1977), 1:214.

12. Cf. Thomas Cleary, trans., *Zen Lessons: The Art of Leadership* (Boston: Shambhala Publications, 1989), 4. According to other sources, Cleary badly misdates the emperor's invitation. For the Chinese text, see CBETA 2020. Q1, T48, no. 2022, 1017a15-19.

13. Dōgen, *Hachidainingaku*. Cf. Thomas Cleary, trans., *Shōbōgenzō: Zen Essays by Dōgen* (Honolulu: University of Hawai'i Press, 1986), 112, and Kazuaki

Tanahashi, trans., *Enlightenment Unfolds: The Essential Teachings of Zen Master Dōgen* (Boston: Shambhala, 1999), 270-71.

14. Cf. Sonja Arntzen, trans., *Ikkyū and the Crazy Cloud Anthology: A Zen Poet of Medieval Japan* rev. 2nd ed. (Melbourne: Quirin Press, 2022), 145-46.

15. Ryūichi Abé and Peter Haskel, trans., *Great Fool: Zen Master Ryōkan; Poems, Letters, and Other Writings* (Honolulu: University of Hawai'i Press, 1996), 196, 120.

16. The late Maezumi Rōshi of the Zen Center of Los Angeles offered a rare treatment of the topic in a commentary on Dōgen's *Hachidainingaku.* See Hakuyu Taizan Maezumi and Bernard Tetsugen Glassman, *The Hazy Moon of Enlightenment* (Los Angeles: Center Publications, 1977), 90-92.

17. In Eido Shimano, ed., *Like a Dream, Like a Fantasy: The Zen Writings and Translations of Nyogen Senzaki* (Tokyo: Japan Publications, Inc., 1978), 30. In a letter four months earlier, Senzaki told a correspondent that the ten or twelve people who joined him for daily zazen were "the happiest and most contented evacuees in this center." *Eloquent Silence: Nyogen Senzaki's Gateless Gate and Other Previously Unpublished Teachings and Letters,* ed. Roko Sherry Chayat (Boston: Wisdom Publications, 2008), 305.

18. I quote Schor from a roundup of related research: John Cassidy, "No Satisfaction," *New Yorker* (January 25, 1999): 90.

19. The U.S. Census Bureau determined that a single-family home in 2015 averaged 2,687 square feet. The average size of new homes in the United States has increased more than a thousand square feet since 1973. Statistics on U.S. vs. European home space: "Alabama, France of the South," *Atlantic Magazine* (September 2004).

20. On "needs" as a clouded factor in environmental debates, see Paul Kingsnorth, *Confessions of a Recovering Environmentalist and Other Essays* (Minneapolis: Graywolf Press, 2017), 48-49.

21. Cass Sunstein discusses this dilemma and others of similar nature in "What Price Is Right?" *New York Review of Books* (June 10, 2021): 27-28. The award figures are from a "Victim Compensation Fund" table for Track A and Track B Claims as of 01/28/2005, accessed at www.justice.gov/archive /victimcompensation/award_amounts.

22. About two-thirds of the 120,000 people incarcerated during the war lived long enough to receive the payments.

23. Sociologist Howard S. Becker explores issues of this nature in *What About Mozart? What About Murder?: Reasoning from Cases* (Chicago: University of Chicago Press, 2014), 144ff.

24. Jack Turner, *The Abstract Wild* (Tucson: University of Arizona Press, 1996), 124. His italics.

25. Odell Shepard, ed., *The Heart of Thoreau's Journals* (New York: Dover Publications, 1961), 144-45 and 121.

26. Ruth Fuller Sasaki et al., trans., *The Recorded Sayings of Layman P'ang: A Ninth-Century Zen Classic* (New York: Weatherhill, 1971), 46.

27. 安心 *anxin* (or *an-hsin*; J., *anjin*). This expression is used, variously interpreted, by several Buddhist traditions. Chan and Zen associate it especially with the founding master Bodhidharma, where it figures in the oft-repeated story in which he brings peace to the heartmind of a desperate inquirer who later would become his successor. Cf. *Wumenguan*, case 41.

28. Wumen's comment, *Wumenguan*, case 1. A double entendre adds punch to this North Asian trope, which refers to the desperate hold that a phantom must maintain to keep from being blown around. In combination, the words I've translated "a wraith, a ghost" may mean "clever." If the traffic on the heartmind highway never lightens, we're liable to get tied up in clever ideas, clinging haplessly to the underbrush of thoughts and emotions.

29. Victor Sōgen Hori, *Zen Sand: The Book of Capping Phrases for Kōan Practice* (Honolulu: University of Hawai'i Press, 2003), items 14.168, 14.424, and 10.416.

30. John Simpson, *The Concise Oxford Dictionary of Proverbs*, 2nd ed. (Oxford: Oxford University Press, 1992), 78, traces first publication of this proverb to Mallory's *Morte d'Arthur*, c. 1470.

31. David Kline, *Great Possessions: An Amish Farmer's Journal* (San Francisco: North Point Press, 1990), 87, and *Scratching the Woodchuck: Nature on an Amish Farm* (Athens, GA: University of Georgia Press, 1999).

32. Marshall Sahlins, *Stone Age Economics* (New York: Aldine de Gruyter, 1972), 1–2.

14. Recognizing the Unrecognized

1. As defined in Paul W. Kroll, *A Student's Dictionary of Classical and Medieval Chinese*, rev. ed. (Leiden: Brill, 2017), 413. Here I also want to acknowledge with gratitude the guidance that Dr. Kroll himself gave me in translating Bodhidharma's initial response to the emperor, which follows.

2. Cf. Thomas and J. C. Cleary, trans., *The Blue Cliff Record* (Boulder, CO: Shambhala Publications, 1977), 1:4.

3. Dōgen, "Genjōkōan."

4. *Denkōroku*, case 32. Cf. Francis H. Cook, trans., *The Record of Transmitting the Light* (Los Angeles: Center Publications, 1991), 148; and T. Griffith Foulk, ed., *Record of the Transmission of Illumination* (Honolulu: University of Hawai'i Press, 2021), 1:323–24.

5. *Wumenguan*, case 47.

6. *Zongmen liandeng huiyao* (or *Tsung-men lien-teng hui-yao*; J., *Shūmon rentō eyō*), *Essential Compilation of the Ancestral Gate Lamp Succession*, ch. 7. Baizhang seems to be paraphrasing a passage from the *Nirvāna Sutra*.

7. *Jingde chuandeng lu* 10. Cf. Sohaku Ogata, trans., *The Transmission of the Lamp: Early Masters* (Wolfeboro, NH: Longwood Academic, 1990), 375.

8. *Jingde chuandeng lu* 10. Cf. Ogata, *Transmission of the Lamp*, 333. Among the many texts that quote the verse is *Wumenguan,* case 12.

9. *Shūmon kattōshū*, case 168 as numbered in Thomas Yūhō Kirchner, trans., *Entangling Vines: A Classic Collection of Zen Koans,* 2nd ed. (Boston: Wisdom Publications, 2013).

10. *Jingde chuandeng lu* 14. Cf. John C. H. Wu, *The Golden Age of Zen* (New York: Doubleday, 1996), 113; Ding-hwa E. Hsieh, "Images of Women in Ch'an Buddhist Literature of the Sung Period," in Peter N. Gregory and Daniel A. Getz, Jr., eds., *Buddhism in the Sung* (Honolulu: University of Hawai'i Press, 1999), 152; and Andrew Ferguson, trans., *Zen's Chinese Heritage* (Boston: Wisdom Publications, 2000), 153. Dr. Hsieh interprets this as a dialogue involving multiple nuns; the others reckon Longtan's interlocutor to be a single nun, as I do.

11. A bow of gratitude to Wendi Adamek for calling this parallel to my attention. The following rendition of the passage hews closely to the translation in Luis Gómez and Paul Harrison, eds., *The Teaching of Vimalakīrti* (Berkeley: Mangalam Press, 2022), 74-75 and 78-79. Since they translated from the Sanskrit, the wording differs in some particulars from translations of the sūtra based on Chinese texts. See, for example, Burton Watson, *The Vimalakirti Sutra* (New York: Columbia University Press, 1996), 87-88 and 91-92.

12. Bassui typically stated the kōan in a fuller form: "Who is the master of hearing that sound?" Cf. Arthur Braverman, trans., *Mud and Water: A Collection of Talks by the Zen Master Bassui* (San Francisco: North Point Press, 1989), 98-105.

13. *Wudeng huiyuan* 5. Another tip of the hat to Ben Brose for chasing down the Chinese text for me.

14. Hsieh offers this suggestion in Gregory and Getz, *Buddhism in the Sung*, 171. She translates the story and analyzes it on pp. 169-70.

15. Appropriately, such efforts have been led by women. The example I know best is that of my own Dharma family, the Diamond Sangha, where a group of women began working in 1979, with Aitken Rōshi's support, to study history, forge ties elsewhere, and found a journal to publish their questions and discoveries. That story is told in *Not Mixing Up Buddhism: Essays on Women and Buddhist Practice* (Fredonia, NY: White Pine Press, 1986). Its title and one of its essays were inspired by the *Wudeng huiyuan* story. I don't know if parity with men has been achieved, but women occupy many leadership positions in U.S. Zen communities today, and more recent books document women's history in our tradition and showcase their newfound prominence. Cf. Grace Schireson, *Zen Women: Beyond Tea Ladies, Iron Maidens,*

and Macho Masters (Boston: Wisdom Publications, 2009) and Florence Caplow and Susan Moon, eds., *The Hidden Lamp: Stories from Twenty-Five Centuries of Awakened Women* (Boston: Wisdom Publications, 2013).

16. Rebecca Giggs, "The Sea, the Sea," *New York Review of Books* (December 22, 2022): 28.

17. Peter E. Gordon, "In Search of Recognition," *New York Review of Books* (June 23, 2022): 46-47.

18. Elizabeth Kolbert, herself a mighty contributor to recognition of our planetary predicament, notes Carson's oversight in *Under a White Sky: The Nature of the Future* (New York: Crown, 2021), 14.

19. Quoted by Elizabeth Kolbert—no coincidence—in "A Little-Known Planet," *New Yorker* (March 20, 2023): 45.

20. *Jingde chuandeng lu* 1. The dialogue continues and is quoted in its entirety, almost verbatim, in Keizan's *Denkōroku*, case 12. Cf. Cook, *Record of Transmitting*, 72; Thomas Cleary, trans., *Transmission of Light* (San Franscisco: North Point Press, 1990), 51; and Foulk, *Record of the Transmission*, 1:179. In his reflections upon the ancient mirror, Dōgen echoes, "In each case, not recognizing is the bare heartmind."

21. *Record of Dongshan*, item 39. Cf. William F. Powell, trans., *The Record of Tung-shan* (Honolulu: University of Hawai'i Press, 1985), 38, and T. Griffith Foulk, ed., *Record of the Transmission of Illumination* (Honolulu: University of Hawai'i Press, 2021), 2:438-39.

22. Dōgen, *Mana Shōbōgenzō*, case 179.

23. Authorship of the verses on the "Five Positions"—五位 *wuwei* (or *wu-wei*; J., *goi*)—is uncertain but conventionally attributed to Dongshan. Translations are numerous. For this verse, see Powell, *Record of Tung-shan*, 61, and Ross Bolleter, *Dongshan's Five Ranks: Keys to Enlightenment* (Boston: Wisdom Publications, 2014), 3 and 61-65.

24. Jason Protass, *The Poetry Demon: Song-Dynasty Monks on Verse and the Way* (Honolulu: University of Hawai'i Press, 2021), 253. In the final sentence, I've replaced Dr. Protass's "men" (for 人) with "people."

15. Hundun the Beneficent, or Chaos Reconsidered

1. For alternative translations of the Hundun story, see Burton Watson, trans., *The Complete Works of Chuang Tzu* (New York: Columbia University Press, 1968), 97; Victor H. Mair, trans., *Wandering on the Way: Early Taoist Tales and Parables of Chuang Tzu* (Honolulu: University of Hawai'i Press, 1994), 71; and Brook Ziporyn, trans., *Zhuangzi: The Essential Writings* (Indianapolis: Hackett Publishing, 2009), 54.

2. Among the accomplished translators who, like Legge, have rendered Hundun as Chaos are Ziporyn, *Zhuangzi*, 54; Thomas Cleary, trans., *Book*

of Serenity: One Hundred Zen Dialogues (Hudson, NY: Lindisfarne Press, 1990), 191, 438; and Hisao Inagaki, *A Glossary of Zen Terms* (Kyoto: Nagata Bunshodo, 1995), 208. Honorable exceptions are Victor Sōgen Hori, who leaves the name untranslated in his *Zen Sand: The Book of Capping Phrases for Kōan Practice* (Honolulu: University of Hawai'i Press, 2003), and Mair, who, in *Wandering on the Way*, gives Hundun's name the alternate reading "Wonton."

3. Legge's note appears in his *Texts of Taoism*, part 1 (Oxford University Press, 1891; New York: Dover Publications, Inc., 1962), 267. The Lin he refers to is Ming Dynasty scholar Lin Xikong. The parenthetical interjections in the quotation are Legge's, the bracketed ones mine. In his chapter-by-chapter synopsis of *Zhuangzi*, Legge singles out the Hundun story for comment (p. 138), expressing incredulity that "according to Taoism they [Shu and Hu] did Chaos an injury!"

4. Hundun (or Hun-tun; J., Konton) may be written in two ways, 渾沌 or more often 混沌. In either case, both graphs carry the abbreviated water radical, 氵

5. Paul W. Kroll, *A Student's Dictionary of Classical and Medieval Chinese*, rev. ed. (Leiden: Brill, 2017), 178. I'm glad Dr. Kroll defines *hundun* as "utterly dark," though why he does so isn't apparent from the graphs. "Murky" seems much better supported.

6. For a more detailed examination of foundational Western accounts of chaos and the dire necessity of overcoming it, I recommend David L. Hall and Roger T. Ames, *Anticipating China: Thinking through the Narratives of Chinese and Western Culture* (Albany: State University of New York Press, 1995), especially pp. 3–12.

7. Shu and Hu are 儵忽. Heedless and Sudden in Legge, *Texts of Taoism*, 267; Brief and Sudden in Watson, *Chuang Tzu*, 97; Lickety and Split in Mair, *Wandering on the Way*, 71; Swoosh and Oblivion in Ziporyn, *Zhuangzi*, 54. In *Student's Dictionary* on p. 420, Kroll points out that the two words often appear together as an idiomatic expression.

8. Pointer to case 45 of the *Congrong lu*. Cf. Cleary, *Book of Serenity*, 191.

9. Pointer to case 3 of *The Blue Cliff Record*. Cf. Thomas and J. C. Cleary, trans., *The Blue Cliff Record* (Boulder, CO: Shambhala Publications, 1977), 1:18.

10. Ziporyn includes this among the commentaries in his translation of *Zhuangzi* on p. 212. I've amended "Chaos" to "Hundun."

11. Commentary on the *Heart Sutra* in Norman Waddell, trans., *Complete Poison Blossoms from a Thicket of Thorn: The Zen Records of Hakuin Ekaku* (Berkeley: Counterpoint Press, 2017), 599. I've taken the liberty of again changing "Chaos" to "Hundun."

12. Waddell, *Complete Poison*, 44. Italics are Waddell's. Here, too, I've switched "Chaos" to "Hundun."

13. Quoted by Michel Mohr, "Imagining Indian Zen: Tōrei's Commentary on the *Ta-mo-to-lo ch'an ching* and the Rediscovery of Early Meditation Techniques during the Tokugawa Era," in Steven Heine and Dale S. Wright, eds., *Zen Classics: Formative Texts in the History of Zen Buddhism* (Oxford: Oxford University Press, 2006), 235.

14. *Weifen* (or *wei-fen*; J., *mibun*): 未分.

15. Linquan Conglun (or Lin-ch'uan Ts'ung-lun; J., Rinsen Shōrin), pointer to case 90 of the *Vacant Hall Collection*, the *Xutang ji* (or *Hsu-t'ang chi*; J., *Kūkoku shū*). Thomas Cleary translates the full case in *Timeless Spring: A Soto Zen Anthology* (Tokyo: Weatherhill, 1980), 86. For another example of the Hundun *wei-fen* terminology, see Thomas Yūhō Kirchner, trans., *Entangling Vines: A Classic Collection of Zen Koans*, 2nd ed. (Boston: Wisdom Publications, 2013), 41.

16. Cf. Sonja Arntzen, trans., *Ikkyū and the Crazy Cloud Anthology: A Zen Poet of Medieval Japan*, rev. 2nd ed. (Melbourne: Quirin Press, 2022), 150, for the Chinese text and her translation.

17. Red Pine gives the Chinese text and his translation in *The Collected Songs of Cold Mountain* (Port Townsend, WA: Copper Canyon Press, 2000), 84–85. See also Robert G. Hendricks, trans., *The Poetry of Han-shan* (Albany, NY: State University of New York Press, 1990), 119.

18. Hall and Ames, *Thinking from the Han: Self, Truth, and Transcendence in Chinese and Western Culture* (Albany, NY: State University of New York Press, 1998), 66. Hall and Ames make this observation in the context of the Hundun story, and I owe a great deal to their analysis.

19. J. C. Cleary and Thomas Cleary, trans., *Zen Letters: Teachings of Yuanwu* (Boston: Shambhala Publications, 1994), 30, lightly emended.

20. Henry Adams, *The Education of Henry Adams* (Boston: Houghton Mifflin Co., 1918), 460 and 451. In this passage and throughout the book, Adams refers to himself in the third person.

21. Adams, *Education*, 460, 460, and 461.

22. William James, *Varieties of Religious Experience*, 2nd ed. (London: Longmans, Green, and Co., 1911), 438–39n1. Freud, lecturing a few years after James's book appeared, took no such unjaundiced view of "chaos," relying on it in describing the dangerous entity he called the id: "We approach the id with analogies: we call it a chaos, a cauldron full of seething excitations....It is filled with energy reaching it from the instincts, but it has no organization, produces no collective will, but only a striving to bring about satisfaction of the instinctual needs subject to the observance of the pleasure principle." Sigmund Freud, *New Introductory Lectures on Psychoanalysis* (published in 1933), p. 106.

23. For a nuanced account of William James's interest in "spiritualism," see Robert. D. Richardson, *William James: In the Maelstrom of American Modernism* (Boston: Houghton Mifflin Co., 2006).

24. Robert Bishop gives a lucid survey of current chaos theory in the online Stanford Encyclopedia of Philosophy, plato.stanford.edu/entries/chaos/.
25. Nathaniel Rich quotes Jacobs in "The Prophecies of Jane Jacobs," *Atlantic* (November 2016): 108.
26. Hans Monderman, quoted by Mark Kingwell in "Talking the Walk," *Harper's Magazine* (July 2013): 88.
27. Adam Kirsch, "Arias of Despair," *New York Review of Books* (February 9, 2023): 19.
28. Nathan Heller, "Mark as Read," *New Yorker* (July 24, 2017): 31.
29. Paul Kingsnorth, *Confessions of a Recovering Environmentalist and Other Essays* (Minneapolis: Graywolf Press, 2017), 222–23.
30. Personal notes, taken at the Western Buddhist Teachers Conference at Mount Madonna, California (May 1995).
31. Jisho Warner et al., eds., *Nothing Is Hidden: Essays on Zen Master Dōgen's Instructions for the Cook* (New York: Weatherhill, 2001), 95. For a translation of the full passage, see Taigen Dan Leighton and Shohaku Okamura, trans., *Dōgen's Extensive Record: A Translation of the Eihei Kōroku* (Boston: Wisdom Publications, 2010), 348, where they note that the master Dōgen quoted was Nāgārjuna.
32. Adams, *Education*, 249.

16. Wuwei and the Power to Desist

1. John R. McRae, *The Northern School and the Formation of Early Ch'an Buddhism* (Honolulu: University of Hawai'i Press, 1986), 11.
2. 信 (trust) and 心 (heartmind). *Ming* 銘 refers specifically to a text engraved on stone.
3. The words I've translated "tie themselves in knots" are 自縛, literally "self bind."
4. For alternative translations, see Ruth Fuller Sasaki et al., trans., *The Recorded Sayings of Layman P'ang: A Ninth-Century Zen Classic* (New York: Weatherhill, 1971), 26, and Victor Sōgen Hori, *Zen Sand: The Book of Capping Phrases for Kōan Practice* (Honolulu: University of Hawai'i Press, 2003), items 10.217-218.
5. It was Pierre Bayle, a French Protestant philosopher and historian, who placed Chan monks—"these speculative [i.e., meditating] Chinese"—in the "*Vu guei Kiao sect*," the sect of the *wuwei jiao* (i.e., *wuwei* teaching). Bernard Faure, *Chan Insights and Oversights: An Epistemological Critique of the Chan Tradition* (Princeton, NJ: Princeton University Press, 1993), 33.
6. *Daodejing* 48. The verse exists in several variants; my translation is based on the Mawangdui texts. Cf. Roger T. Ames and David L. Hall, trans., *Daodejing:*

Making This Life Significant (New York: Ballantine Books, 2003), 151. In citing the *Daodejing* here and later the *Zhuangzi*, I don't mean to imply that I'm presenting *the* Daoist line on wuwei. For a strict Daoist construction of wuwei as an ethical response to ecological problems, I recommend Russell Kirkland, "'Responsible Non-Action' in a Natural World" in N. J. Girardot et al., *Daoism and Ecology: Ways within a Cosmic Landscape* (Cambridge, MA: Harvard University Press, 2001).

7. *Jingde chuandeng lu* 14. Carl Bielefeldt translates the dialogue in *Dōgen's Manuals of Zen Meditation* (Berkeley: University of California Press, 1988), 147n27. In each instance, the Chinese phrase I've translated as "not doing" is a variant form of *wuwei*: 不為 *buwei*.

8. Personal notes, from a meeting of the American Zen Teachers Association in August, 2011, held at San Francisco Zen Center.

9. *Yi* is open to many interpretations and has often been translated as "rightness" or "duty."

10. *Mengzi* 2A. For other translations, see D. C. Lau, trans., *Mencius* (London: Penguin Books, 1970), 78, and David Hinton, trans., *Mencius* (Washington, DC: Counterpoint, 1998), 40-41.

11. David L. Hall, "From Reference to Deference: Daoism and the Natural World," in N. J. Girardot et al., *Daoism and Ecology*, 257.

12. *Denkōroku*, case 24. Cf. Thomas Cleary, trans., *Transmission of Light: Zen in the Art of Enlightenment* (San Francisco: North Point Press, 1990), 105; Francis H. Cook, trans., *The Record of Transmitting the Light* (Los Angeles: Center Publications, 1991), 121; and T. Griffith Foulk, ed., *Record of the Transmission of Illumination* (Honolulu: University of Hawai'i Press, 2021), 1:266. The term that I've translated "liberative benefit," 功德, Cleary and Cook translate as "virtue" and "merit," respectively. According to Paul W. Kroll in *A Student's Dictionary of Classical and Medieval Chinese*, rev. ed. (Leiden: Brill, 2017), 134, it refers to "pious works, meritorious actions." Robert E. Buswell Jr. and Donald S. Lopez Jr. in *The Princeton Dictionary of Buddhism* (Princeton, NJ: Princeton University Press, 2014) give it as Chinese for two different Sanskrit words, *anuśaṃsa* (p. 54) and *guṇa* (p. 336), while a third word, *puṇya* (p. 681), means "merit."

13. *Zhuangzi* 12.11. Cf. Burton Watson, trans., *The Complete Works of Chuang Tzu* (New York: Columbia University Press, 1968), 134, and Victor H. Mair, trans., *Wandering on the Way: Early Taoist Tales and Parables of Chuang Tzu* (Honolulu: University of Hawai'i Press, 1994), 111.

14. Quoted in Roger Shattuck, *Forbidden Knowledge: From Prometheus to Pornography* (New York: St. Martin's Press, 1996), 29. As his title indicates, Shattuck surveys the question of appropriate limits across a huge range of settings and topics, and his inquiry goes beyond knowledge per se to

experiences, technologies, and actions such as the atomic bombing of Japan and modification of DNA. Wide-ranging, erudite, and valuable as it is, his discussion is based on European, British, and U.S. sources, omitting Asian thought almost entirely.

15. William Blake, "Proverbs of Hell" in *The Marriage of Heaven and Hell* (c. 1793).

16. Mary Shelley, *Frankenstein*, chapter 20. Shelley's italics.

17. Ralph Waldo Emerson, "Ode, Inscribed to W. H. Channing."

18. Henry David Thoreau, *Walden*, ch. 1. Robert D. Richardson observes in his *Henry Thoreau: A Life of the Mind* (Berkeley: University of California Press, 1986), 227-28, that Thoreau had a knack for machinery, so to dismiss this statement as a product of blind prejudice against tools would be mistaken.

19. Yanagi Sōetsu, *The Unknown Craftsman: A Japanese Insight into Beauty*, adapted by Bernard Leach (Tokyo: Kodansha International Ltd., 1972), 206. The quotation is from an essay dated 1927.

20. Robert Burns, "To a Mouse, on Turning Her Up in Her Nest with the Plough, November 1785."

21. Bill Joy, "Why the Future Doesn't Need Us," *Wired* (April, 2000): 254 and 258.

22. Ivan Illich's books include *Blasphemy: A Radical Critique of Our Technological Culture* (Morristown, NJ: Aaron Press, 1995) and full-scale critiques of modern systems of education and medical care: *Deschooling Society* (New York: Harper & Row, 1971) and *Medical Nemesis* (New York: Pantheon, 1982).

23. Ivan Illich, *Tools for Conviviality* (Berkeley: Heyday Books, 1973), 84-85. E. F. Schumacher, *Small Is Beautiful: Economics as if People Mattered* (New York: Harper & Row, 1973), 52, quotes Ananda K. Coomaraswamy drawing a similar distinction.

24. Illich, *Tools for Conviviality*, xv.

25. On the nature, demands, pleasures, and necessity of work of this kind, Wendell Berry has been a steady source of inspiration for me, through his essays, fiction, poems, conversation, and modest example. I also recommend Matthew B. Crawford's books *Shopcraft as Soulcraft* and *The World Beyond Your Head*. The final chapter of the latter is especially delightful, evoking skillful practice of "the useful arts" and "the stochastic arts," as Crawford calls them, and connecting that practice to the experience and vitality of an old tradition, organmaking.

26. Illich, *Tools for Conviviality*, 85.

27. "Expensive tastes" is a term of art in philosophical discourse, I understand, used in reference to social, political, aesthetic, and environmental "goods" such as free public education as well as to material goods like comfortable dwellings and protein-rich diets. I use it here in both those senses,

to encompass not just fine wines, high-end art, yachts, and so on but also many things that citizens of wealthy nations assume to be normal.

28. If Schumacher's subtitle doesn't make his orientation clear, in his later book, *A Guide for the Perplexed* (1977), Schumacher propounds the medieval Christian concept of a Great Chain of Being, which ranks humans above all other earthly beings.

29. Joy, "Why the Future Doesn't Need Us," 246. More typical is his question, "And if our own extinction is a likely, or even possible, outcome of our technological development, shouldn't we proceed with great caution?"

30. For a voluminous and deeply informed anthology of Western writings that celebrate and advocate for the other-than-human (with a small sampling of texts from their East Asian counterparts), see Robert M. Torrance, ed., *Encompassing Nature: A Sourcebook* (Washington, DC: Counterpoint, 1998).

31. Aldo Leopold, "The Land Ethic," *A Sand County Almanac: With Essays on Conservation from Round River* (New York: Ballantine Books, 1970), especially p. 240.

32. Jimmy Carter, "Crisis of Confidence," July 14, 1979, accessed at cartercenter .org/news/editorials_speeches/crisis_of_confidence.

33. Gernot Wagner, *But Will the Planet Notice? How Smart Economics Can Save the World* (New York: Hill and Wang, 2011). Save the world? Hmmm. See chapter 10.

34. Sometimes given with the character pairs in reverse order—*wanxiang senluo*—as in both the examples that follow. For the source of this phrase, see Robert Sharf, *Coming to Terms with Chinese Buddhism: A Reading of the Treasure Store Treatise* (Honolulu: University of Hawai'i Press, 2002), 191 and n149.

35. Cf. Hori, *Zen Sand*, item 21.17.

36. Brose and Foster, unpublished manuscript, lines 116-19.

Selected Bibliography

Primary Sources

Congrong lu (or *Tsung-jung lu*; J., *Shōyōroku*). Kōans selected by Hongzhi, his accompanying verses, and commentary on both the kōans and verses by Wansong. Cf. Cleary, *Book of Serenity*.

Daodejing (or *Tao-te ching*), attributed to Laozi. Translations abound. I recommend *Daodejing: Making This Life Significant*. Translated by Roger T. Ames and David L. Hall. New York: Ballantine Books, 2003.

Denkōroku, by Keizan Jōkin. Cf. Cook, *The Record of Transmitting the Light*, and Foulk, *Record of the Transmission of Illumination*.

Jingde chuandeng lu. Cf. Whitfield, *Records of the Transmission of the Lamp*, the only complete English translation to date; Chang, *Original Teachings of Chan Buddhism* (selected records); and Ogata, *The Transmission of the Lamp* (a translation of the first third of the text).

Lunyu. The Confucian *Analects*. Of the many available translations, I recommend Roger T. Ames and Henry Rosemont, Jr. *The Analects of Confucius: A Philosophical Translation*. New York: Ballentine Books, 1988, and Burton Watson. *The Analects of Confucius*. New York: Columbia University Press, 2007.

Zhaozhou lu. Cf. Green, trans., *The Recorded Sayings of Zen Master Joshu*, and Hoffman, trans. *Radical Zen*.

Zhongyong (or *Chung-yung*). Attributed to Confucius and often referred to under the title *The Doctrine of the Mean*. Cf. Roger T. Ames and David L. Hall, trans. *Focusing the Familiar*.

Zhuangzi. Cf. Watson, *The Complete Works of Chuang Tzu*, and Mair, *Wandering on the Way*.

Secondary Sources

Ames, Roger T., and David L. Hall, trans. *Focusing the Familiar: A Translation and Philosophical Interpretation of the* Zhongyong. New York: Ballantine Books, 2003.

Buswell, Robert E., Jr. and Donald S. Lopez Jr., *The Princeton Dictionary of Buddhism*. Princeton, NJ: Princeton University Press, 2014.

Chang, Chung-Yuan. *Original Teachings of Chan Buddhism*. New York: Pantheon, 1969.

Cleary, J. C., and Thomas Cleary, trans. *Zen Letters: Teachings of Yuanwu*. Boston: Shambhala Publications, 1994.

Cleary, Thomas, and J. C. Cleary, trans. *The Blue Cliff Record*. Boulder, CO: Shambhala Publications, 1977.

Cleary, Thomas, trans. *Book of Serenity: One Hundred Zen Dialogues*. Hudson, NY: Lindisfarne Press, 1990.

———, trans. *Zen Lessons: The Art of Leadership*. Boston: Shambhala Publications, 1989.

Cook, Francis H., trans. *The Record of Transmitting the Light*. Los Angeles: Center Publications, 1991.

Ferguson, Andrew, trans. *Zen's Chinese Heritage*. Boston: Wisdom Publications, 2000.

Foulk, T. Griffith, ed. *Record of the Transmission of Illumination*. Honolulu: University of Hawai'i Press, 2021.

Green, James, trans. *The Recorded Sayings of Zen Master Joshu*. Boston: Shambhala Publications, 1998.

Hall, David L., and Roger T. Ames. *Thinking from the Han: Self, Truth, and Transcendence in Chinese and Western Culture*. Albany: State University of New York Press, 1998.

Hoffman, Yoel, trans. *Radical Zen: The Sayings of Jōshū*. Brookline, MA: Autumn Press, 1978.

Hori, Victor Sōgen. *Zen Sand: The Book of Capping Phrases for Kōan Practice*. Honolulu: University of Hawai'i Press, 2003.

Kirchner, Thomas Yūhō, trans. *Entangling Vines: A Classic Collection of Zen Koans,* 2nd ed. Boston: Wisdom Publications, 2013.

Kroll, Paul W. *A Student's Dictionary of Classical and Medieval Chinese*, rev. ed. Leiden: Brill, 2017. A third edition was published in 2022.

Leighton, Taigen Dan, and Shohaku Okamura, trans. *Dōgen's Extensive Record: A Translation of the Eihei Kōroku*. Boston: Wisdom Publications, 2010.

Mair, Victor H., trans. *Wandering on the Way: Early Taoist Tales and Parables of Chuang Tzu*. Honolulu: University of Hawai'i Press, 1994.

Ogata, Sohaku, trans. *The Transmission of the Lamp: Early Masters*. Wolfeboro, NH: Longwood Academic, 1990.

Red Pine, trans. *The Collected Songs of Cold Mountain*. Port Townsend, WA: Copper Canyon Press, 2000.

Rohsenow, John. *ABC Dictionary of Chinese Proverbs*. Honolulu: University of Hawai'i Press, 2002.

Sasaki, Ruth Fuller, trans., and Thomas Yūhō Kirchner, ed. *The Record of Linji.* Honolulu: University of Hawai'i Press, 2009.

Sharf, Robert. *Coming to Terms with Chinese Buddhism: A Reading of the Treasure Store Treatise.* Honolulu: University of Hawai'i Press, 2002.

Waddell, Norman, trans. *Complete Poison Blossoms from a Thicket of Thorn: The Zen Records of Hakuin Ekaku.* Berkeley: Counterpoint Press, 2017.

Watson, Burton, trans. *The Complete Works of Chuang Tzu.* New York: Columbia University Press, 1968.

———, trans. *The Zen Teachings of Master Lin-chi.* Boston: Shambhala Publications, 1993.

Whitfield, Randolph S., trans. *Records of the Transmission of the Lamp*, 8 vols. Books On Demand, 2014-2020.

Yampolsky, Philip B. *The Platform Sutra of the Sixth Patriarch.* New York: Columbia University Press, 1967.

Index

activating words, 147, 263n34
Adams, Henry, 198, 200, 207
Aitken Rōshi (Robert Aitken), xv, 1, 5, 27-28, 29, 38, 96, 206
Ames, Roger, 197, 200
Amitābha, 120, 259n62
Analects, 21, 28, 32, 66-67, 96, 140, 245n21, 265n5, 265n6. *See also* Confucius
Ancestral Gate of Entangling Vines, 178. *See also Shūmon kattōshū*
anthropocentrism, 84
antinomianism, 30-31, 34
anxin, 166-67, 267n27
Āryasimha, 215
Aśvaghosa, 187
Avalokiteśvara, 176. *See also* Guanyin (a.k.a. Guanshiyin)

Baisaō, 25-26, 109-10
Baizhang Huaihai, 88, 94, 148, 177
Bankei Yotaku, 60-61
bao, x, xi
baozang, xi, 25, 240n15
Baozhi, 174, 175, 176, 177
Bassui Tokushō, 182, 269n12
Bellow, Saul, 98-99
Blake, William, 221
Blue Cliff Record (Yuanwu), 15, 21, 146, 258n54
  on beginnings, 147
  on Bodhidharma, 175-76, 177

  on Hundun, 194
  on Lazy Zan, 155
  on light and dark, 129
  yaojin in, 255n28
Blyth, R. H., 94, 100
Bo Juyi, 79-80, 110
Bodhidharma, 21-22, 106, 141, 255n19
  anxin and, 267n27
  on Chan transmission, 10
  Emperor Wu and, 24, 174-76, 177, 186
  "I've come as rootstock . . ." verse, 133-34, 149-50
bodhisattva ideal, 117-18
Book of Songs, 68. *See also Shijing*
Bringhurst, Robert, 78
Burns, Robert, 223

Canetti, Elias, 78-79, 81
Cantong qi, 24-25
Caodong lineage, 15, 22, 34. *See also* Sōtō Zen
Caoshan Benji, 84
Carson, Rachel, 184-86
Carter, Jimmy, 229
Changqing Da'an, 88
Changsha Jingcen, 91, 178
Changsheng, 46
charitable activity, 117-19
Chen, Ellen, 152
cheng, 54, 67-68, 244n7, 244n14
Chuang-tzu. See *Zhuangzi*
Chuanzi Decheng, 258n58

| 281